The Vision of Kings

The Vision of Kings

ART AND EXPERIENCE IN INDIA

Michael Brand

NATIONAL GALLERY OF AUSTRALIA

Edited, designed, typeset and produced by the Publications
Department of the National Gallery of Australia, Canberra.
Colour separations by Pep Colour.
Proudly printed in Australia by Inprint Ltd.

Cataloguing-in-Publication data
Brand, Michael, 1958–
The vision of kings: art and experience in India.
Bibliography.
ISBN 0 642 13039 6.
I. Art, India – Exhibitions. I. National Gallery of Australia. II. Title.
709.540749471

Distributed by:
Thames and Hudson (Australia) Pty Ltd,
11 Central Boulevarde, Portside Business Park,
Port Melbourne, Victoria 3207, Australia

Thames and Hudson Ltd,
30–34 Bloomsbury Street, London WC1B 3QP, UK

Thames and Hudson Inc.,
500 Fifth Avenue, New York, NY 10110, USA

ISBN in USA 0-500-97438-1
Library of Congress 95-61906

This catalogue is published on the occasion of an exhibition
held at the National Gallery of Australia, Canberra,
25 November 1995 – 4 February 1996.
National Gallery of Victoria, Melbourne,
23 February 1996 – 28 April 1996.

Proudly sponsored by

Supported by
the Australia-India Council

Indemnified by the Australian Government through
the Department of Communications and the Arts.

Front cover image:
PAYAG (active c.1595–1655)
The Emperor Humayan seated in a landscape (detail)
Mughal dynasty, c.1650
Arthur M Sackler Gallery, Smithsonian Institution,
Washington D.C.

Contents

Foreword

The National Gallery of Australia in Canberra and the National Gallery of Victoria in Melbourne have great pleasure in hosting *The Vision of Kings: Art and Experience in India.*

This outstanding exhibition features a selection of over one hundred masterpieces created throughout a period of two thousand years for Hindu, Buddhist, Jain and Muslim patrons. The exhibition illuminates the extraordinary history and achievement of Indian culture.

The works of art in this exhibition have been drawn from some of the world's greatest public and private collections of Indian art. We are indebted to these lenders for providing the Australian public with an unparalleled opportunity to view their works.

This exhibition was developed with the generous assistance of many people and in the spirit of cultural co-operation encouraged by the Cultural Exchange Agreement between Australia and India which was signed in 1971, and the Memorandum of Understanding on Cultural Exchanges between Australia and India signed in May 1993.

For their assistance in negotiating this exhibition in India we are particularly grateful to the Minister for Human Resource Development, the Hon Shri Madhav Rao Scindia and his predecessor, the Hon Shri Arjun Singh; the Hon Shri Laloo Prasad Yadav, Chief Minister of Bihar; the Hon Ms Jayalalitha, Chief Minister of Tamil Nadu; Dr Sitakant Mahapatra, Secretary of the Department of Culture, Ministry of Human Resource Development; and Shri Ashok Vajpeyi, Acting Director of the National Museum of India. We also received the generous support of the Indian High Commissioner to Australia, His Excellency Mr Gopalaswamy Parthasarathy and his predecessor, His Excellency Mr Akbar Mirza Khaleeli.

The National Gallery of Australia wishes to thank especially the Australia-India Council for its help, and acknowledges the important role played by the former Chairman of the Council, the late Graham Feakes, and the continuing support of our good friend, Michael Abbott QC.

The support received from the Australian Government was vital, and we would like to thank the Hon. Michael Lee, Minister for Communications and the Arts, Senator the Hon. Gareth Evans QC, Minister for Foreign Affairs, and Senator the Hon. Bob McMullan, Minister for Trade for their keen personal interest and support for the project.

As with all major undertakings, we rely on corporate sponsorship. On this occasion Telstra has joined with us to present this outstanding exhibition, and will be associated with an exhibition of Australian Aboriginal art which will travel to India in 1996. We thank Telstra for its support of this important cultural exchange.

We would also like to congratulate Dr Michael Brand, Curator of Asian Art at the National Gallery of Australia, who has excelled in bringing this fine exhibition together. Michael's scholarship in the area is internationally recognised and this exhibition has afforded him an opportunity to present some of the wonders of Indian culture to an Australian audience.

Betty Churcher
Director
National Gallery of Australia, Canberra

Timothy Potts
Director
National Gallery of Victoria, Melbourne

Acknowledgments

This book accompanies the first major exhibition of Indian art to be held in Australia. In bringing this project to fruition I have had to rely upon the generous assistance of many colleagues and their institutions. Most important among these are the art institutions and private collectors in India, Europe, the United States and Australia who have so kindly agreed to share parts of their collections with the Australian public. Central to the project has been the establishment of an extremely cordial working relationship with our prime collaborator, the National Museum in Delhi. For this, I would like to offer my sincerest thanks to Shri Ashok Vajpeyi, who has been Acting Director of the National Museum as well as Joint Secretary of the Department of Culture. Other individuals who deserve special recognition are Dr George Michell, the doyen of Australian scholars of Indian art and architecture, and a highly productive consultant to this project; Ross Owen Feller, who designed the exhibition's magnificent installation at the National Gallery of Australia in Canberra; John Gollings, who photographed all the works of art borrowed from Indian collections (except two later additions) with his usual combination of aesthetic rigour and extraordinary attention to detail; and, at the National Gallery of Australia, Gary Hickey, the Assistant Curator of Asian Art, and Anne McDonald, who both provided tireless support for the project. Graham Feakes, Australian High Commissioner to India from 1984 to 1990, then Chairman of the Australia-India Council from 1992 until just before his death in December 1994, along with his wife Nicola provided unparalleled support for all Australians involved in strengthening our ties with India. I am among many people who deeply regret that he did not live to see this exhibition.

Without all those listed below this project would never have happened.

INDIA
Delhi
Dr G.N. Pant (Director, National Museum Institute of History of Art, Conservation and Museology), who acted as a highly efficient and generous Project Coordinator in Delhi; Dr R.C. Sharma (former Director), Dr L. Asthana, K.R. Bamhania, Dr Daljeet, J.E. Dawson, Anju Sachdeva, Manikuntala Sarkar, Jayshri Sharma, Rita Sharma and Tejpal Singh at the National Museum; G. Venkataramani, whose friendly support and advice during this project was particularly appreciated, Shri Rangarajan and Dharam Pal at the Department of Culture within the Ministry of Human Resource Development; also Jasleen Dhamija, Dr Geeta Kapur, Aman Nath and Francis Wacziarg.

Darren Gribble (High Commissioner), David Evans (former High Commissioner), Gavan Bromilow, Pera Wells, Brett Martin, Asha Das and Anjali Kumar at the Australian High Commission in Delhi all played crucial roles in ensuring the success of this project.

Calcutta
Dr S.S. Biswas (Director), Dr Sakti Kali Basu, Mangala Chakrabarty, Dr Dibakar Das, Dr Jñan Ranjan Haldar, Dr Dolly Mukherjee, Dr Anusua Sengupta and P.K. Bannerjee at the Indian Museum.

Madras
M. Ramu (Director), S. Thangavelu, Dr N. Devasahayam and R. Balasubramaniam at the Government Museum; and Dr R. Nagaswamy.

Patna
Dr Naseem Akhtar, Director of Museums, Government of Bihar; Prashant Kumar Jaysval (Director), Parvez Akhtar, O.C. Dvivedi and Parashuram Pande at the Patna Museum.

Vijayanagar
Dr John M. Fritz, Dr Anna Dallapiccola and Dr George Michell — my time with them in the midst of one of India's greatest sacred archaeological sites provided crucial intellectual inspiration and critical feedback.

EUROPE
Geneva
Prince Sadruddin Aga Khan, and Mme Liliane Tivolet at His Highness's Secretariat.

London
Dr Robert Anderson (Director), J.R. Knox and T. Richard Blurton at the British Museum; Dr Alan Borg (Director), Elizabeth Esteve-Coll (former Director), Dr Deborah Swallow, John Guy and Rosemary Crill at the Victoria and Albert Museum; Sir Howard Hodgkin and Ann Marchini, his assistant; Robert Skelton; Nikos Stangos and Tim Evans at Thames and Hudson; and Michael Letendrie and Peter Grove-White at Wingate and Johnston.

UNITED STATES OF AMERICA
Boston
Dr James Cuno (Director), Stuart Cary Welch (who gave me the first opportunities to work with and appreciate Indian paintings many years ago and has been a constant source of support ever since), Craigen Bowen, Jane Montgomery, Maureen Donovan, Ada Bortoluzzi, Elizabeth Gombosi and Miriam Stewart at the Harvard University Art Museums; Dr Malcolm Rogers (Director), Dr Darielle Mason, Jean-Louis Lachevrie and Robin Weiss at the Museum of Fine Arts; and Dr Eric Rosenberg.

Boulder, Colorado
Professor James L. Wescoat, at the Department of Geography, University of Colorado, Boulder, has been an inspirational colleague during the course of our Mughal garden project in Lahore, and has shown extraordinary patience while this exhibition distracted my attention from our own publications.

Chicago
Woodman Taylor at the University of Chicago.

New York
Philippe de Montebello (Director), Daniel Walker, Martin Lerner, Stefano Carboni, Steven Kossak, Nestor Montilla and Minora Pacheco at the Metropolitan Museum of Art; Dr Vishakha N. Desai (Director), Dr Denise Patry Leidy and Amy McEwan at the Asia Society Galleries; Terence McInerney; and David B. Epstein of Masterpiece International Ltd.

Washington
Dr Milo C. Beach (Director), Dr Thomas W. Lentz Jr, Dr Vidya Dehejia, Rocky Korr, Jane Norman and Bruce Young at the Arthur M. Sackler Gallery, Smithsonian Institution; and Dr Massumeh Farhad.

AUSTRALIA
National Gallery of Australia, Canberra
The National Gallery Council, Betty Churcher (Director), Alan Froud (Deputy Director), Kevin Munn and Jan Meek have supported this project from its inception. My most profound gratitude is reserved for the members of *The Vision of Kings* Project Team, who offered such sound professional advice and solid support over the last twelve months: Alan R. Dodge (co-Chair), Suzanna Campbell, Emma Cheshire, Gary Hickey, Jos Jensen (who provided unstinting support during the exhibition design process), Anne McDonald, Geoffrey Major, Kirsty Morrison (who also designed the catalogue with her usual flair and sensitivity), Peter Naumann, Brian Parkes, Harijs Piekalns, Renfred Pryor, Warwick Reeder, Inge Rumble, David Sequeira and Margaret Shaw (who also prepared the catalogue's bibliography). Particular thanks are due to Pauline Green and Theresa Willsteed who edited the catalogue, and to Joy McCleary who keyed in all the corrections; Andy Jorritsma and his entire staff, who built the exhibition installation for the Canberra showing; and Winifred Mumford who prepared the map for this catalogue.

Other members of staff at the National Gallery of Australia who played significant roles are Valerie Alfonzi, Jeni Allenby, Lesley Arjonilla, Sue Bioletti, Barbara Brinton, Erica Burgess, Ellen Cordes, Gillian Currie, Micheline Ford, Morrie Harding, Bruce Howlett, Trevor Hoyne, Willi Kemperman, Brenton McGeachie, Michelle McMartin, Jenny Manning, Bruce Moore, Mark Nash, Pam Owen, Margaret Parkes, Richard Pedvin, Helen Power, Ron Ramsey, Sarah Rennie, Beata Tworek-Matuszkiewicz and Kathryn Weir.

Also in Canberra, I would like to thank Dr Chris Gregory and Dr Yogendra Yadav at the Australian National University; Padma Menon, Artistic Director of the Kailash Dance Company; and Durga Vishwanathan.

Adelaide
Michael and Mary Abbott, who have always been among the most generous supporters of Asian art at the National Gallery of Australia, and Dick Richards, Art Gallery of South Australia.

Melbourne
Dr Timothy Potts (Director), Dr Mae Anna Pang, Gordon Morrison, Janine Bofill, Thomas Dixon, Catherine Millikan, Lindsay Knowles, Daryl West-Moore and Fiona Wright at the National Gallery of Victoria; Richard Gilmour at Thames and Hudson; and Dr Kelleson Collyer, for sharing her expert knowledge about the Hoysala temples of Karnataka.

Sydney
Joan Bowers of Joan Bowers Antiques, who lent a number of wonderful architectural elements that considerably enhanced the installation of the exhibition in Canberra; Dr Sugandha Johar; and Alex and Jo Wodak.

Antonio Martinelli in Paris, Bharath Ramamrutham in Bombay, and Dr Joanne Punzo Waghorne and Dick Waghorne at the University of North Carolina at Chapel Hill have all generously allowed us to reproduce some of their excellent photographs.

I also add my thanks for their generous support to Dr Sanjay Modak, Charles Buttrose and Jill Lester at Telstra; Michael Abbott (a second time), Ian Wille, Keith Gardner and Ian Black at the Australia-India Council; Genevieve Prieto of the Oberoi Group of Hotels; Doug Alexander of Inprint Limited; and Gary J. Willemsen of Willemsen Constructions and The Griffin.

I feel certain that the late Professor A.L. Basham would have been especially pleased to see a major exhibition of Indian art in Australia. He is the teacher who set me on the path of looking seriously at Indian art while I had the good fortune to study with him at the Australian National University in Canberra from 1976–1979. I would hope that Professor Oleg Grabar, now at the Institute of Advanced Studies in Princeton, under whom I previously had the privilege of studying at Harvard University, would recognise his role in inspiring me to seek new perspectives from which to view Indian art.

Tina Gomes Brand has shared the whole experience with extraordinary enthusiasm, even as she took on numerous extra responsibilities. My final thanks go to Isabel and Claudia.

Michael Brand
Curator of Asian Art
National Gallery of Australia, Canberra
November 1995

Because no diacriticals have been used in this publication, certain Sanskrit names will appear in different forms. 'Siva' will appear for 'Śiva', for example, in quotes from works that do include diacriticals. In this text, 'Śiva' is also transliterated as 'Shiva'.

Certain catalogue entries for works of art in the collection of the National Gallery of Australia are based on my entries in the introduction to our collection which I edited earlier this year (*Traditions of Asian Art: Traced through the Collection of the National Gallery of Australia*, Canberra: National Gallery of Australia, 1995). Additional information about objects belonging to the National Gallery of Australia is included in the relevant endnotes.

Dimensions are given as height x width x depth.

Some works in this catalogue are on display only at the National Gallery, Canberra. These are: no. 79, *Krishna lifting Mount Govardhan*; no. 94, *The Emperor Akbar with a lion and calf*; no. 96, *The Emperor Shah Jahan nimbed in glory*; and no. 98, *Rosette (shamsa) with the name and titles of the Emperor Shah Jahan*. Catalogue no. 89, *Maharana Jagat Singh II attending a Rasalila performance* is not included in the exhibition in Canberra — the National Gallery of Victoria has discovered that much of their collection of Indian paintings is now too fragile to travel.

Michael Brand
November 1995

Michael and Mary Abbott, Adelaide

Prince Sadruddin Aga Khan, Geneva

Asia Society Galleries, New York

British Museum, London

Government Museum, Madras

Sir Howard Hodgkin, London

Indian Museum, Calcutta

Terence McInerney, New York

Metropolitan Museum of Art, New York

Museum of Fine Arts, Boston

National Gallery of Australia, Canberra

National Gallery of Victoria, Melbourne

National Museum, Delhi

Patna Museum, Patna

Arthur M. Sackler Gallery, Smithsonian Institution, Washington D.C.

Victoria and Albert Museum, London

and anonymous private collections

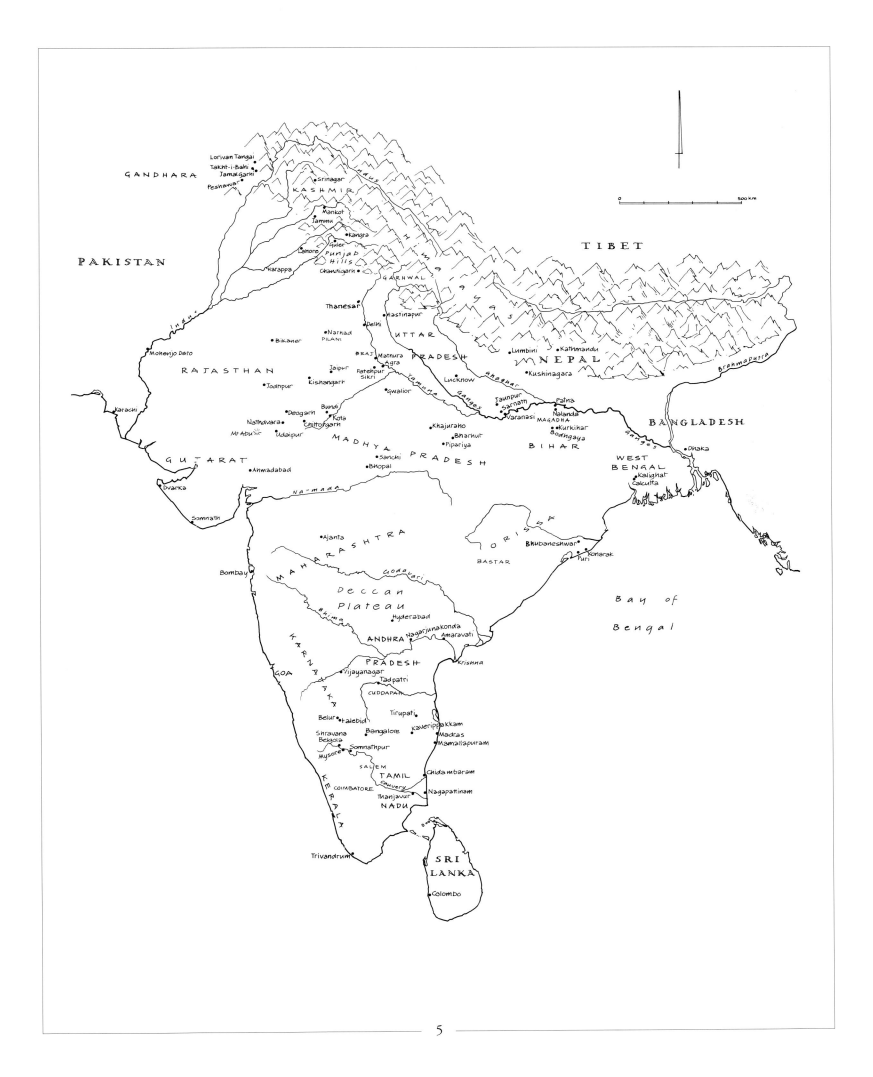

Introduction

King Narasimha I worshipping the Puri trinity. Sun Temple, Konarak, Orissa, 1238–58 (detail) (see Catalogue no.1b)

See the god!
See him who is higher than the gods!
See him who is Sanskrit of the North
and southern Tamil and the four Vedas!
See him who bathes in milk and ghee,
see the Lord, see him who dances, holding fire,
in the wilderness of the burning-ground,
see him who blessed the hunter—saint!
See him who wells up as honey
in the heart-lotus of his lovers!
See him who has the unattainable treasure!
See Shiva! See him who is our treasure! . . . [1]

Seeing is an essential part of ritual practice in India. Vision transmits both spiritual and political power. In Hinduism, for example, the sacred image is viewed literally as the god, and eye contact is exchanged. In the political realm, where the presence of the ruler legitimises authority, some Muslim emperors ceremonially showed themselves to their subjects daily at a special viewing window. In both cases the word used to describe the ritual is *darshana*, literally 'seeing' or an 'auspicious sight'.

For Hindu, Buddhist, Jain and Muslim patrons, Indian artists over many centuries have created a range of highly distinctive imagery. It serves both religion and royalty, connecting the realm of the sacred with the ambitions of the patrons and the devotional needs of worshippers. The images are closely related to the sacred and political architecture of India — great ritual spaces in which ideals of cosmic order are made manifest. *The Vision of Kings* explores the nature of the visual power of the Indian image and the experience of viewing Indian art.

Civilisation in India can be traced back as far as the third millennium BC. The ruined cities of the Indus or Harappan civilisation (*c.*2250–1750 BC) have provided evidence of sophisticated systems of writing (not yet deciphered), urban planning and irrigation, as well as a small number of extraordinarily refined sculptures. Around 1500 BC, a radical shift in the course of Indian civilisation occurred when the Aryan or Vedic peoples entered the subcontinent. In their Indo–European language, these people composed the hymns and prayers of the Vedas which form the basis of much of what later came to be known as Hinduism. Subsequent cultural shifts of major significance occurred with the rise of Buddhism and Jainism from the sixth century BC, the arrival of various Muslim groups from the eighth century onwards and the establishment of British colonial authority in the mid-eighteenth century. It is a remarkable feature of Indian civilisation that earlier cultures have never been fully eclipsed by later ones.

The depth of Indian civilisation is reflected in the richness of its imagery. Within a sophisticated aesthetic system, sacred and political ideals have been represented both symbolically and figuratively. Principally artists have employed the human figure (incorporating codified gestures and physical attributes) to represent a startling array of divine concepts, philosophical ideals and political ambitions. Some gods combine human and animal forms; some possess multiple heads and arms. A god might be depicted as a universal monarch (*chakravartin*), imposing cosmic order from a royal court, or as an ascetic *yogi* smeared with cremation-ground ashes and residing in the isolated heights of the Himalayas (the Abode of Snow). Many paintings show rulers seeking the blessing of mystics — a symbolic reconciliation between political and spiritual authority.

Vision as an experience in Indian art is diverse. Images of the Hindu gods, Buddhist and Jain saviours, auspicious guardians and historical kings all engage the gaze of the viewer in different ways. In Hinduism, sculptures of gods are portrayed with their eyes wide open in order to engage worshippers in a highly charged exchange of glances (*darshana*); while images of the Buddha most frequently have their eyes cast downward in meditation as they aid worshippers in the visualisation of philosophical ideals. In their portraits, the Mughal emperors of India were generally painted in profile, averting their gaze from the viewer; however some of these Muslim rulers presented themselves to their subjects each morning framed architecturally at a specially constructed '*darshana*-window' facing the rising sun.

Meaning in Indian art is closely related to architectural context. Sculptures of one and the same god can function totally differently according to their position in a temple. Some images are truly sacred and are worshipped directly, some have a protective purpose, others serve a more didactic function. Within pictorial space the meaning of royal images is dependent on symbolic connections with the palace and the landscape; while a king's individual portrait can take on distinctively cultic significance according to the way the king presents himself in certain palace rituals. Whatever the setting, the experience of viewing art in India is further mediated by the performance of music and dance, the chanting of sacred scriptures and the recitation of poetry.

The vision of the patron was also central to the creation of art in India. Patrons were usually, but not exclusively, kings and nobles. In the case of the royal patron, the architectural monuments in which images were installed or housed were, in themselves, important symbols of the king's worldly and other-worldly aspirations.

1a *King Narasimha I with his guru*

Sun Temple, Konarak, Orissa
Eastern Ganga period, 1238–58
stone (chloritic schist); 78.5 x 43.0 x 23.0 cm
On loan from the Board of Trustees of the Victoria and Albert Museum, London (IS 938)

In its great monuments the power of India's art is enacted. It is in these temples and palaces that the complex relationships between sacred and political authority, between gods and kings and, finally, between the image and the devotee as viewer come to life. These relationships are articulated with singular clarity at the Sun Temple of King Narasimha I at Konarak (in Orissa on the Bay of Bengal). Narasimha, named after the 'man-lion' incarnation of the Hindu god Vishnu, ruled Orissa and neighbouring regions of eastern India from 1238 to 1264. Although he called himself an emperor (*maharajadhiraja*), it was a form of the god Vishnu, known as Purushottama (the Supreme Being) or Jagannatha (the Lord of the World), who was regarded as the supreme ruler of the kingdom. Narasimha's official role was that of *rauta* or subordinate ruler. He described himself as a devout worshipper of Shiva, and as the son of Purushottama, Shiva and the goddess Durga.[2] While some of these distinctions are no more than symbolic, the intention to forge an ambiguously close relationship between the king and the divine is clear. It is a pattern that finds many parallels throughout Indian history. Its representation was a primary concern of Indian art.

In 1258 the great festival in honour of Surya, the Hindu sun god, fell on a Sunday — a highly auspicious conjunction occurring only once every seven years. A month prior to this Sunday in 1258, *brahman* priests had been brought together at Konarak by the order of King Narasimha to commence a ritual of rare importance. After at least twenty years of planning and construction, the king's extraordinary new Sun Temple was almost complete.[3] Final construction work on this massive stone edifice had been continuing at a feverish pace to ensure that the temple was ready for consecration at dawn on the auspicious day. On the Saturday preceding the solar festival, the ceremonies approached their climax and two-thousand-year-old Vedic hymns were chanted through the night. At dawn on the Sunday, the first *puja* (ceremony of worship) was performed on schedule after the priests had carried out their final and most important act, the consecration of the presiding stone image of Surya in the temple's dark inner sanctum. After purifying the image they would have infused it with *prana* (the breath of life) by the utterance of a sacred *mantra*.

Finally, a priest would have opened the god's eyes by removing with a golden needle a specially applied coating of honey and ghee.[4]

The sculptural program at Konarak covers all four aspects of the Indian conception of life: *dharma* (sacred law and duty), *artha* (polity and material gain), *kama* (sensual enjoyment) and *moksha* (liberation from the cycle of rebirth in this world). During the planning of the Sun Temple, Narasimha ordered his architects to incorporate images of himself within a standard iconographic program of gods and auspicious guardians, as well as a slightly less common series of erotic sculptures. The royal sculptures, a number of which have long since been removed from their original niches on the temple, illustrate the two roles adopted by the king: as the warrior king, he hunts within the royal lands and worships at a major dynastic shrine; in other examples he is shown as a devotee, submitting himself to the authority of his religious preceptor or guru.

In this Konarak sculpture, now in the collection of the Victoria and Albert Museum in London, Narasimha is depicted with his guru, probably the *yogi* Acharyaraja.[5] As king, Narasimha held political control over the region in which the Sun Temple was constructed and was the actual patron of the temple, yet he is shown as smaller than his guru. Reverence for the teacher has always been a central feature of Indian culture and it was only the guru, after all, who was able to provide the key to understanding particularly esoteric religious concepts. The guru sits cross-legged, with one arm raised in a gesture of explanation. The bearded king, seated in the centre of the sculpture, is stripped of all royal symbols. His sword lies on the ground in front of him. Instead of a weapon he holds a palm-leaf manuscript, the original medium for transcribing sacred texts in India. Behind the king are two attendants: one sits reading from a palm-leaf manuscript; the other stands with his hands joined together in a demonstration of reverence. On the lower register, in smaller scale, four warriors stand with shields and weapons. The message is clear: here at the temple even the king must defer to the status of priestly intermediaries if he is to partake of the benefits of divine power and favour.

9

fig. 1: Sun Temple, Konarak, Orissa, 1238–58 (detail) (Photo: George Michell).

The architectural form and space of the Hindu temple is a highly sophisticated amalgam of geometry and symbolism, a microcosm of the universe wrought in stone. Unique among major temples in India, the Sun Temple at Konarak (fig. 1) was given the form of a giant chariot. With twelve elaborately carved wheels (measuring three metres in diameter), six on each side of the platform, it is 'pulled' by seven stone horses set at the front of the structure. The twelve wheels symbolise the twelve signs of the zodiac as well as the twelve months of Surya's annual journey through the heavens.

Though now partly in ruins, the temple at Konarak is clearly one of the most ambitious religious structures ever constructed in India; fabled in early European maritime charts as the 'Black Pagoda', it is comparable in grandeur to Angkor Wat completed in Cambodia just a century earlier. The temple was commissioned by Narasimha while he was crown prince, after a successful military campaign at the head of his father's army. Work commenced in earnest once he ascended the throne in 1238, financed by a combination of personal wealth and booty collected during his military expedition to the south. It took almost thirteen years to build under the supervision of Sadashiva Samantaraya Mahapatra in his position as the *sutradhara* ('holder of the thread' — the creator and designer).

The Sun Temple stands on a four-metre-high platform in the centre of a large compound measuring approximately 260 by 165 metres. The plan of the temple (fig. 2) is designed on a grid; the structure consists of a pillared hall (*jagamohana*) and a sanctum (*deul*) laid out along an east–west axis on top of the platform. The hall, on the east, is about twenty-nine metres square with walls five metres thick.

Its corbelled ceiling is supported on massive iron beams, some of which are over ten metres long. The sanctum of a Hindu temple, known more generally as the 'womb-chamber' (*garbha griha*), is not intended as a congregational space — the dark, unadorned interior of the Konarak sanctum is just under ten metres square. It once contained the presiding stone image of Surya, but this image of the god, seated cross-legged in the *padmasana* pose, is now missing. Smaller sub-shrines housing secondary images of Surya are attached to the sanctum on the south, north and west. To the east stands a detached dance pavilion (*natamandir*) with the remains of a platform for musicians nearby. Featuring images of female dancers and musicians, its interior would once have been used by temple dancers to stage sacred performances as entertainment for the sun god.

The elevation of an Orissan style Hindu temple can be divided into four main zones: the platform (*pitha*), the perpendicular walls (*bada*), the superstructure (*gandi*) and the crowning elements (*mastaka*). At Konarak, the roofs of the hall and sanctum are built in different styles. The *jagamohana* hall is crowned by a pyramidal roof of the *pidha* type rising to a height of thirty-eight metres. The superstructure of the sanctum features a spire in the *rekha* style. Although most of the spire collapsed in the seventeenth century it would have soared approximately sixty-seven metres above the platform. A hollow stone vessel (*kalasha*) filled with jewels and a metal lotus finial studded with rubies originally crowned the *mastaka* section at the very top of this spire, but these precious items were plundered in the seventeenth century.

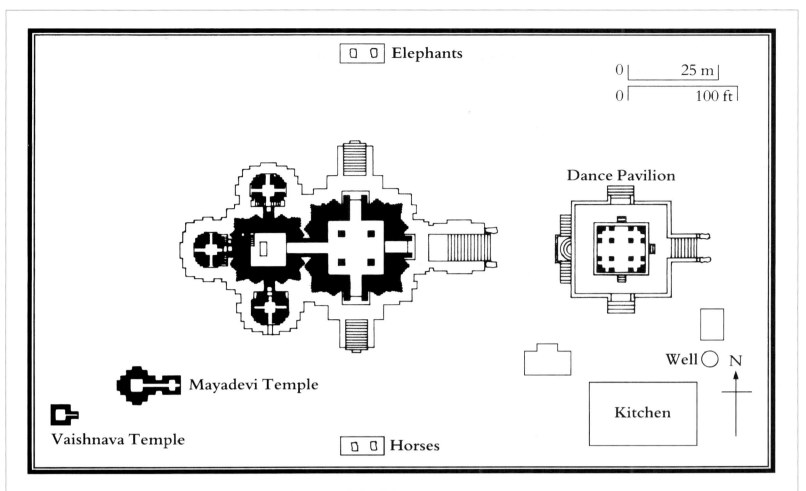

fig. 2: Plan, Sun Temple, Konarak, Or.ssa, 1238–58 (after George Michell, *Monuments of India*, Vol. I).

The placement of sculptures on and within a Hindu temple follows strict canons laid out in the same ancient Sanskrit texts that prescribe the actual form of the temple itself. Apart from the image of the presiding deity in the sanctum, other particularly auspicious sites for sculptures of various deities include niches on the exterior walls of the sanctum, the lintel of the doorway leading into the sanctum and lintels above doorways to other important halls. Virtually nothing can be classified as purely decorative. For example, the multiple images of auspicious guardians such as fertility figures, doorkeepers and mythical animals play important roles protecting the temple from evil. Among the most brilliant pieces of sculpture at the Sun Temple is a huge frieze of the nine planets that was once installed over the door to the *jagamohana* hall. A single slab of stone six metres long and over a metre high, it was lifted into place by pulleys worked by both humans and elephants. Other images include a set of monolithic free-standing stone sculptures of animal guardians and numerous erotic sculptures whose exact function remains a matter of debate. Texts refer to the existence of portable metal images, now lost, including two sculptures of Surya that would have been bathed, dressed and anointed during major ceremonies. The identities of the artists who created the majority of sculptures on and within Indian temples are unknown. However, in the case of the Sun Temple, a later text mentions a sculptor by the name of Ganga Mahapatra who was rewarded with a pair of silk cloths, two earrings and a generous amount of gold for creating an image featuring King Narasimha.[6]

1b *King Narasimha I worshipping the Puri trinity*
Sun Temple, Konarak, Orissa
Eastern Ganga period, 1238–58
stone (chloritic schist); 89.0 x 47.0 x 23.0 cm
National Museum, Delhi (50.182)

Most of the surviving Konarak sculptures featuring King Narasimha can be divided into two groups; both sets appear to have been placed in highly conspicuous locations within the Sun Temple. It has been suggested that the sculpture of Narasimha with his guru (see catalogue no. 1a) was one of a series of images originally set into niches on the exterior walls of the *jagamohana* hall. Seven more images featuring Narasimha have been assigned to niches on the exterior walls of the sanctum (*deul*), beneath a series of religious cult images.[7]

This sanctum sculpture, now in the collection of the National Museum in Delhi, shows King Narasimha worshipping a group of Hindu images within a temple, probably the Jagannatha temple at the holy city of Puri on the Bay of Bengal just to the south of Konarak.[8] This famous temple at Puri is dedicated to Krishna (one of the ten incarnations of the god Vishnu) under the name Jagannatha (Lord of the World). Its construction was commenced in 1136 at the order of Narasimha's ancestor, King Anantavarman Chodaganga, who was primarily a worshipper of the Hindu god Shiva, but as a self-described *chakravartin* (universal monarch) he also regarded himself as a partial incarnation of Vishnu. The Jagannatha cult at Puri synthesised the cults of Shiva, Vishnu and the goddess Durga, and it is these deities that Narasimha worships in this sculpture from Konarak.

Narasimha shows his respect to the deities by bowing slightly and joining his hands together. While in the image of Narasimha and his guru (no. 1a), the king is shown as a diminutive figure without royal accoutrements, here he is larger than all the other figures and wears the symbols of royalty, including a tiara-shaped 'crown' and a large sword in a scabbard. The figure in the centre holding a garland of flowers probably represents a temple priest — at a Hindu temple a priest always mediates the ritual contact between the devotee and the deity. In the lower register, a procession of priests welcomes the royal visitor. The temple itself is resplendent. The roof, reminiscent of the *pidha*-type roofs over the *jagamohana* halls at both Puri and Konarak, is crowned by an auspicious *kalasha* pot flanked by sculptures of rearing lions, with birds resting on either side. The eaves of the holy structure are decorated with garlands of jewels and fabric awnings. Hanging just above the king's head is a set of bells.

The three Puri gods stand on a pair of elaborate thrones with legs carved in the form of lions. On the far left is the goddess Durga, shown brandishing a sword in her form as the Slayer of the Buffalo Demon (see also catalogue no. 13). The severed head of the buffalo just slain lies at her feet, with a demon emerging from its neck. On the right, behind the priest, is a small *linga*. This aniconic or non-human image of the god Shiva is rich in sexual symbolism: the phallic-shaped *linga* is embedded within a circular base or *yoni*, a symbol of the female generative power. Between Durga and the *linga* is a representation of the unusual wooden image of Krishna as Jagannatha that is housed in the sanctum of the Jagannatha temple in Puri. This archaic image, similar to rough-hewn wooden 'pillar' gods that have long been popular in Orissa, is probably of aboriginal origin (a reminder that 'tribal' or aboriginal culture remains as a parallel force in India). Within the Puri temple, Jagannatha is flanked by images of his brother, Balarama, and his sister, Subhadra. These images of Jagannatha and his siblings are taken in procession each year carried in huge chariots.

In the design of the Sun Temple at Konarak, the relationship between the god, the patron and the devotee is clearly articulated. On the macrocosmic level, Narasimha constructed a temple at an auspicious site in honour of Surya, the Hindu sun god, and gave it the form of the sun god's twelve-wheeled chariot. Inside its dark womb-chamber, an image of Surya was installed as the primary focus of worship, one of the forms of which was *darshana*, the ritual exchange of glances between deity and devotee. On the microcosmic level, Narasimha inserted his own person into the cosmological symbolism of the temple through a series of sculptures set into niches on its exterior walls. In these images the king was depicted both deferring to the spiritual authority of the priesthood and offering his prayers to the forms of the Hindu deities from whom he claimed descent. Three different types of Hindu images are represented: the aniconic (Shiva in the non-human form of the *linga*); the anthropomorphic (Durga in human form as the Slayer of the Buffalo Demon); and the localised (Krishna as Jagannatha in a form unique to the temple in Puri).

2 *Seated Vishnu*

Kongunadu, Coimbatore and Salem districts, Tamil Nadu
Chola period, *c.* 950
cast bronze; 35.0 x 26.0 x 24.5 cm
Courtesy of the Trustees of the British Museum, London (OA 1967.12–15.1)

Hindu worship focuses on gods who personify cosmic forces, not on historical teachers or prophets (although some historical saints are worshipped as deities). The many gods of Hinduism reflect what can be termed a fluid polytheism. According to one tradition, Hindu gods number 330 million — and a single god (*deva*) is often worshipped under a variety of names and forms. However, most Hindus also recognise that each god is a manifestation of the same Absolute. The two most important gods, Shiva (literally, the Auspicious One) and Vishnu (the Preserver), each are generally recognised by their followers to incorporate the significant attributes of the other. The concept of the Hindu triad casts the gods Brahma, Vishnu and Shiva as the three main manifestations of the Absolute, and assigns them, respectively, the symbolic functions of creation, preservation and destruction. Hindu deities are discussed in the section *Gods and Goddesses*.

Hindu practice also accords recognition to a wide variety of related demi-gods, nature-spirits, fertility figures and guardians. As auspicious figures, they feature in the sculptural programs of temples, both independently and as attendants in the spaces surrounding individual sculptures. These types of figures, which also feature prominently in Buddhist and Jain art, are discussed in the section *Auspicious Guardians*.

The central act of Hindu art has been to give each of the many deities an individual visual form. Many of these forms have been codified in sacred texts (*shilpashastras*) but others exist without textual authority. The canons of Hindu iconography allow for variations of the form for each god, with some forms tied to a particular temple. Village and tribal deities exist outside the realm of textual Hinduism and its corpus of iconographical prescriptions and usually represent an amalgam of the local and the pan-Indian worlds.

This magnificent cast bronze image of Vishnu from the Kongu region of Tamil Nadu in south India[9] provides a fine example of the ways a sculpture of a Hindu god functions. As a *murti* (image), it serves as more than a symbol of Vishnu, or a likeness; when originally consecrated in a Hindu temple it was seen as an actual manifestation of Vishnu. Because such a *murti* is a manifestation of the god and not just a symbol, it offers worshippers a direct encounter with the deity.

Images of Hindu gods such as this Vishnu function largely through the eyes; and the opening of the god's eyes with a golden needle is the final act in the ritual consecration of the image. Because the god's first glance must fall on something auspicious, the newly-consecrated image is sometimes provided with a mirror within which it can contemplate its own perfection.[10] Here, Vishnu's eyes gaze straight ahead towards the viewer, allowing the devotee to 'take' the *darshana* (literally 'seeing' or 'auspicious sight') 'given' by the god. Apart from taking *darshana*, the devotee would also honour the image in a number of ways, sometimes in a very domestic manner clearly motivated by affection. In a Hindu temple, this bronze image of Vishnu would have been ritually bathed, clothed and adorned, as well as 'fed' and entertained with music and dance.

A Hindu image also communicates symbolically. This Vishnu has four arms which stress the supra-human qualities of the god and facilitate the expression of compound symbolic messages through hand gestures and physical attributes. In his true right upper hand he holds a *chakra* (discus), an ancient weapon that came to symbolise celestial and cosmic order; and in his true left a conch-shell, originally used as a war trumpet but later as a means of awakening a deity during worship. His lower right hand displays the gesture of charity (*varada mudra*). In Hinduism gods are not just seen as *yogis*, but also as metaphorical kings (with their temples described as palaces). Seated in the yogic posture known as *lalitasana*, with an elegantly tall crown and sumptuous jewellery, this Vishnu presents himself as a universal monarch (*chakravartin* — literally 'the turning of the wheel', usually meaning the wheel of the ruler's chariot as it moves across his territory). Through this metaphor it became common for Indian kings to relate their earthly power to Vishnu's cosmic role.[11]

The concept of the *chakravartin* is not limited to Hinduism. The historical Buddha, usually portrayed in the ascetic garb of a monk, is sometimes portrayed in the role of a divine king setting the wheel of law into motion. The later Mughal emperors, on the other hand, described themselves as the 'shadow of god on earth', (*al-zill Allah*) and adopted titles such as Shah Jahan (literally 'King of the World'), and, like their Rajput counterparts in north India, had their portraits painted with a glowing halo.

3 *The Buddha with a statue*

ancient Gandhara, Pakistan
Kushana period, 2nd–3rd century
stone (schist); 30.2 x 15.2 cm
Lent by The Metropolitan Museum of Art, New York,
Purchase, The Christian Human Foundation Gift,1987 (1987.218.9)

The sacred art of India has derived signficant inspiration from historical figures: enlightened saviours who strove to liberate their followers from the endless cycle of rebirth. During the sixth century BC, the sacrificial culture of early Hinduism and the dominance of the priestly *brahman* class over the warrior and princely *kshatriya* class was challenged by a number of preachers and philosophers. Chief among these were the Buddha (the Enlightened One) and his slightly older contemporary Mahavira (the Great Hero), the last of the twenty-four Jinas — the 'victors' or 'conquerors' revered by followers of the Jain religion. Magnificent contemplative images of these enlightened beings were later created by Indian artists in the service of Buddhism and Jainism. As Buddhism spread from India throughout Asia, the image of the Buddha in human form became one of the first truly international icons.

Unlike the sculptures installed in Hindu temples, Buddhist and Jain images are not manifestations of gods; they are symbols of the perfection of a philosophical ideal. While eye contact is exchanged with the image of a Hindu god, Buddhist and Jain images do not return the viewer's gaze. They act instead as a focus of meditation for the worshipper. Nevertheless, Buddhist and Jain images do share many common features with images of Hindu gods such as the use of symbolic gestures and attributes — but, unlike Hindu and Buddhist images, those of Jinas are never shown with more than one head or two arms.

This sculptural relief from the region of Gandhara in the north-west of the subcontinent illustrates the subtle manner in which Buddhist art blends the historical with the ideal and the iconic with the narrative. In the lower section a standing Buddha holds a sculpture in his right hand — possibly referring to the moment when the Buddha sanctioned the veneration of his image. At first, the Buddha was represented exclusively by symbols: these included the *bodhi* tree (under which he attained Enlightenment) and the *stupa* (a sacred relic mound). Five centuries after his death, images of the Buddha in human form gained popularity. Originally based on earlier sculptures of *yakshas* (nature-spirits), they came to incorporate up to thirty-two special symbols (*lakshanas*), including the distinctive *ushnisha* — a protrusion on the top of the Buddha's head that originally represented a princely hair-style or turban but later came to symbolise his superior wisdom.

Stories of the Buddha's previous lives on this earth (*jatakas*) were popular as subjects for illustration and played an important didactic role. It has been suggested that the scene depicted in this sculpture might represent the occasion when King Udayana commissioned a sandalwood image to worship during the Buddah's temporary ascent to heaven.[12] Upon his return, the Buddha is said to have approved the veneration of such images. The king is not shown, but the bearded figure at the far right holding a symbolic thunderbolt can be identified as Indra, the early Hindu king of the gods who also figures prominently in both Buddhism and Jainism. The characterisation of Indra's face and the treatment of the robes worn by all the figures point to the influence of Hellenistic art on Gandharan art of the Kushana period.

As the rationalism of early Buddhism gave way to more devotional forms of worship, new cults developed around the ideal of the *bodhisattva* (one whose essence is Enlightenment). These compassionate beings postpone indefinitely their own attainment of *nirvana* (release from the cycle of rebirth in this world) and Buddhahood in order to help others achieve this goal. Framed architecturally in the upper section of this relief is an iconic image of one such *bodhisattva*, identifiable as Maitreya, the Future Buddha, by the small water flask he holds. Seated in meditation on a stylised lotus base he faces straight ahead, unlike the Buddha below whose gaze is fixed inwards, within the narrative.

Buddhas, *bodhisattvas* and Buddhist goddesses, along with images of some of the twenty-four Jinas are discussed in the section *Enlightened Saviours*. While the initial inspiration for Buddhist and Jain art can be traced to historical individuals or events, other images represent the personification of highly theoretical ideals. Interest in the historical sphere is not limited to Buddhist and Jain art. It will also be seen, in the section *Gods and Goddesses*, that a number of historical Hindu saints became widely popular in south India during the rise of *bhakti* devotionalism between the fifth and ninth centuries. Eventually, these saints became worshipped as deities, their images an essential part of the iconography of south Indian Hindu temples. Much later on, portraits of contemporary Muslim saints were painted at the Mughal court in north India; these depictions were not objects of veneration in their own right (idol worship is prohibited by Islam) but generally part of a royal narrative. The tombs of these deceased saints became the primary object of veneration for mystical Islam in India.

4 Designed by BASAWAN (active *c*.1560–1600); painting by NAND OF GWALIOR (active *c*.1584–1596)
The Emperor Akbar on pilgrimage to Ajmer by foot
page from a manuscript of the *Akbarnama* (*The History of Akbar*)
north India, Mughal dynasty, *c*.1590
opaque watercolour and gold on paper; 38.0 x 25.0 cm
On loan from the Board of Trustees of the Victoria and Albert Museum, London (IS 2–1896–77/117)

By 1569 the Mughal emperor Akbar (the Great) was facing a major crisis. He had already ruled northern India for thirteen years, but lacked an heir. A Muslim, Akbar was a devotee of the mystical saint Shaykh Salim al-Din Chishti (1479–1572). Shaykh Salim had foretold the eventual birth of three sons, and on 30 August a son was born and named Salim in honour of the saint. Shortly after this momentous event Akbar decided to make a unique pilgrimage by foot to the tomb of the founder of the Chishti order to which Shaykh Salim belonged. The shrine of Khwaja Muin al-Din Chishti (d.1236) is located at Ajmer, adjacent to the Hindu holy city of Pushkar in Rajasthan, 350 kilometres to the west of the Mughal capital at Agra. Upon reaching Ajmer after a sixteen-day journey, Akbar went straight to the shrine and prostrated himself in front of the saint's tomb and sought his blessing. Akbar returned to Agra via Delhi on horseback, hunting deer by moonlight during the final stages of the journey.

This painting illustrating this event, from the first imperial manuscript of Abul Fazl's *Akbarnama* (*The History of Akbar*), focuses on a portrait figure of the emperor striding through the Indian landscape towards Ajmer (with two lines of Persian text to be read from right to left against the direction of the pictorial action).[13] Akbar is dressed immaculately in court robes and wears a golden sword and dagger at his waist. The red-roofed palanquin in the lower centre conceals a member of the royal harem. In the far right background (receding pictorial space is read from bottom to top in Mughal paintings), white domes represent the Chishti shrine in Ajmer; the rocky landscape is typical of the region. With the Mughal royal standards carried behind him, Akbar is depicted as the perfect symbol of royalty in action. The landscape is his stage.

This image of Akbar on pilgrimage to Ajmer is one of well over one hundred illustrations painted for the first imperial copy of the *Akbarnama*. To facilitate the timely completion of such ambitious projects, a system of workshop production was established in the Mughal atelier with up to three artists working on each illustration. An inscription at the bottom of this page gives the names of two artists: Basawan, praised by Abul Fazl as one of the four greatest painters to have worked at Akbar's court, was responsible for the overall design; while Nand of Gwalior completed the actual painting. Both artists have Hindu names. It has never been essential in India for artists to belong to the same religion as their patrons.

The painting traditions of north India constructed a richly-layered vision of kingship. The palace and the landscape, the present and the historical past, were all reconciled in activities that focused on the person of the emperor. The Muslim Mughals and the Hindu Rajputs ruled contemporary states with complex social and political connections. Sometimes they were bitter rivals. Sometimes they were allies. What the Mughals and Rajputs had in common was that they inhabited the same Indian landscape. In the section *The Royal Image*, the Mughal and Rajput approaches to giving visual form to political and spiritual goals are compared and contrasted.

Just one year after returning to Agra from his pilgrimage to Ajmer, Akbar ordered the construction of a huge new palace complex at Sikri near the establishment of Shaykh Salim who had predicted the birth of Prince Salim (the future Emperor Jahangir). Renamed Fatehpur (City of Victory), it not only commemorated military achievements but also the birth of Prince Salim. Near the new city's congregational mosque, Akbar constructed a unique '*ibadatkhana* (House of Worship) in which he debated the finer points of religion and philosophy every Friday night with Muslims, Hindus, Zoroastrians, Jews, Jains and Jesuits. At Fatehpur–Sikri, Akbar took another very unusual step for a Muslim ruler in India: on the eastern facade of his palace he commissioned the construction of a special window at which he sat each morning after praying to the sun. As the sun rose in the east, the emperor was illuminated before his subjects in a ritual described by Abul Fazl as *darshana*, the very term used for the ritual of viewing a sacred image in a Hindu temple. Not only did Akbar become a living portrait but also a visual embodiment of spiritual and political authority.

Gods and Goddesses

5 *Shiva as Nataraja (the Lord of Dance)*
Tamil Nadu
Chola period, *c.*950–1000
cast bronze; 86.0 x 48.0 x 24.5 cm
National Gallery of Australia, Canberra (1994.1409)

Around the image of a Hindu deity is woven a web of interconnecting relationships between the divine, the worshipper, the temple, the city and the landscape. An almost limitless number of gods represent the all-encompassing cosmic unity of Hinduism. They assume many different forms: gods can be peaceful or violent, young or old, male or female — a single god can even combine the two sexes. The image (*murti*) through which a deity manifests itself to the worshipper can be in human form, or it can be an aniconic or non-human symbol. The Hindu temple in which the image is installed is itself a spatial symbol of the cosmos. Laid out in the form of a *mandala* (sacred diagram), the temple is a sacred site (*tirtha*) where images, hymns, poetry and local myths combine to bring the worshipper closer to god. With a temple at its centre, the city itself could also take on the form of a cosmic *mandala*; while myths connected to the presiding deity often transform the surrounding countryside into a sacred geography with its own patterns of pilgrimage.

The image of Shiva in the form of Nataraja (the Lord of Dance) is the perfect embodiment of the cosmic ambitions of Hindu art — a unique visualisation of time and place, sound and motion. This creation was given its most expressive form by the master sculptors of south India during the reign of the imperial Cholas (850–1279). In the great temple cities of the Chola-mandalam (corresponding to the modern state of Tamil Nadu), these artists cast extraordinary bronze images of Shiva Nataraja in which apocalypse and creation are fused together in human form. Hindu philosophy proposes a cyclical rather than linear model of creation and existence: where cycles begin and end, creation is simultaneous with destruction. While Shiva is considered the god of destruction and Vishnu the god of creation within the Hindu triad of gods, worshippers of Shiva regard their deity as the lord of both destruction and creation. He must destroy the universe in order for it to be reborn.

Dating from the second half of the tenth century, this bronze sculpture of Shiva as Nataraja exemplifies the manner in which Chola artists gave visual form to this cosmic ideal. Apart from many Chola metal images, large stone versions can also be found on Chola temples connected with the patronage of Queen Sembiyan Mahadevi (active 941–1001). This sculpture represents a particular iconography of Nataraja's Dance of Bliss (*anandatandava*) which was developed early in the Chola period and perfected during the tenth century.[1] It shows how Shiva sets the cycle of creation into motion during his Dance of Bliss: starting from the top left, creation is energised by the beat of the small drum held in Shiva's upper right hand; his other right hand signals protection through the gesture of reassurance (*abhaya mudra*) with the palm facing forward; ignorance is dispelled by his right foot trampling on the dwarf Apasmara (who represents ignorance); solace is granted by the outstretched left hand pointing at the raised left leg (in the *gajahasta mudra* or elephant-hand gesture); and, finally, the destruction of the universe is assured by the flames in his upper left hand.

The image of a Hindu god is enhanced in the mind of the viewer through association with literary descriptions. Gazing at this Nataraja, for example, the devotee might recall poetic evocations of Shiva's coral-coloured body smeared with milk-white ash (poets have also described how streams of ash fly from Shiva's arms as he rotates them wildly during the Dance of Bliss). Here, Shiva has a cobra coiled around his lower left wrist (its hood is just visible to the left of the hand). A century and a half before this Chola image of Nataraja was cast, a similar image prompted the poet Ratnakara to write:

His [Shiva's] fire-fierce gaze fell on His wrists

as He danced

and the snakes there

writhed in the pain of its heat

and showed their yellow bellies —

acquiring the beauty

of golden bracelets.[2]

This solid bronze image was cast in three separate sections. Remarkably, the four-armed god and the dwarf on which he stands were cast as a single piece. Weighing almost thirty-five kilograms, it slots into a separate twelve kilogram base. The vertical lugs on either side of the base originally supported an arch in the form of a ring of flames. The representation of Shiva himself, poised on one leg with the other raised elegantly in dance, is a masterpiece of the lost-wax metal casting technique perfected by Chola artists. Sculptures cast in this way possess a beauty of form and intricate detail due in part to the method of production. The original image is created in wax, then encased in clay and fired. The firing causes the wax to evaporate, leaving a perfect void in the form of the sculpture which is then filled with molten metal through an opening in the casing. The artists who created these images usually worked within a temple complex, and important stages of their work were accompanied by the chanting of hymns and prayers.

Early Hinduism focused mainly on sacrificial rituals (*yajna*). However, as devotion (*bhakti*) became a greater motivation, worship (*puja*) became more important than sacrifice. The worship of the manifested deity prescribed by ancient texts includes 'taking' *darshana* (the 'seeing' of a god), bathing, dressing, adorning, touching, honouring and entertaining the image, as well as circumambulation (*pradakshina*) of the central shrine. The features of this Shiva's face have been worn away by the touch of devotees during worship, but the eyes have not been recut in order to facilitate eye contact during *darshana*, as so often happens with old images in south Indian temples.

Hindu rituals fall into two main categories: daily worship (*nityapuja*) and festivals (*utsava*). Daily worship of a deity is concentrated on the central immovable image (the *mula murti* or 'root image')

fig. 3: The *utsava murti* (festival image) of Shri Venkatesa Perumal, with those of the goddesses Shridevi and Bhudevi. They are emerging from the Bairagi Madam Shri Venkatesha Temple to begin a procession around the streets of Georgetown in Madras (Photo: Dick Waghorne).

in the womb-chamber or sanctum of the temple. Such images are usually sculpted from stone on a comparatively large scale. During festivals attention shifts to smaller festival images (*utsava murti*), such as this Chola Nataraja, which are usually cast in metal and housed in subsidiary shrines within the temple. These images, which can represent related deities or saints as well as the presiding deity itself, are carried around the temple in procession and out into the surrounding town on palanquins or giant wooden chariots (fig. 3). The movement of these festival images helps to unite the divine space of the temple with the secular space of the city. In a similar manner, the clockwise circumambulation of the central shrine is often extended beyond the temple to include pilgrimage to related sacred sites in the surrounding countryside.

Shiva in the form of Nataraja was the family deity of the Cholas, and many bronze images of Shiva Nataraja were commissioned during their imperial rule from the ninth to thirteenth centuries. Based in what is now the modern Indian state of Tamil Nadu, at times their political influence reached as far as Sri Lanka and Sumatra. The Chola kings endowed a number of huge stone temples dedicated to Shiva in cities such as Thanjavur, Chidambaram, Darasuram and Gangaikondacholapuram (the latter commemorating a triumphant military campaign extending to the banks of the river Ganga in north-eastern India). Most Shiva temples in this part of India from the Chola period onwards have a subsidiary shrine housing a bronze festival image of Shiva Nataraja as well as the central image in the form of a stone *linga* (see catalogue no. 8).

Chidambaram (235 kilometres south of Madras) is a particularly auspicious site because it is thought that Shiva won a victory in a forest of *tillai* trees there in a dance contest with the fierce goddess Kali. The Cholas endowed a massive temple at Chidambaram (fig. 4) in honour of Shiva Nataraja. Several Chola kings were crowned in this temple, the earliest parts of which date from the ninth century; most of the surviving temple dates from the twelfth and thirteenth centuries. The Nataraja temple, also known simply as 'The Temple' or 'Tillai' (after the trees of the forest where Shiva danced to victory over Kali) sits in the centre of Chidambaram with the town's markets reaching up to its walls. The broad avenues along which the huge wooden chariots carry sacred images during the major festivals stretch out from the temple into the city.

The Chola temples of south India are vastly more complex than a temple such as the one King Narasimha built in honour of the sun god at Konarak (see pp. 9–13). The sacred heart of the Nataraja temple at Chidambaram sits in the innermost of four enclosures; the whole compound covers approximately twenty-two hectares. Coconut groves and flower gardens predominate in the outer enclosure. Pyramidal gateways (*gopuras*) in the centre of each wall of the third enclosure soar to a height of forty-two metres and dominate the surrounding countryside. While festival images of Nataraja are usually installed in the sub-shrines of Shiva temples, at Chidambaram a cast bronze Nataraja is the central image. The sanctum in which this Nataraja is housed in the central

fig. 4: Nataraja Temple, Chidambaram, Tamil Nadu, 12th–13th century and later, with monumental temple gateway at right (Photo: Bharath Ramamrutham).

enclosure is known as the Chit Sabha or Chit Ambalam (hence the name Chidambaram). The walls of the Chit Sabha are made of wood but the roof is covered with gilded copper tiles. Within the Chit Sabha the goddess Shivakamasundari stands to the left of Nataraja. To the right is one of the five famous 'elemental' *lingas* of south India, the 'space' or *akasha linga* (the others represent earth, water, fire and wind). Known as the Chidambaram Rahasya (secret), it is simply an empty space shrouded by a curtain — a void at the centre of the cosmos.

A Shiva *linga* with a face of the god (*mukha linga*) and a pair of Shiva's sandals (*padukas*) are also kept within the Chit Sabha, but the sandals spend each night with the goddess in 'Shiva's bedroom' in the north-west of the temple compound (travelling backwards and forwards in a palanquin). A dance hall sits on an axis with the Chit Sabha in the second enclosure, while the temple's festival images are kept elsewhere in the Deva Sabha. An image of the bull Nandi, Shiva's animal 'vehicle' (*vahana*), is installed in a pavilion to the south of the Chit Sabha. Highlighting the catholicism of Hindu worship, an image of the god Vishnu also resides in a shrine within the innermost enclosure.

Chidambaram was also of special significance for the Shiva-worshipping saints (*nayanmar*) of south India. Sambandar, Appar and Sundarar, the three saints from the seventh and eighth centuries whose hymns are compiled in the *Tevaram* (the most important Shaivite text of south India) all sang eloquently about the Dance of Bliss at Chidambaram. The saint Manikkavachaka who lived in the late seventh and early eighth

century is said to have attained spiritual liberation there (see catalogue no. 11). Images of these four saints are featured in the four soaring gateways at Chidambaram: Sambandar in the south, Appar in the west, Sundarar in the north and Manikkavachaka in the east. Cast metal images of the full group of sixty-three *nayanmar* are set in a row along the north wall of the temple's second enclosure.

The benign smile seen on Nataraja's face while he performs the Dance of Bliss was an inspiration for many of the hymns composed by these saints. Other hymns mentioned his gracefully arched eyebrows and the beauty of his raised foot. A poem by Appar dedicated to 'The Temple' at Chidambaram claims that viewing the image of Nataraja is such a great pleasure that it is worth foregoing release from rebirth on this earth:

> If you could see
>
> the arch of his brow,
>
> the budding smile
>
> on lips red as the *kovvai* fruit,
>
> cool matted hair, the milk-white ash on coral skin,
>
> and the sweet golden foot
>
> raised up in dance,
>
> then even human birth on this wide earth
>
> would become a thing worth having.[3]

6 *The Hindu triad (trimurti)*
North West Frontier Province (probably Swat), Pakistan
9th century
cast bronze inlaid with silver; 13.3 x 17.2 cm
Lent by The Metropolitan Museum of Art, New York
Purchase, Edith Perry Chapman and Rogers Funds, 1980 (1980.118)

This small bronze altarpiece from the Swat Valley in northern Pakistan illustrates many of the philosophical bases of Hinduism and the conventions of Indian art. According to Hindu philosophy, all existence is derived from a cosmic Absolute which is both transcendent and immanent. All manifestations of Hindu deities are merely facets of this indefinable and neutral reality. This bronze represents a combined form of three of the most important divine manifestations of Hinduism: the four-headed Brahma on the left, Shiva on a slightly higher lotus base in the middle, and Vishnu on the right. In the Hindu triad, known as the *trimurti* (literally 'having three forms'), each god has been assigned a major function in the cosmic cycle of existence. Brahma (seldom worshipped in his own right) is the creator, Vishnu is the preserver, and Shiva is the destroyer.

Shown side by side within double halos, the three gods each have four arms with hands either holding symbolic attributes or presenting symbolic gestures. The eyes have been drilled and then inlaid with silver. The small figures of goddesses who sit on the laps of the gods are known as *shaktis* — the female personification of a male god's divine power and a form of the Great Goddess.

The gods sit upon the animals that are their vehicles (*vahana*): Brahma rides the goose (a symbol of knowledge in India), Shiva rides a bull named Nandi (the Happy One), and Vishnu rides Garuda, half bird and half man. The slightly recessed base of the altarpiece has a spout on the right to carry away offerings poured over the images during worship.

7 *Self-born linga (svayambhu linga)*
Narmada River, central India
age unknown
polished stone; height 57.0 cm
National Gallery of Australia, Canberra
Gift of Phillip Goldman, London, 1977 (1977.798)

Shiva reveals himself to his worshippers in three continuous stages of manifestation, from formless transcendency to visible matter. The unadorned phallic-shaped *linga* (literally 'sign' or 'mark') is regarded as the purest representation of the transcendent reality of Shiva (*paramashiva*). In this formless (*nishkala*) aspect of Shiva 'all beings merge at the time of dissolution, and . . . re-emerge at the time of creation'.[4]

This ovoid boulder is of a type that occurs naturally in the sacred Narmada River in central India. Considered the most auspicious

of all *lingas,* naturally occurring *svayambhu* ('self-born') *lingas* do not need to be consecrated before worship. Polished, but otherwise untouched by an artist's hand, the 'self-born' *linga* is one of the most potent of all Hindu sacred images. When installed in a Hindu temple as an aniconic representation of the god Shiva, the male *linga* is set within a circular stone base (called the *yoni* or *pitha*) which symbolises the female generative organ and female sexual energy. Combined, the *linga* and *yoni* represent Shiva and his *shakti*. The coloured stripes in this type of 'self-born' *linga* are interpreted as representing the female energy that inspires Shiva's urge to create.

8 *Five-faced linga (panchamukha linga)*
Joti, Cuddapah district, Andhra Pradesh
Vijayanagar period, *c.*16th century
stone (granite); 129.0 x 31.0 x 31.0 cm
Government Museum, Madras (2612)

Early carved *lingas* are quite obviously shaped like a phallus, but gradually the forms became less specific. As well, the purely aniconic *linga* representing Shiva in his formless transcendence was frequently transmuted by the addition to its shaft of one or more faces of the god. This type of *linga* is called a *mukha linga* (face linga) and represents an aspect of Shiva described as *sakala-nishkala* (formless with form). On the *panchamukha linga* (five-faced *linga*), four of the Shiva faces point in the cardinal directions. The fifth face is not actually represented; philosophical theory implies its presence, pointing upwards from the top of the *linga*. The four sculpted faces represent the elements — air, water, fire and earth — while the implied fifth face at the zenith represents space. The *mukha linga* is the image of Shiva most commonly installed in the sanctum of a Shiva temple.

This Shiva *linga* incorporates the Hindu triad: the square base represents Brahma, the octagonal central portion, Vishnu, and the cylindrical top part, Shiva himself. When this sixteenth century *linga* was installed in a temple, the lower square and octagonal sections would have been set into the *yoni* or *pitha* base representing female sexual power. Only the upper section with its faces representing Shiva would have been visible to the worshipper. All four heads have Shiva's vertical third eye; the *jatamukuta*, comprised of piled-up strands of hair; and the three beautifying folds of flesh (*trivali*) around the neck. The only face differentiated from the others is the face with fangs protruding from the corners of its mouth. It represents Bhairava (the Frightful), a violent manifestation of Shiva as the ascetic who dances in cremation-ground ash.[5]

9 *Sadashiva (Eternal Shiva)*
Tamil Nadu
Chola period, late 10th century
stone (granulite); 162.5 x 75.0 x 54.0 cm
Gift of Mrs John D. Rockefeller, Jr.
Courtesy Museum of Fine Art, Boston (42.120)

As the final stage in the unfolding of his cosmic reality Shiva manifests himself in human form (*sakala*). Shiva must assume form in order to act. This image of Sadashiva (Eternal Shiva) is the supreme representation of this aspect of Shiva.[6] Sadashiva's five faces are highly symbolic. As well as the five elements and Shiva's five primal *mantras* (sound formulas with sacred power), the faces also symbolise the five cosmic actions so brilliantly represented in the image of Shiva Nataraja dancing the universe around the cycle from destruction to creation and back again.

Only four of Sadashiva's five faces are actually depicted in this massive sculpture from the Chola period. As in the case of the five-faced *linga* (see catalogue no. 8), the fifth face is implied, facing upwards at the summit of the god's head. The face at the rear is not as well finished as the other three depicted.

Moving clockwise from the lower left, three of Sadashiva's hands each hold a lotus bud in the *kakata mudra* gesture, they also display the gesture of reassurance (*abhaya mudra*) and hold a rosary, while the lower hand at the right is shown in the gift-bestowing gesture (*varada mudra*).

Following Indian convention, Sadashiva is depicted as an adolescent: 'Crystal in colour and calm', according to a later religious text, 'he is a lovely, tranquil smiling sixteen-year-old'.[7] According to the Shaiva Siddhantha school of Hindu philosophy, supported by the Chola kings who ruled south India from the ninth to thirteenth centuries, Sadashiva is the visual focus for the final stages of meditation leading from the cycle of rebirth to liberation (*moksha*).[8] But in this dualistic system, the soul aims for equality with Shiva rather than union — liberated souls do not merge with the godhead, but share his bliss and wisdom.

10 *The saint Sambandar*
Tamil Nadu
Chola period, 12th century
cast bronze; height 55.9 cm
National Gallery of Australia, Canberra (1989.347)

Sambandar, who lived in the late seventh century, is one of the most important of the sixty-three south Indian saints (*nayanmar* or 'leaders') who popularised personal devotion (*bhakti*) to Shiva through music and dance. He spent his short life singing hymns while making pilgrimages to all the major Shiva temples in the Tamil Nadu region; when he was just sixteen years old he vanished into a glowing radiance created by Shiva. Sambandar's many hymns (along with those of the saints Appar and Sundarar) form a major part of the *Tevaram*, the primary scripture of Tamil Shaivism. He is also famous for having converted one of the Pandyan kings of Madurai from Jainism — a major turning point in the return of the Tamil country to Hinduism. Although Sambandar's hymns are primarily in praise of Shiva and the goddess Parvati, the last verse is often a stinging attack on Jainism and Buddhism.

Images of the sixty-three *nayanmar* are found in almost all temples dedicated to Shiva in Tamil Nadu. They are often in special shrines where they are worshipped as deities. In rarer cases they are depicted in bands of relief sculpture on the walls of Shiva temples. Sambandar is the only one worshipped as a child.[9]

This twelfth-century bronze sculpture shows the child–saint with a cup in his left hand, symbolising the milk of the goddess Parvati with which he was nourished miraculously at the age of three. Sambandar wears a necklace with tigers' claws (as a child's protective ornament) and a miniature trident, in homage to Shiva. Sambandar's right hand is shown in the *vismaya mudra*, a gesture symbolising wonderment and praise.[10]

11 *The saint Manikkavachaka*

Tamil Nadu
Chola period, 12th century
cast bronze; height 47.5 cm
National Museum, Delhi (75.353)

Manikkavachaka, who lived in the late seventh to early eighth centuries, is revered as one of the four most important Shaivite saints of south India (along with the poet–saints Sambandar, Appar and Sundarar whose hymns were compiled in the *Tevaram*). This saint was also a prime minister at the court of the Pandyan king, Varaguna.

Manikkavachaka is the author of the *Tiruvachagam* — a collection of fifty-one hymns in praise of Shiva, still recited daily by worshippers of Shiva in Tamil Nadu. His poems are highly charged with emotion and powerful imagery; in one hymn he reproaches his beloved Shiva for having forsaken him and taunts him as a 'Madman clad in wild elephant as skin and "The Mighty God gone wrong"'.[11] Manikkavachaka also sang in praise of Shiva Nataraja at the temple in Chidambaram, where he disappeared into Shiva's radiant light at the end of his life.

Manikkavachaka is depicted in this twelfth-century Chola bronze with his eyes wide open, as if staring at Shiva in wondrous bliss. His hair is arranged in an ornate halo-like circle of curls; and he wears the sacred thread, indicating his status as a member of the priestly *brahman* class, draped over his left shoulder. In his left hand Manikkavachaka holds a palm-leaf manuscript. Inscribed on its cover are the five sacred symbols of the *panchakshara mantra*: '[Om] Namah Shivaya' (Praise be to the name of Shiva).[12] His right hand is depicted in the *chin* or *vyakhyana mudra* of discourse, a gesture symbolising Manikkavachaka's role as a preacher.

12 *Mahakali, the Destroyer of Time*
Tamil Nadu
Chola period, 11th century
cast bronze; height 58.1 cm
National Gallery of Victoria, Melbourne
Felton Bequest 1975 (AS20-1975)

The Great Goddess is both the *shakti*, the personification of the male god's power, and the focus of numerous different Hindu cults. Occasionally she is referred to simply as Devi (the Goddess); at other times she is approached through more specific names and forms such as Parvati, Durga, Kali (all connected with Shiva) and Lakshmi (connected with Vishnu). Such is the power of the *shakti* that, according to one saying playing on Shiva's name, 'Shiva without his *shakti* is a corpse (*shava*)'.[13] Kali ('the Power of Time' or, more literally, 'the Dark One') stands above all other goddesses in the ferociousness of her individual powers.

Kali or Mahakali (the Great Kali) is described as being black as collyrium and notorious for her love of flesh and blood. North Indian representations of Kali emphasise her most gruesome attributes (see catalogue no. 26), but images from south India, such as this eleventh-century Chola bronze, often combine a ferocious face with a beautiful body. Kali's iconography is closely related to Shiva's: here (moving clockwise from the left) Kali's hands hold Shiva's trident, an elephant goad, a noose and a skull cup. Her flaming headdress is surmounted by a skull, a snake and a crescent moon, and the third eye in the centre of her forehead also connects her with Shiva. At the end of time it is Kali who is the active agent of destruction.

13 *Durga as the Slayer of the Buffalo Demon*
(mahishasuramardini)
South Arcot district, Tamil Nadu
Vijayanagar period, 15th–16th century
stone (granite); 117.0 x 42.0 x 34.0 cm
Government Museum, Madras (1284/59)

Durga is another fierce aspect of the Great Goddess. In one story Durga had to borrow weapons from the incapable male gods in order to rid the world of the buffalo demon, Mahisha, who threatened the cosmic order. Before the battle began, the demon exploded with rage: '… the ocean, lashed by his tail, overflowed on all sides; the clouds, pierced by his swaying horns, were broken into fragments; and mountains fell from the sky by the hundreds, cast down by the blast of his breath'.[14] Many images show Durga decapitating the buffalo, and the demon emerging in human form from the neck of the carcass (see, for example, the small image within catalogue no. 1b). Here, however, the artist has abandoned the traditional narrative to create a static icon of victory over disorder, showing the six-armed Durga standing on a buffalo head representing the slain demon. In her hands she holds some of the weapons lent to her by the other gods, such as Vishnu's discus (*chakra*). The palm of her lower right hand is raised in the gesture of reassurance (*abhaya mudra*), signalling that cosmic order has been restored.

This sculpture of Durga would have been installed in a niche on the exterior wall of a Shiva temple, following a standardised iconographic program that is still intact at many sites. According to this system, when circumambulating the temple clockwise in the ritual of *pradakshina*, the worshipper encounters a number of Shaivite images, starting with Ganesha (the elephant-headed son of Shiva and Parvati) and ending with Durga slaying the buffalo demon. A Shiva *linga* would have been installed in the sanctum of the temple to which this sculpture of Durga once belonged.

14 *Sita*

Karnataka
Vijayanagar period, 15th–16th century
cast bronze; height 68.0 cm
National Gallery of Australia, Canberra (1991.1)

The goddess Sita is the heroine of the *Ramayana*, one of the two great epics of Hindu India. In this vast Sanskrit work of 50,000 lines, Sita is married to Rama, the heir to the throne of Ayodhya and one of the ten incarnations (*avataras*) of the god Vishnu. After Rama and Sita have been exiled to the jungle for fourteen years, Sita is abducted by Ravana, the evil ruler of Lanka, who holds her captive for several years before she is rescued with the help of Hanuman and his monkey army. Because she had dwelt in the house of another man, Rama must reject Sita as his queen. Once her innocence is established, however, she is hailed as the embodiment of chastity and conjugal fidelity.

This bronze sculpture of Sita would have been commissioned as a subsidiary image for a temple during the time of the Vijayanagar empire (1336–1546), the last great Hindu kingdom in South India.[15] With broad hips, narrow waist, full breasts, a moon-shaped face and leaf-shaped eyes, this depiction of Sita embodies many of the Indian ideals of classical feminine beauty. Her right hand is shown in the 'ring' gesture of holding a flower (*kataka mudra*). It is likely that this image of Sita once would have formed part of a group of figures with Rama and his loyal brother, Lakshmana. In such groups Sita normally stands to her husband's true left, while Lakshmana stands to Rama's right.[16]

15 *Vishnu in the form of Trivikrama*
Shialdi, Dhaka district, Bangladesh
Pala period, early 12th century
stone (phyllite); height 162.5 cm
National Gallery of Australia, Canberra (1989.1365)

Recognised by his devotees as the Supreme Being, and worshipped as the preserver of *dharma* and cosmic order, Vishnu is the Hindu god most closely connected to ideals of kingship. In this four-armed image, Vishnu displays his standard attributes in the order connected with the form of Trivikrama, the solar god who crosses the sky each day with 'three great strides'. In three of his hands Vishnu holds a *chakra* (a discus-shaped weapon), a battle mace and a conch shell, while the fourth hand is shown in the gesture of charity (*varada mudra*) with a small lotus bud in its palm.[17]

Carved virtually in the round and almost standing free from the back of the stela, Vishnu is shown here as the crowned universal monarch (*chakravartin*). The god is flanked by smaller figures of Lakshmi (the goddess of prosperity, shown holding a royal flywhisk) and Sarasvati (the goddess of learning, playing a stringed musical instrument known as the *vina*). In contrast to Vishnu's rigidly upright pose, the two goddesses are shown in the sensuously curved *tribhanga* (triple-bend) pose. A small figure of the man-bird Garuda (Vishnu's *vahana* or 'vehicle') crouches below the god's feet. Various celestial figures and animals (both real and mythical) are carved in shallow relief surrounding the god. A *kirttimukha* (face of glory) is set at the top of the stela.

The stone for such sculptures was transported to Bengal by boat along the Ganges. Because Pala dynasty temples in Bengal were built of terracotta brick, there are virtually no architectural remains on which to base a contextual study of Pala sculpture; however, it is quite likely that an image of this extraordinary quality was installed inside the main sanctum of a Vishnu temple as the principal focus of worship.

16 *Vishnu's discus (chakra purusha)*
Pipariya, Satna district, Madhya Pradesh
Gupta period, *c.*510–20
sandstone; height 42.0 cm
National Museum, Delhi (78.1001)

The *chakra* or discus is one of the most popular symbols associated with Vishnu and his worship. It is an early Indian steel weapon with a hole in the middle and a sharp edge. In battle, it was twirled around the forefinger and hurled at the enemy, or flung like a deadly frisbee. From the time of the Vedas approxiately three thousand years ago, the discus was also regarded as a solar symbol. As one of Vishnu's attributes (see catalogue no. 15) it is a symbol of that god's universal dominion.

This fragment of a larger sculpture shows Vishnu's discus personifed as Sudarshana (Fair to See), who represents the infinite power of Vishnu's mind. The discus is depicted behind Sudarshana's head. The hand on top of Sudarshana's head belongs to the large image of Vishnu (to which this fragment once belonged); the god's other hand would undoubtedly have held a personified image of Vishnu's battle-mace.[18] Both the discus and the battle-mace (the latter symbolising the god's ability to impose cosmic order) were occasionally the focus of their own cults.

17 *Vishnu as Shrinivasa with consorts*
Sirupanaiyur, Thanjavur district, Tamil Nadu
Chola period, late 10th century
cast bronze; height 44.0 cm (Vishnu); 34.0 cm (Shridevi and Bhudevi)
Government Museum, Madras (28)

Some Hindu temples house an image of a god which is unique to the site. Special manifestations of Vishnu are linked with a number of major temples in south India: one of the most popular of these Vishnu manifestations is known as Shrinivasa or Shri Venkateshvara (or Venkatesha). The main image, housed in a temple in the Seven Hills of Tirumala (700 metres above Tirupati in southern Andhra Pradesh), is encrusted with jewels and coated with precious metals. Only the face is visible to devotees. This shrine was a major dynastic centre for the kings of Vijayanagar, whose final capital in the sixteenth century was just eleven kilometres away at Chandragiri.

Numerous bronze images of Shrinivasa were cast in Tamil Nadu during the Chola period. This group of three images, representing Shrinavasa and his two consorts, has been dated to the time of the great Chola queen Sembiyan Mahadevi (an active patron of

the temple arts from 941 until shortly before her death in 1006.[19]) Shrinivasa images combine three standard iconographical features connected with Vishnu (here, the discus and the conch shell in the upper hands, and the lower right hand displaying the gesture of reassurance or *abhaya mudra*) with the distinguishing feature, the lower left hand resting horizontally against the upper thigh, suggesting that 'the ocean of mundane activities (*samsara*) is only thigh deep to his devotees'.[20] Vishnu's senior wife, Shridevi or Lakshmi (the goddess of prosperity), stands to the right of the god; his second wife, Bhudevi (the earth goddess), stands on his left wearing a distinctive breastband. The sensuous stance of the goddesses in the *tribhanga* (triple-bend) pose contrasts with Vishnu's rigidly vertical stance. (For a later set of images dressed for a festival and carried on a chariot, see fig. 3).

18 *Priests worshipping Krishna as Shri Nath-ji*
Kota, Rajasthan
*c.*1840
opaque watercolour, ink, silver and gold on cotton; 188.5 cm x 144.5 cm
National Gallery of Australia, Canberra (1993.1137)

Vishnu manifests himself through ten special incarnations or *avataras* (literally 'descents'), including Rama (the hero of the epic *Ramayana*) and Krishna (the Black One). Like Vishnu himself, Krishna has become manifest in a number of special images connected with specific sites and temples. This painting represents one such image, said to have been found by the philosopher Vallabhacharya (1479–1532) on Mount Govardhan (in the Braj country around Mathura in Uttar Pradesh). Carved in deep relief on a black stone stela and popularly known as Shri Nath-ji, the image is of a childlike Krishna with his left arm raised in the gesture of holding up Mount Govardhan to shelter the cattle-herders and their families from a storm.

Between 1669 and 1671 the Shri Nath-ji image was moved to Nathdvara (Portal of the Lord) in Rajasthan, to protect it from the increasingly iconoclastic and anti-Hindu policies of the Mughal emperor Aurangzeb (a painting of Krishna lifting Mount Govardhan, commissioned by Aurangzeb's more tolerant great-grandfather, appears at catalogue no. 79). In the Nathdvara temple, which is laid out more like a palace than a traditional Hindu temple, the Shri Nath-ji image is fed, bathed, clothed and entertained as if he were a human king.[21] Painted cloths (*pichhavais*) are used extensively in these rituals, and elsewhere by devotees to recreate the temple setting.

This painting shows Shri Nath-ji dressed in a silver gown (most of the pigment is now missing) being worshipped by two priests during the autumn harvest festival known as *annakut* (mountain of food).[22] During this festival the background of the stela is always covered with an orange cloth. The *picchavai* surrounding the temple image of Shri Nath-ji has floral designs on either side (painted here in a lively dot-form).

19 *The infant Krishna floating on the cosmic ocean*
Nathdvara, Rajasthan
*c.*1840
opaque watercolour, silver and gold on paper; 30.4 x 20.4 cm
Courtesy Arthur M. Sackler Gallery, Harvard University Art Museums, Private Collection

Krishna's *lila* (divine play) in the Braj country around Mathura, which included amorous adventures with the local milkmaids, is seen as a manifestation of Vishnu's eternal *lila*. The prime example of this 'effortless effort' is Vishnu spontaneously dreaming the world into existence. As he lay asleep on the coils of the snake, Ananta, floating on the waters of the cosmic ocean, a lotus bud carrying the god Brahma sprouted forth from his navel. Brahma then created the universe.

This creation myth is transformed and elucidated in the legend of the sage Markandeya who came across Vishnu, in the form of the child Krishna, lying on a banyan leaf floating on the cosmic ocean.

The radiant Krishna was sucking his big toe in the ultimate act of divine insouciance. While addressing the startled elder, the young god alluded to his role in the cyclic nature of existence: 'I am the Primal Cosmic Man, Narayana [another name for Vishnu] . . . I am the Lord of Waters . . . I am the cycle of the year, which generates everything and again dissolves it.'[23]

In this painting from Nathdvara, the Rajasthani town sacred to Krishna in the form of Shri Nath-ji (see catalogue no. 18), the infant Krishna is depicted with golden hair and extravagant jewellery. His chartreuse-green leaf floats on a silver ocean which has become tarnished and abraded with time.

20 *The musical mode Raga Megha-Malhara*
from a manuscript of the *Ragamala* (*Garland of Ragas*)
Bundi, Rajasthan
*c.*1760
opaque watercolour and gold on paper; 27.0 x 17.0 cm
National Museum, Delhi (51.67/1)

The *raga* is an Indian musical mode, comprised of a particular series of notes. Over the centuries the main *ragas* have been classified according to the season in which they should be played and whether at day or night. They have also been personified and given visual forms through metaphors relating to both nature and the divine. The *raga* Megha-Malhara is a melody of clouds and rain favoured at night during the monsoon season (*megha* means 'cloud'). It is visualised in the form of the god Krishna (the Dark One) playing a stringed musical instrument known as the *vina*.

This representation of the *raga* Megha-Malhara was originally part of a manuscript of the *Ragamala* (*Garland of Ragas*),

illustrated in the Rajasthani state of Bundi in about 1760.[24] Nature is painted freely with raw power, while Krishna and his five consorts are depicted in the most intricate detail. The dark monsoon clouds have been built up with bold washes of blue and purple, and the snake-like lightning flashes are amplified by the brilliant gold of Krishna's costume. To the left of Krishna three of the attendants clap, dance and play a drum. A crescent moon rises in the sky, just to the left of the blue-skinned god, who has been described in related musical texts as having 'a complexion like the blue lotus and a face like the moon'.[25]

21 *The wedding of Krishna and Rukmini*
Garhwal or Kangra, Himachal Pradesh
*c.*1820
opaque watercolour and gold on paper; 35.6 x 49.6 (folio); 34.1 x 48.2 (painting)
National Gallery of Australia, Canberra (1991.1325)
Gift of Robert Skelton through the Gayer-Anderson Gift, 1954 (1991.1325)

The mythical lives of Hindu gods are commonly depicted in the context of a royal court. According to the most popular tradition, Krishna was a prince of the Yadava clan. His father, Vasudeva, smuggled him out of the palace as a child to protect him from the evil Kamsa, who had usurped the throne of Mathura from his father, King Ugrasena. Krishna later killed Kamsa, but had to to flee with the Yadavas to Dvarka (on the coast of the Arabian Sea in Gujarat) to avoid retribution. There is no text on the verso of this painting, but it probably once belonged to a vernacular work based on a section of the *Bhagavata Purana* (*The Ancient Story of Vishnu*) which tells of Krishna's marriage to Rukmini in his palace at Dvarka.[26]

Three events are set in a continuous narrative within stage-like openings in an otherwise flat picture plane typical of early nineteenth-century painting from the courts of Garhwal and Kangra (in the hills to the north-west of Delhi). At the lower right, King Ugrasena, in a light yellow robe, and Vasudeva, in mauve (identified by small labels in Devanagari script) watch a dance performance. In the chamber above, Krishna is having his hair washed and dressed, an essential pre-nuptial ritual, in the company of Ugrasena, who casts an offering in Krishna's direction, and Vasudeva. Rukmini has her hair dressed in a chamber at the lower left. In both pre-nuptial scenes, priests recite hymns from sacred texts which commence (in tiny letters), with homage to the elephant-headed god, Ganesha.

22 *Surya, the Sun God*
Orissa
Eastern Ganga period, 13th century
stone (chloritic schist); 97.0 x 51.5 x 25.8 cm
Courtesy of the Trustees of the British Museum, London (OA 1872.7-1.100)

Not all images of gods in a Hindu temple are objects of direct worship (as discussed in the introduction at pp. 7–19). Apart from the main image of the sun-god Surya in the sanctum of the great thirteenth-century temple at Konarak, for example, Surya is also depicted in other parts of the temple — including the extraordinary six-metre lintel over the eastern door of the *jagamohana* hall.

Sun worship in India stretches back at least three thousand years to the time of the Vedas. Often, as in the case of the Konarak lintel, the sun is also worshipped as Ravi, one of the nine 'planets' (*navagraha*): Ravi (the sun), Soma (the moon), Mangala (Mars), Budha (Mercury), Brihaspati (Jupiter), Shukra (Venus),

Shani (Saturn), Rahu (the ascending node of the moon) and Ketu (the descending node of the moon or a comet). The *navagrahas* protect the natural world and are worshipped at times of danger.

This image of Surya is very closely related to that of Ravi at the far left of the Konarak lintel.[27] It is one of ten related planet images from Orissa now in the collection of the British Museum.[28]

Surya is shown seated in the lotus pose (*padmasana*) in a niche surrounded by the stepped outline of a temple tower. He holds a large lotus flower in each hand. A mythical *kirttimukha* (face of glory) is incorporated at the front of his crown.

23 *Ganesha with Shakti*
probably Konarak, Orissa
Eastern Ganga period, 13th century
stone (chloritic schist); 102.0 x 59.0 x 38.0 cm
Courtesy of the Trustees of the British Museum, London (OA 1872.7-1.60)

The elephant-headed god Ganesha is the son of Shiva and his consort, the goddess Parvati, and chief of their dwarf attendants (the *ganas*). Also known as Vighneshvara or Vinayaka (the Remover of Obstacles), he is worshipped at the beginning of all ventures. After Shiva cut Ganesha's head off in a rage, Parvati pleaded to have him revived. Shiva agreed to replace Ganesha's head with that of the first creature to walk by — which happened to be an elephant.

There are very few temples devoted solely to Ganesha. In temples dedicated to other gods, his image is sometimes associated with doorways. In other cases, it is installed in its own subsidiary shrine (particularly in temples dedicated to Shiva or the goddess Durga).

At times Ganesha is shown with his *shakti* (a form of the Goddess) seated on his lap.[29] This imposing example featuring a five-headed Ganesha stela appears to have been part of the Sun Temple at Konarak.[30] Ganesha is shown seated under a *kalpa* tree in the *lalitasana* pose with his right leg hanging down from his throne. The base of the throne is supported by small figures of *ganas*. Ganesha's ten hands hold a diverse group of attributes including a pomegranate and his own broken tusk in his main front hands; and an elephant goad, a bow, a trident, a discus, a lotus flower and a noose. He is shown wearing a jewelled crown, but his belly is girded by a serpent (see catalogue no. 24). Ganesha's rat vehicle waits beneath the throne.

24 *Ganesha*
Tamil Nadu
Vijayanagar period, 15th–16th century
cast bronze; height 41.0 cm
National Gallery of Australia, Canberra (1993.1933)

The iconography of Hindu images reflects a vast array of myths and legends. Those connected with Ganesha accentuate his playful and auspicious qualities. His favourite round sweets (the one he holds in his lower left hand in this bronze is about to be plucked up by his trunk) are regarded as the seeds of the universe, offered to Ganesha by other gods and devotees; when represented within his belly they symbolise the innumerable universes of existence. He wears a snake tied around his middle because, when riding on his rat vehicle one day, the rat tripped on a snake and Ganesha tumbled to the ground. His belly was ripped open in the process,

and the sweets that spilled out had to be put back inside his belly, which was then tied up with the snake. The fragment of tusk Ganesha holds here in his lower right hand is the legacy of another incident in which he broke off one of his tusks and threw it at the moon after it laughed at him.

In this Vijayanagar-period bronze with its typically crisp modelling, Ganesha holds an elephant goad with his upper right hand and a noose with his upper left. Bronze images of Ganesha were cast in south India for use as festival images (*utsava murtis*) in temple festivals and processions.

25 *Ganesha*
Kalighat, Calcutta, Bengal
*c.*1880
watercolour and silver paint on paper; 42.5 x 27.0 cm
National Gallery of Australia, Canberra
The Gayer-Anderson Gift 1954 (1991.1317)

Pilgrims to Hindu temples often carried home images of deities. This rapidly-executed painting of Ganesha shows the elephant-headed god wearing a stylised crown of peacock feathers and accompanied by his rat vehicle. It is of a type mass-produced for pilgrims in the European watercolour medium by artisans (*patuas* or *chitrakars*) in the bazaars around the Kalighat temple in Calcutta dedicated to the goddess Kali.[31] Calcutta, which served as the colonial capital of British India from 1773–1911, derived its name from this famous temple site, which was incorporated into the city as it expanded in the nineteenth century.

The earliest Kalighat paintings date from around 1830. The Kalighat *patuas* eventually faced competition from the makers of coloured lithographs and even cheaper chromolithographs (the forerunner of the ubiquitous, multi-coloured bazaar prints of today). Earlier this century, Kalighat paintings became an important source of inspiration for Indian artists seeking a more nationalistic form of modern art.

26 *Kali*
Kalighat, Calcutta, Bengal
*c.*1880
watercolour and silver paint on paper; 44.0 x 27.5 cm
National Gallery of Australia, Canberra
The Gayer-Anderson Gift 1954 (1991.1315)

This representation of the goddess Kali belongs to the same Kalighat tradition of pilgrim images as the painting of Ganesha (see catalogue no. 25). Kali is the *shakti* or consort of the god Shiva. As a symbol of eternal time, this violent form of the great Indian goddess both gives life and destroys it. Kali is especially popular in the Indian state of West Bengal, where a famous temple was dedicated to her in 1809 at Kalighat (now a suburb of Calcutta).

The traditional *patua* artists painted the goddess with four arms, a prominent tongue and a garland of human heads around her neck. In this painting these heads have been simplified to quickly drawn semi-circles. Foreigners in India often misunderstood the positive nature of ferocious Hindu deities; at the bottom of this painting is an English inscription reading 'Black Mother or Kali — Hindoo devil'.

27 *Bhairon Deo*

Muria tribe, Bastar district, Madhya Pradesh
early 20th century
cast bell metal; 30.5 x 10.0 x 8.0 cm
National Museum, Delhi (87.647)

The aboriginal (*adivasi*) cultures of India have co-existed with newer cultures ever since the first Aryan invasions in the middle of the second millenium BC. While some aboriginal groups have become assimilated within Hindu society, others maintain their separation. Shamans usually communicate with and represent deities in aboriginal religious beliefs; images, therefore, are of lesser importance.

The Murias are a sub-group of the Gond tribe who live in the Bastar district in the far south-east of Madhya Pradesh. Their religious life focuses on three main cults: the Earth, the Clan-God, and the Village Mother. Some groups, however, also worship images of local deities who have become connected with Hindu gods (in forms not found within the canons of classical Hindu iconography).

This cast metal image is said to represent Bhairon Deo, a Muria god related to the ferocious form of Shiva known as Bhairava. The identity of the small figures on his shoulders is not known. According to one Muria tradition, Bhairon Deo was born deaf and is worshipped as a general protector — but tribal mythology is very fluid.[32] This image might be attributed to the Bison-horn Murias, during whose ritual dances men wear a special head-dress (*tallagulla*) featuring a pair of bison-horns[33]. Muria images are made by a separate group of Hindu metal casters called Ghadwas (or Gharuas) using a lost-wax technique called *dhokra*. In this technique, an image is built up on a clay core using long strips of beeswax (note the distinctive horizontal stripes on the chest of this image). This is then covered with fine clay plaster and a coarser coating of clay mixed with paddy husks. When molten metal is poured into the casing through a special channel, the wax melts and a metal image forms in its place.[34]

28 *Aiyanar on an elephant*
Thogur, Thanjavur district, Tamil Nadu
16th century
cast bronze; height 57.0 cm
Government Museum, Madras (317)

Aiyanar (the Lord) is one of the most popular village gods (*gramadevatas*) of south India. He is linked with the mainstream Hindu pantheon as the son of Shiva. Simple shrines dedicated to Aiyanar are established on the south side of rural villages, usually in association with a grove of trees and a pond (shrines dedicated to the fierce goddess Kali protect the north side of villages). Aiyanar's shrines, presided over by non-brahman priests, feature a stone image of the god and large groups of terracotta horses, up to three metres tall, standing in the open air.[35] At least two horses must be offered to Aiyanar each year, so that he can patrol the village nightly with the demon, Karuppan (the Dark One). Aiyanar is worshipped with offerings of rice, fruit and flowers, but during certain festivals blood sacrifices are carried out for Karuppan within Aiyanar's shrines.[36]

This sixteenth-century bronze image of Aiyanar riding an elephant with double tusks is extremely rare.[37] Where it was originally worshipped is uncertain — it is unlikely that a bronze of this quality was commissioned for a village shrine, but there is no evidence of Aiyanar being worshipped in major Shiva temples. Cast separately from his elephant mount, Aiyanar wears three Shaivite symbols in his hair: a snake on the left, a skull in the centre, and a crescent moon on the right. Holding a lotus flower in its trunk, the elephant is elaborately decorated with lotus medallions on the top of its head and *kirttimukhas* (faces of glory) on its fore knees. The small figure of the elephant driver behind Aiyanar holds a goad and is surrounded by a garland of skulls.

29 *The Buddha 'calling the earth to witness' his victory over Mara*

Kurkihar, Bihar
Pala period, 9th century
cast bronze; 33.0 x 16.0 x 11.0 cm
Courtesy of Patna Museum, Patna and Directorate of Museums, Government of Bihar (Arch. 9789)

The rise of Buddhism and Jainism in India in the sixth century BC was part of a widespread reaction against the sacrificial cults of early Hinduism. *Shramanas*, or wanderers, set out to find paths towards new spiritual goals; among them were the men later known as the Buddha (the Enlightened One) and Mahavira (the Great Hero and last of the twenty-four Jain saviours). These enlightened saviours from the warrior and princely *kshatriya* class were also challenging the spiritual power of the priestly *brahman* class, the custodians of the Vedic sacrificial lore.

The Buddha was born as Siddhartha Gautama in *c.*563 BC at Lumbini (the present day Rummindai in southern Nepal). The son of a local king, he was also known as Shakyamuni ('the sage of the Shakya clan'). At twenty-nine he renounced his royal privileges to adopt the life of a wandering mendicant in search of a path towards spiritual liberation. Six years later, he attained Enlightenment (*bodhi*) while seated under a *pipal* tree (the *ficus religiosa* with distinctive heart-shaped leaves) at a site now known as Bodhgaya in the north-east Indian state of Bihar. It was at this point in *c.*528 BC that Shakyamuni became a *buddha*, an 'enlightened' or 'awakened' being: 'My emancipation is assured', the Buddhist scriptures quote him as exclaiming. 'This is my last birth, There will be no more re-becoming!'[1] Shortly afterwards he began his teaching mission with the Sermon on the Turning of the Wheel of Dharma (doctrine) in which he expounded upon the Four Noble Truths and the Noble Eightfold Path leading to *nirvana* and the end of rebirth. After the Buddha died in *c.*483 BC, he entered the state of total extinction (*parinirvana*); his body was cremated and his ashes interred in eight burial mounds known as *stupas*.

There are a number of ways of seeing the Buddha. His physical body (*rupakaya*), for example, can be seen by the 'eye of flesh' (*mamsachakshu*) while the 'body' of his teachings (*dharmakaya*) can be 'seen' by the 'eye of wisdom' (*prajnachakshu*). Once the Buddha's physical body had been cremated, only his teachings remained and some devotees felt the need to make the Buddha present in their world once more by means of visualisation and other ritual practices.[2] At first they paid homage to the *stupas* in which his ashes had been interred, and they venerated other relics of the Buddha such as sets of his footprints. Then, from the first century of the present era, images of the Buddha in human form were created: the Buddha's human body, it was felt, possessed 'much magic power to lead men to Enlightenment'.[3]

This image of the contemplative Buddha can be ranked among the supreme creations of Indian art, and is one of the first truly international icons. The Buddhist image can symbolise both the Buddha himself and his teachings, as well as specific events in his life and the sites at which these events were enacted.

This ninth-century bronze sculpture, discovered in 1930 as part of the famous hoard found in the ruins of a Buddhist monastery at Kurkihar, is a magnificent example of one of the most enduring types of Buddha image. Pala kings, during whose reign this image was cast, were the guardians of most of the sacred sites of Buddhism in north-east India from the eighth century until they were overrun by Muslim invaders in the twelfth century. Here the Buddha is shown seated cross-legged on a stylised lotus incorporated within an elaborate throne. His eyes, half-closed, are focused inwards in meditation. Dressed in a simple monastic robe, the Buddha touches the ground with his right hand in the gesture of 'calling the earth to witness' (*bhumisparsha mudra*) his victory over Mara (the god of evil) just prior to attaining Enlightenment at Bodhgaya. By touching the ground the Buddha summoned the earth goddess who wrung out her wet hair and, with it, swept away Mara and his army of evil. The earliest surviving examples of this iconographic type date from the Kushana period (first to third centuries) but it was not until the sixth century that it took hold in north-eastern India. By the tenth century it was almost the exclusive form used there for representing the Buddha.[4]

In this image, the body of the Buddha bears some of the thirty-two marks (*lakshanas*) that identify him as a *mahapurusha* (Great Man). These include the *ushnisha* (a 'bump' on the top of his head that gives it the shape of a royal turban), the *urna* (a hairy mole between his eyes), and the eight-spoked wheel or *chakra* depicted on the upturned palm of his left hand and the soles of his feet. Other of these marks are blue eyes and skin the colour of gold (many such bronzes were in fact gilded).

The Buddha's elongated but unadorned earlobes are symbols of his upbringing as a prince when he wore heavy ear ornaments.

The elaborate throne back, cast separately and contrasting noticeably with the unadorned form of the Buddha, heightens the sanctity of the image. In its centre, a halo surrounded by cloud-like flames frames the Buddha's head. Right above it is a stylised animal face known as a *kirttimukha* (face of glory), from whose mouth issue forth two fronds of *pipal* leaves representing the tree under which the Buddha attained Enlightenment. The shaft rising above the *kirttimukha* would have held a circular canopy or umbrella (*chattra*), a symbol of royalty. A number of auspicious animals — both real and mythical — flank the throne and provide protection for the Buddha: recumbant elephants, rampant lions (two more lions support the base of the throne) and, on either side of the halo, a *kinnara* (a primitive sub-deity with a human head and the body of a horse). The throne's main cross-beam ends with heads of the aquatic *makara*, a mythical 'crocodile' shown with its mouth wide open.

fig. 5: Rock-cut *chaitya* hall with seated Buddha and votive *stupa*, Cave 26, Ajanta, Maharashtra, late 5th century (Photo: Antonio Martinelli).

The kneeling figure at the front right of the base, with his hands held together in a gesture of respect, presumably represents the patron who donated the image to the temple or monastery. He was a lay devotee identified in an inscription elsewhere on the sculpture as one Nagendravarman of Kanchi, a major religious centre in south India hundreds of kilometres from Kurkihar.[5]

The acquisition of merit is an important concern for Buddhists. Constructing monasteries and temples, and donating sacred images for use within them, were considered highly meritorious acts. The first great Buddhist patron of sacred architecture was the Emperor Ashoka (r.*c*.265–232 BC) of the Mauryan dynasty. Striving for the status of a *chakravartin* (the wheel-turning universal monarch said to share the thirty-two marks of a Great Man with the Buddha), Ashoka's vision of a Buddhist empire first led him to exhume the Buddha's remains from seven of the original eight *stupas* and distribute them between 84,000 new *stupas* constructed throughout the Indian subcontinent. Recalling events from the Buddha's life is also a meritorious act, and Ashoka made a pilgrimage to all thirty-two sacred sites connected with the Buddha 'to honour the places where the Blessed One lived, and mark them with signs as a favour to posterity'.[6]

The Buddhist community constructed four main types of sacred structures. The first was the *stupa* (pp. 82–83), a solid hemispherical mound which might contain bodily relics and objects used by the Buddha, or commemorate incidents in his life. The second was the monastery (pp. 50–51), where monks and wandering ascetics could retreat from the everyday world during their quest for salvation. The third, the *chaitya*, was a circular or apsidal hall set up for the worship of *stupa*, often cut into a cliff-face (fig. 5). The fourth was the Buddhist temple, which differed very little in form from Hindu and Jain temples in India. All four types of structures eventually incorporated images of the Buddha in human form within their sacred spaces along with references to earlier symbols such as the *bodhi* tree.

The *bodhi* tree at Bodhgaya (most likely a direct descendent of the original tree under which the Buddha attained Enlightenment) continues to attract pilgrims from throughout the Buddhist world. As early as the third century BC, the Emperor Ashoka is said to have constructed an elaborate stone throne platform next to the *bodhi* tree in order to commemorate this sacred site. A slightly later replacement of this throne still stands there. Adjacent to the tree rises the Mahabodhi Temple (fig. 6), almost the only monumental temple constructed of brick to survive in north India. The earliest layer of construction dates to the seventh century but the temple was extensively restored by Burmese Buddhists in the nineteenth century. The tower reaches a height of fifty-five metres and is crowned by multiple *chattras*. In the central sanctum is a large stone sculpture dating from the late tenth century showing the Buddha 'calling the earth to witness' his victory over Mara.

fig. 6: Mahabodhi Temple, Bodhgaya, Bihar, 7th century and later (Photo: Antonio Martinelli).

The function of Buddhist and Jain images is fundamentally different from those of Hinduism. A Hindu deity is all-encompassing, a cosmic presence that can manifest itself to worshippers through a sacred image. By exchanging eye-contact during the ritual of *darshana* the devotee obtains direct access to the power of the deity. The enlightened saviours of Buddhism and Jainism cannot establish a direct relationship with worshippers because they left this world forever once they had achieved mental perfection and release from the endless cycle of rebirth. After the third century, images of the Buddha generally have their eyes half-closed and focused inwards, their countenance a perfect expression of inner Enlightenment. Buddhist worshippers make offerings to these images as symbols of the Buddha's spiritual perfection and show respect by walking around them, or the sacred structures in which they are housed, in a clockwise direction. Sometimes the image transcends symbolism alone and it becomes an object energised with its own magical power (thought to be derived from the accumulated strength of the worship directed at it[7]). In viewing an image of the Buddha it is hoped to achieve a mental disposition favourable to spiritual progress and, ultimately, *nirvana.*

Buddhist philosophy continued to evolve from the time of the Buddha's death in the fifth century BC right up until the twelfth century, when most of the sacred sites of Buddhism in north India were laid waste by Muslim armies. The progression from Theravada to Mahayana and then Tantrayana or Vajrayana Buddhism gave rise to an expanded pantheon of compassionate bodhisattvas, gods and goddesses personifying philosophical concepts, and even multiple Buddhas of a purely symbolic nature. By the Pala period (eighth to twelfth century) rituals of Buddhist worship had also grown more complex and often focused on the magical powers of certain *mantras* (verbal invocations) and *mandalas* (mystical diagrams). Throughout this expansion of Buddhist imagery and practice, however, the form of the Buddha seated cross-legged in meditation and wearing a simple monastic robe never lost its power to inspire.

30 *Women worshipping the footprints of the Buddha*
Amaravati, Andhra Pradesh
Satavahana period, late 2nd century
limestone; 80.0 (image 40.0) x 81.0 x 14.0 cm
Government Museum, Madras (297)

The Buddha was represented exclusively by symbols for the first five centuries after his death in *c.*483 BC. Long after images of the Buddha in human form were created, however, symbolic representations retained their importance. The Buddha's footprints (*buddhapada*), for example, are viewed as a sign of his presence in our world; the place where the transcendent meets the earthly. In Buddhist art they represent the Buddha in narrative scenes, but also became cult-objects in their own right, equal in power to physical relics of the Buddha.

This fragmentary sculpture of four women worshipping the Buddha's footprints comes from the ruins of the great *stupa* at Amaravati in Andhra Pradesh (near the central east coast of India).

The Amaravati *stupa* is one of the greatest achievements of early Indian architecture. Construction started in the second century BC and continued in various stages until the second century AD. Mounted on a high platform, the solid dome measured forty-nine metres in diameter, and was originally covered in carved panels.[8] This sculpture is the broken base of an upright post of the stone railing, built around the *stupa* in the late second century AD to mark the path of circumambulation.[9] In this fragment the Buddha's footprints are set on a low throne. Each footprint is marked with a *chakra* symbolising the Buddhist Wheel of Doctrine.

31 *Votive stupa*
eastern India (Bihar or Bengal)
Pala period, *c.*11th century
sandstone; 97.0 x 43.0 x 43.0 cm
Courtesy of the Trustees of the British Museum, London
(OA 1880.4085)

The *stupa* is a domed mound holding Buddhist relics. Even after the first anthropomorphic images of the historical Buddha were created almost two thousand years ago, the *stupa* remained the preferred symbol for the ideal of the transcendental Buddha. During the Pala period, from the eighth to the twelfth centuries, numerous small votive stupas were added to major Buddhist sites in eastern India. They were commissioned by wealthy pilgrims as means of gaining religious merit. At least two hundred of these stone stupas survive around the Mahabodhi temple at Bodhgaya, representing only a small proportion of the original number at the site.[10]

On one side of the base of this eleventh-century votive stupa are the seven 'treasures' (*saptaratna*) that come into existence when a *chakravartin* (universal monarch) is born: from left to right are an elephant, jewel, general, wheel, minister, queen, and horse. Above, on the next level four small niches contain Buddha figures: two are of the Buddha taming an elephant; while the others show his miraculous birth and, on the opposite side, his death. The domical superstructure features four more niches with seated figures: the Buddha calling the earth to witness, two images of the compassionate bodhisattva Padmapani (the Lotus Bearer) and one of the saviouress Tara. At the very top are eight *chattras* (circular parasols or canopies) symbolising both royal prestige and the eight stages in the meditative progress of a bodhisattva travelling towards Enlightenment.

32 *Standing Buddha*
Sarnath, Uttar Pradesh
Gupta period, *c.*430–50
sandstone; 97.0 x 50.0 x 19.0 cm
National Museum, Delhi (59.527/2)

The image of the historical Buddha Shakyamuni in human form remains one of India's most enduring contributions to world art. Some forms, such as the seated Buddha 'calling the earth to witness' his victory over Mara prior to his Enlightenment at Bodhgaya, represent both an event and a sacred site (see catalogue no. 29). Standing images of the Buddha carry a more generalised message concerning the Buddhist ideal. In the Gupta empire in the fourth and fifth centuries a new type of Buddhist image emerged, in which a spiritual vision of worldly detachment prevails. With his eyes half closed in meditation, this Gupta Buddha from Sarnath represents the inner experience of Enlightenment. Originally, a halo

would have framed his head, and his true right hand would have been raised in the gesture of reassurance (*abhaya mudra*). The Buddha's thin, monastic robe is only visible at the hems. It is tied around his waist with the belt of the Sarvastivadin sect.[11]

The Buddha preached his first sermon at the deer park at Sarnath, just ten kilometres from the Hindu holy city of Varanasi, thereby setting the 'Wheel of Dharma' in motion. The site is marked by the famous Dhamekh (*dharmachakra*) *stupa*. Sarnath was one of the major centres of Gupta art; the buff coloured sandstone from nearby Chunar was the preferred medium in this period, rather than the pink Sikri sandstone favoured in Mathura.

33 *Standing Buddha*
Nagapattinam, Tamil Nadu
Chola period, 11th century
cast bronze: 73.5 x 28.0 cm
Government Museum, Madras (19)

Buddhism once had a very strong presence in south India, from where many Buddhist ideals spread to Southeast Asia. Nagapattinam, on the coast of Tamil Nadu, was a major port on the maritime trade route between the Middle East and China; it was known to the Greek geographer Ptolemy (as Nikama) and visited by Marco Polo in 1292. A cosmopolitan Buddhist community existed at Nagapattinam long after Hinduism had regained ascendancy in south India, and at least two Buddhist temples were built there under the patronage of the Shailendra kings of Sumatra.

This image of the Buddha standing on a stylised lotus is one of more than 350 Buddhist bronzes uncovered at sites in Nagapattinam since 1856.[12] It is one of the most beautiful Buddhist images to have survived in south India. The Buddha wears a monastic robe draped over both shoulders. His right hand, with webbed fingers (one of the Buddha's marks), is raised with the palm towards the viewer in the gesture of reassurance (*abhaya mudra*); his left hand displays the *kataka mudra*, symbolising the holding of a flower. The *ushnisha* in the shape of a flame is a typical south Indian feature that later became popular in Sri Lanka and Southeast Asia. There are two pairs of hooks at the sides of the base. The pair of hooks facing upwards would once have supported an elongated nimbus behind the figure of the Buddha. The two lower hooks suggest that the image was carried beyond its temple in special processions (a practice more commonly associated with Hindu festival images).

34 *Crowned Buddha*
Kurkihar, Bihar
Pala period, 11th–12th century
cast bronze with silver inlay; 66.0 x 22.0 x 17.0 cm
Courtesy of Patna Museum, Patna,
and Directorate of Museums, Government of Bihar (Arch. 9793)

The Buddha is generally depicted wearing monastic robes, with no jewellery or other outward signs of worldly power. In some instances, however, the Buddha is represented as a *chakravartin* (universal monarch) wearing a jewelled crown and necklaces. It is thought that these images are related to texts that describe the Buddha's Enlightenment as a coronation in a realm beyond time, rather than as an historical event at Bodhgaya (as represented in catalogue no. 29).[13] The crowned Buddha had a brief period of popularity towards the middle of the eleventh century in north-east India, during the Pala dynasty. Three other crowned Buddhas from Kurkihar bear inscriptions dating them to the reign of King Vigrahapala III (*c.*1058–85).[14]

This Buddha stands erect in the rigid *samabhanga* pose — the most common pose for images of *chakravartins*. He wears a crown with three triangular panels, attached at the back by ribbons that fall to the shoulders. One row of curled hair protrudes from underneath the crown. The tall nimbus behind the Buddha (cast separately), his crown and necklaces were all originally set with jewels and semi-precious stones; the whole image may once have been gilded. The Buddha's right hand is raised in the gesture of reassurance (*abhaya mudra*), and his left hand holds the hem of his diaphanous monastic robe. The nimbus is surmounted by a *kirttimukha* (face of glory) with a lotus finial that once would have supported a *chattra*, the circular parasol of royalty.

35 *Stupa gable*
ancient Gandhara, Pakistan
Kushana period, 2nd–3rd century
stone (schist); 80.6 x 40.0 cm
National Gallery of Australia, Canberra (1989.345)

During the Kushana period, many narrative scenes involving the Buddha were sculpted for inclusion on sacred Buddhist structures. In the Gandhara region around Peshawar (in the north-west of present-day Pakistan), on the trade route linking the Gangetic plain with central Asia, sculptures carved in grey schist borrowed heavily from the Greco-Roman tradition. There are no intact architectural sites in Gandhara, and most of these sculptures have now been removed to museums. This gable would have been attached to the domed superstructure of a small *stupa* within a monastery complex (the two holes in the bottom register and one near the top would have been used to attach it to the *stupa*).

The relief carving on the gable, with its profile based on early Indian wooden architecture, is a mixture of the hieratic and the narrative. The two upper registers feature two images of the Buddha seated in meditation among standing and kneeling devotees. The lower register, beneath a decorative band of Greco-Roman acanthus leaves, features a narrative scene with a standing Buddha flanked by four figures in smaller scale. It probably represents an episode in the *Dipankara Jataka*, one of the popular stories concerning the previous lives of the historical Buddha Shakyamuni. The figure to the right holding a *vajra* (stylised thunderbolt) is Vajrapani. Six small female heads peer over projecting balconies at the scene below. The inscription on the base of the gable in Kharoshti script translates 'of dharma buddha'.

36 *White dog barking at the Buddha*
Jamalgarhi, ancient Gandhara
North West Frontier Province, Pakistan
Kushana period, *c.*2nd century
stone (schist); 19.3 x 61.4 x 7.5 cm
Indian Museum, Calcutta (G34/A23292)

Relief sculptures on *stupas* and their plinths were read from right to left as the worshipper circumambulated the monument in a clockwise direction during the ritual of *pradakshina*. The various scenes, sometimes with a continuous narrative, were divided by representations of architectural elements such as columns. Even though all but one head is missing, this panel with three figures of the Buddha (identifiable by the halos behind the two missing heads) is a masterpiece of Gandharan carving. The scene on the left is an episode from the Buddha's life involving a white dog. It is first shown cowering under a table when the Buddha, at the far left, recognises the dog as the reincarnation of its owner's greedy father. The dog is also shown on top of the table barking at the Buddha.[15] The identity of the nude figure to the right of the Buddha in the centre of the panel is unknown.

This relief is from a ruined monastery at Jamalgarhi, about fifty-five kilometres to the north-east of Peshawar in Pakistan's North West Frontier Province, and less than fifteen kilometres to the east of the famous monastery at Takht-i-Bahi (pp. 50–51). The Jamalgarhi monastery had four parts: a circular court, with cells housing images around the base of a *stupa* (seven metres in diameter) adorned with seated Buddhas; a rectangular court surrounded by niches with votive *stupas* and more cells for images; residential cells for monks; and a meeting hall thirty metres to the east.[16]

37 *Great Decease of the Buddha*
(mahaparinirvana)
ancient Gandhara, Pakistan
Kushana period, *c*.2nd century
stone (schist); 22.4 x 40.4 x 8.5 cm
Indian Museum, Calcutta (2543/A23223)

The Buddha died at the age of eighty around 483 BC after he had fallen ill during one of his many journeys. His death, referred to as the *mahaparinirvana* (the great liberation from suffering), occurred in a small grove of *shala* trees near Kushinagara. Representations of this ultimate form of *nirvana*, which ended the Buddha Shakyamuni's individual existence in this world, are among the four most important images included in cycles representing the Buddha's life (with his birth, his Enlightenment, and the first sermon preached in the deer park at Sarnath).

Here the scene is framed by two columns with luxuriant pseudo-Corinthian capitals.[17] The Buddha's corpse (with a halo and larger in scale than the other figures included in the scene)

lies on a camp bed between two *shala* trees. The lightly clothed figure by the head of the bed is Vajrapani, holding a symbolic thunderbolt (*vajra*). The figure on the right with a staff over his shoulder is probably the disciple Mahakashyapa, usually depicted with a staff holding his travel kit. The figure seated in front of the bed with his back to the viewer can be identified as Subhadra, the last person to have been ordained into the Buddhist community by the Buddha himself.[18] To Subhadra's left is a water bag hanging from crossed sticks. At the very top, clasping his head in mourning, is one of the Malla princes who rushed out from Kushinagara to pay homage to the ailing Buddha.

38 *Frieze with pipal leaves*
Loriyan Tangai, ancient Gandhara
North West Frontier Province, Pakistan
Kushana period; *c.*2nd century
stone (schist); 41.0 x 22.2 cm
Indian Museum, Calcutta (5452/A23459)

Certain trees such as the *pipal* (*ficus religiosa*) and the *shala* (*Shorea robusta*) feature prominently in the narrative of the Buddha's life: Enlightenment was attained while seated under a *pipal* tree (see catalogue no. 29) and the Great Decease took place in a grove of *shala* trees (see catalogue no. 37). Other auspicious vegetal forms are used on Buddhist monuments to unite the different figural elements of the sculptural programs. Among the most commonly used are the lotus flower, either as an individual flower or attached to long stalks, and the acanthus-leaf friezes of Greco-Roman origin (all appear in the upper section of catalogue no. 35). Acanthus leaves also feature on capitals of the pseudo-Corinthian columns used to divide narrative scenes (see catalogue no. 37).

In this small fragment from a ruined monastery at Loriyan Tangai, the sacred *pipal* tree plays a more decorative role, its distinctive heart-shaped leaves grouped together within circles of swirling tendrils. Whether used vertically, perhaps as part of a doorjamb, or horizontally around the base of a structure, the auspicious nature of these leaves would have been immediately apparent to any Buddhist worshipper. Loriyan Tangai is in the most northern part of the Peshawar Valley, near one of the passes leading up into the Swat Valley.

39 *Panel from a stupa with auspicious symbols*
Nagarjunakonda, Andhra Pradesh
Ikshvaku period, 3rd century
limestone; 123.0 x 78.0 x 12.0 cm
National Museum, Delhi (50.20)

Buddhist *stupas* were decorated with numerous auspicious symbols. This limestone panel was once part of a frieze running around the domical superstructure of a *stupa* at Nagarjunakonda, above a band of individual narrative friezes. Based on the evidence of representations of similar stupas found at Amaravati, about 120 kilometres to the east (see catalogue no. 30), there were usually lotuses and clusters of garlands depicted further up on the dome and, at the summit, a mast with symbolic umbrellas.[19]

This fragment from Nagarjunakonda starts at the bottom with a band of running leonine animals, and then continues with *triratna* symbols representing the 'Three Jewels' of Buddhism: the Buddha (the teacher), the *dharma* (the doctrine), and the *sangha* (the monastic order). Next follow bands of *stupas* and *purnaghatas*,

'urns of plenty', filled with lotuses, symbolising fertility and wealth. Finally, a heavy garland is carried, with considerable effort, by human figures. At the centre is a *dharmachakra*, representing the 'wheel' of the Buddhist doctrine.

Nagarjunakonda was the capital of the Ikshvaku dynasty in the third and fourth centuries. In its ruins are numerous Buddhist monasteries, with residential halls and large *stupas* covered with limestone panels or plaster. Most of these now lie under a lake formed by a new dam. The Ikshvakus succeeded the Satavahana kings, during whose reign many of the stupas at Amaravati were built. Nagarjunakonda contains the last major examples of Buddhist architecture in south India.

40 *Bodhisattva*

ancient Gandhara, Pakistan
Kushana period, late 2nd century
stone (schist); 109.5 x 36.0 x 17.5 cm
Helen and Alice Colburn Fund.
Courtesy Museum of Fine Arts, Boston (37.99)

Theravada Buddhism, representing the earliest system of Buddhist thought and monastic practice, was gradually supplanted in India by another system known as Mahayana (the Great Vehicle). Mahayana Buddhism promoted the possibility of achieving *nirvana* in this lifetime with the help of compassionate beings known as bodhisattvas (those whose essence is Enlightenment). Bodhisattvas, who are capable of achieving Enlightenment but delay their attainment of Buddhahood in order to assist other beings, act as both a model of Buddhist action and as a source of compassionate assistance. The historical Shakyamuni Buddha (the main focus of Theravada Buddhism) is regarded as having been a bodhisattva prior to his attaining Enlightenment at Bodhgaya, but no other bodhisattva is based on an historical person.

In contrast to the Buddha who wears nothing but monastic robes (see catalogue nos 32 and 33), bodhisattvas are usually depicted as princes, with elaborate robes and fine jewellery. Early images of bodhisattvas show them to be men of action as well as idealised representations of compassion. The halo (now broken) behind this Gandharan image of a bodhisattva highlights its exalted status. The heavy drapery of his double robe shows clearly the Gandharan interest in Greco-Roman models. His jewellery includes a bulky necklace with figures of two cherubs, and a diagonal chain with amulets. The projecting right hand was evidently carved separately and slotted into the groove in his arm. Because the sculpture is now without hands (and, therefore, gestures and attributes), it is not possible to identify which bodhisattva this image represents. On the front of the base is a scene showing four monks worshipping what appears to be a *stupa*.

41 *Figure of a bodhisattva*
Mathura, Uttar Pradesh
Kushana period, 2nd century
sandstone; 86.5 x 32.0 x 19.0 cm
National Gallery of Victoria, Melbourne
Purchased through the
Art Foundation of Victoria and with assistance of
Hari N. Harilela OBE, Fellow, and Mrs Padma Harilela,
and Brenmoss Investment Pty Ltd, Fellow 1982 (AS28.1982)

The dramatic difference between this Kushana bodhisattva from Mathura and the previous example (see catalogue no. 40) from Gandhara show how style played a secondary role to meaning in early Indian art. Not only did two different styles flourish at these two urban poles of the Kushana empire, but there were also different conceptions of the bodhisattva at these two centres. In Gandhara, these compassionate saviours were conceived as separate objects in their own right; in Mathura, bodhisattvas were often depicted as attendants on either side of images of the Buddha. These attendants stand in the *tribhanga*, or triple-bend pose, while the Buddha is depicted as either standing rigidly or seated.

Though missing its head and arms, this sensuous figure sculpted from the typical mottled pink sandstone of the Mathura region can be identified as a bodhisattva (but not enough of it remains to conclude which one).[20] Originally, it probably flanked an image of the Buddha. The missing right hand was probably raised up to the shoulder, holding a flywhisk (a symbol of both royalty and compassion). It was thought that giving sacred images of this type to a Buddhist establishment would result in the accumulation of religious merit, and many Kushana-period Buddhist images in Mathura have inscriptions naming their donors. Some were Buddhist monks or nuns, while other donors were lay devotees. As an example of the spirit of Mahayana Buddhism, an inscription on a sculpture to a Buddhist establishment (donated a couple of centuries later) includes the wish that 'Whatever merit may accrue from this [gift], let it be for the attainment of supreme knowledge by all sentient beings.'[21]

42 *The bodhisattva Avalokiteshvara*
north-west India
*c.*700
cast bronze inlaid with silver; height 50.0 cm
National Gallery of Australia, Canberra (1978.532)

As the philosophy of Mahayana Buddhism developed in its complexity, sculptures of bodhisattvas were created in many new forms. This exceedingly rare twelve-armed bronze is one of the earliest multi-armed figures known of the bodhisattva Avalokiteshvara (the Lord who Looks Down [with Compassion]).[22] He is depicted in the guise of a wandering ascetic, rather than as a prince, and is devoid of any jewellery, with his hair gathered up into a knot. His twelve hands display his various qualities in either symbolic form, such as the lotus (representing his compassion), or in gestures (*mudra*), such as those of reassurance and charity. Cast in one piece by the lost-wax method, this is a masterpiece of the Indian metalworker's art.

From top to bottom, the bodhisattva's left hands hold a manuscript, display the forefinger and thumb touching (perhaps originally holding a noose), hold a fruit, an unidentifiable stem, an ascetic's water pot, and the stem of a lotus flower. Also from top to bottom, his right hands display the gesture of adoration (with a distinctive web between thumb and forefinger), flames between the four fingers (a unique feature of uncertain meaning), the gesture of reassurance, the thumb and forefinger arching towards each other (probably once holding a small necklace), the gesture of charity and, finally, the same gesture with a jewel in the palm of the hand. The small image of a seated Buddha 'calling the earth to witness' on the top of the bodhisattva's forehead could represent the Conqueror Buddhas Akshobhya or Amitabha (see catalogue no. 43). Avalokiteshvara's eyes are inlaid with silver.

43 *Akshobhya Buddha in lotus mandala*
eastern India (Bihar or Bengal)
Pala period, 12th century
cast bronze with silver and copper inlay and traces of gilding; 21.5 x 14.5 x 14.5 cm
Courtesy of the Trustees of the British Museum, London (OA 1982.8-4.1)

Out of Mahayana Buddhism emerged a more esoteric system known as Vajrayana Buddhism (the Vehicle of the Thunderbolt). This new system was based on a greatly expanded repertoire of complex sacred rituals, many involving the use of the *vajra*, a stylised thunderbolt symbolising the Absolute. In Vajrayana Buddhism, the primacy of the historical Buddha gave way to conceptions of a more transcendent and timeless Buddhahood. According to this splendidly visualised system, five 'conqueror' or Jina Buddhas emerge from the meditations of the Supreme Buddha Vajrasattva (the Being of the Thunderbolt). In the centre of this cosmic *mandala* of Buddhas sits Vairochana (the Resplendent), surrounded by Akshobhya (the Imperturbable) in the east, Ratnasambhava (the Jewel-Born) in the south, Amitabha (Boundless Light) in the west, and Amoghasiddhi (Infallible Success) in the north.

This remarkable eleventh-century bronze, once used in a temple as an aid for meditation, represents a *mandala* focused on Akshobhya Buddha. It is constructed in the form of a lotus bud supported underneath by celestial deities, some of whom remain seated in meditation while others dance among swirling tendrils. When the eight lotus petals are opened they reveal an image of Akshobhya Buddha 'calling the earth to witness' (the only other figure to use this gesture is Shakyamuni Buddha) and wearing an unusual headdress inlaid with copper and silver. Akshobhya's *vajra* lies in front of him. On the inner surface of each of the lotus petals is a crowned and jewelled bodhisattva. An inscription on the base records a dedication by a Buddhist layman named Dantanaga.[23]

44 *Tara, the Saviouress*
Kurkihar, Bihar
Pala period, mid-9th century
cast bronze; 32.0 x 22.0 x 15.0 cm
Courtesy of Patna Museum, Patna, and Directorate of Museums, Government of Bihar (Arch. 9795)

The goddess Tara (the Saviouress) is said to have been born out of a lake formed by a tear fallen from the eye of the bodhisattva Avalokiteshvara. A female counterpart of a bodhisattva, Tara manifests herself in a number of forms differentiated by colour. This magnificent bronze represents Green Tara (*shyama tara*), the *shakti* or female companion of Amoghasiddhi, one of the five Conqueror Buddhas. Images of Tara date back to at least the fifth century and can be connected not only with the rise of Mahayana Buddhism but also with the popularity of the Hindu Great Goddess.[24] In Vajrayana Buddhism, worshippers aim to transform themselves literally into the object of their meditation.[25] Images of deities personifying qualities such as compassion or wisdom serve as the visual focus for this practice.

This ninth-century image shows Tara seated in a decidedly languid version of the *lalitasana* pose. Her right foot is supported by a lotus flower, which grows from underneath the throne. Cast separately from the rest of the sculpture, the throne's back incorporates a large, flame-fringed halo behind Tara's head; this halo originally would have been surmounted by a *kirttimukha* face and a *chattra*. Tara's eyes and the *tilaka* mark in the middle of her forehead are inlaid with silver. Her right hand displays the gesture of charity (*varada mudra*), while her left hand holds a lotus flower, described as blue in iconographic texts. The lion-throne is almost identical to the one on which the Buddha sits in another Kurkihar bronze discussed previously (see catalogue no 29).

45 *Prajnaparamita, the Goddess of Wisdom*
Orissa
Eastern Ganga period, 12th century
stone; height 60.0 cm
National Gallery of Australia, Canberra (1990.531)

Wisdom (*prajna*) is seen by all Buddhists as one of the supreme virtues. The Buddhist scripture known as the *Prajnaparamita Sutra* (the Sutra of the Perfection of Wisdom) came to be personified by a goddess with the same name. Like the saviouress Tara, Prajnaparamita is extremely popular in both the Mahayana and the later Vajrayana traditions of Buddhism. According to a related text, 'Perfect Wisdom spreads her radiance . . . She brings light to the blind . . . she is the mother of bodhisattvas . . . the Perfect Wisdom of the Buddhas, she turns the Wheel of Law.'[26]

Images of Buddhist goddesses were an essential part of the sculptural programs of later Buddhist temples. This carved stone stela from a temple niche features an image of Prajnaparamita seated on a lotus throne, with her two upper hands in the preaching gesture (*dharmachakra mudra*).[27] The lower right hand points downward in the gesture of charity (*varada mudra*), while the missing fourth hand presumably would have held the stalk of the lotus (rising to the right of the goddess). Within the flower is a small palm-leaf manuscript representing the *Prajaparamita Sutra*. The goddess is surrounded by attendant sub-deities, including garland-bearing *vidyadharas* in the top corners. Directly above the cut-out back of the throne, and fringed with bands of jewels and stylised flames, is a *kirttimukha* exhaling scrolls of vapour. At the bottom is a frieze depicting devotees and an array of ritual utensils and offerings.

46 *Marichi, the Goddess of Dawn*
Bihar
Pala period, 11th century
stone; 55.4 x 28.3 x 12.9 cm
Indian Museum, Calcutta (4614/A25192)

In Vajrayana Buddhism, human emotions and natural powers are personified and given visual form. Marichi (literally 'shining' or 'ray of light') is the Buddhist goddess of dawn. Worshipped at sunrise, she symbolises the power of the sun and rides through the heavens on a chariot drawn by seven pigs (the exact symbolism of which is unknown).[28] Marichi is considered to be an emanation of the Conqueror Buddha Vairochana, whose small, seated figure appears at the very top of this stela. She is also regarded as a manifestation of Tara.[29]

This eight-armed image of Marichi would have been installed in a wall niche in a Buddhist temple, probably connected spatially with an image of Vairochana Buddha. Marichi is shown crowned and has three faces. According to Vajrayana iconography, the principal face radiates passionate love; the left, a sow's face, displays terrible wrath; while the third face is peaceful in disposition.[30] Her body is carved almost free from the back of the stela, joined only at her shoulders, hands and feet. Against a background of flames, Marichi is depicted in an aggressive stance known as *pratyalidha*, based on a position used when shooting with bow and arrow. Her two lower hands hold a needle and thread with which she sews up the mouths and eyes of the wicked. Marichi is surrounded by four miniature sow-faced attendants in the same *pratyalidha* stance. Her female charioteer sits between her feet astride Rahu, the god of the solar eclipse. The seven pigs that her pull her chariot are depicted at the base.

47 *Altarpiece with the twenty-four Jinas (chaubisi)*
Gujarat
Sultanate period, 15th century
cast bronze; 35.7 x 24.0 x 11.0 cm
National Museum, Delhi (47.109/171)

Like Buddhism, Jainism was part of an ascetic tradition that developed in India in the middle of the first millennium BC in opposition to the sacrificial rituals of early Hinduism. Twenty-four Jinas ('conquerors' or 'liberators'), also known as Tirthankaras ('forders'), are revered by Jains. The final two of the twenty-four are historical figures. Vardhamana Mahavira (*c.*599–527), the twenty-fourth Jina and a contemporary of the Buddha, taught that an austere path of ascetic practices must be followed to gain liberation for the soul from the continuing cycle of rebirths. Because they have attained complete liberation and no longer have material bodies, the Jinas are actually powerless to help their followers; Jain images serve instead as a focus for meditation, by reminding the worshipper of the qualities required to achieve liberation.

This altarpiece, known as a *chaturvimshati patta* (twenty-four figure plaque) or, in more vernacular forms, *chovisi* or *chaubisi*, represents all twenty-four of the Jinas in the symmetrical and literal manner typical of Jain art. Among the eight essential 'chief attendants' (*ashta-maha-pratiharyas*) included here are the three-tiered umbrella under which the central Jina is seated (representing spiritual sovereignty), his lion-throne, the radiating halo behind his head and the *dharmachakra* wheel below the throne (here, flanked by tiny deer). Most Jinas are depicted in an identical manner, but can often be identified by their accompanying emblems. The central figure here, cast separately from the rest of the altarpiece, might be identified as the second Jina, Ajitanatha (the Invincible), on the basis of the small elephant heads under the throne.[31] He is surrounded by twenty-three other Jinas, one standing on either side of him, the others seated in rows to the sides and above.

48 *Standing Jina*
Karnataka
11th–12th century
cast bronze; 45.0 x 14.5 x 3.3 cm
Courtesy of the Trustees of the British Museum, London
(OA 82.10-10.26)

The Jain religion is divided into two main sects. The Shvetambaras (White Clad) were confined to north India but the Digambaras (Sky Clad) established a strong presence both there and in the south. The Digambaras were the more austere of the two sects and, as their name suggests so poetically, did not even sanction the wearing of clothes (except by nuns). In south Indian images, the Jinas are always shown nude, as was the Jain saint Bahubali, the subject of the famous eighteen-metre high monolithic sculpture at Sravana Belgola in Karnataka (dating from 948.)

Jain texts stipulate that Jinas should be depicted as young men with long arms stretching to the knees, calm countenances and, like the Buddha, with long earlobes and hair arranged in tight rings. While the eyes are depicted open, the gaze is directed inwards — a Jina image does not return the gaze of its devotees. Apart from the fact that this bronze image of a nude Jina was obviously cast for a Digambara patron, it is not possible to identify which Jina it represents.[32] He stands in the unique Jain meditative posture of body-abandonment known as *kayotsarga*.

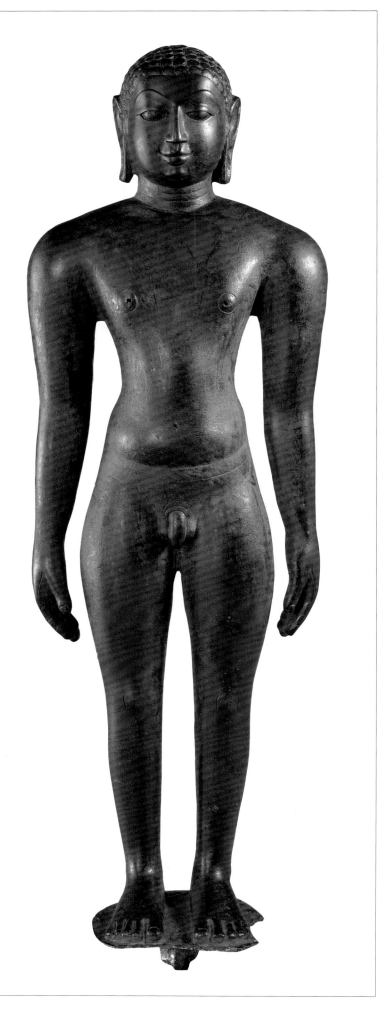

49 *Neminatha, the twenty-second Jina*
Narhad, Pilani district, Rajasthan
Chahamana period, 12th century
stone (basalt); 119.0 x 37.0 x 22.0 cm
National Museum, Delhi (69.132)

Most Jinas are depicted in an identical manner, but often the presence of the Jina's special emblems within the image allows it to be identified. This image of a Jina standing in the body-abandonment posture of *kayotsarga* can be identified as Neminatha, the twenty-second of the twenty-four Jinas, by the presence of his conch-shell emblem at the centre of the base. According to Jain tradition, Neminatha was a cousin of the Hindu god Krishna.

This clothed image of Neminatha would have been commissioned for a Shvetambara Jain temple at a time in the twelfth century when Jainism was at its peak in Gujarat and Rajasthan in western India. In 1192, however, the Chahamana Rajput king, Prithviraja III, was defeated and killed near Delhi by Muhammad Ghuri, who had invaded India from the north-west. Four centuries of struggle were to ensue between the Rajputs of what is now known as Rajasthan and the various Muslim rulers of Delhi.

Although it is carved to be almost freestanding, this magnificently polished image of Neminatha with the auspicious *shrivatsa* symbol on his chest was conceived to be seen from the front only — the back of the sculpture is quite roughly finished. There is a wealth of fine detail, such as the bifurcated lips, the whorls within the nipples and the decorative border of the Jina's fine cloth wrap. Most spectacular are the gracefully attenuated fingers. Two flywhisk bearers (among the eight chief attendants of a Jina) stand by Neminatha's legs, along with smaller figures of the donor and his wife kneeling in reverence.

50 *Neminatha, the twenty-second Jina*
Dilwara, Mount Abu, Rajasthan
Solanki period, 1160
stone (marble); 58.5 x 48.5 x 24.0 cm
The Jina Collection, Courtesy of the Arthur M. Sackler Gallery,
Smithsonian Institution, Washington D.C. (LTS 1991.31)

White marble was available for sculpture only in western India. In this comparatively rare example, the twenty-second Jina Neminatha is shown seated in the lotus position (*padmasana*) with his hands in the gesture of meditation (*dhyana mudra*). This image of Neminatha probably would have had larger enamel eyes attached to it when under worship in a temple. Although the actual Jina is not present in the stone image, worshippers imagine themselves to be in the presence of the preaching Jina who can witness their spiritual progress.[33] The slight vertical extension of Neminatha's head is probably related to the Buddha's *ushnisha,* and the small strip of cloth emerging from between his legs indicates that the Jina is clothed.

The almost illegible inscription on the front of the elaborate cushion gives the date 1160 and (1217 Samvat). Stylistically, this image can be related to those found at Dilwara on the thousand-metre high Abu Plateau in southern Rajasthan.[34] This site is famous for its white marble temples, especially those dedicated to the Jinas Adinatha (in 1032) and Neminatha (in 1230), in which ornate decoration contrasts so strikingly with the purity of representations of the Jinas' bodies. Although the goals of worship differ, the general form of a Jain temple is based on that of Hindu temples: a dark sanctum houses the principal image of the presiding Jina. This inner sanctum is surrounded by a cloistered corridor with sub-shrines for all twenty-four Jinas and fronted by a number of halls, both open and closed. The Dilwara temples were intended as replicas of a celestial assembly hall (*samavasarana*). They feature heavily carved columns and profusely decorated corbelled domes.

51 *Head of a Jain image*
Aluara, Dhanbad district, Bihar
Pala period, 12th century
cast bronze; height 14.5 cm
Courtesy of Patna Museum, Patna, and Directorate of Museums, Government of Bihar (Arch. 10698)

This small but brilliantly stylised bronze head with curvilinear eyelids was part of a hoard of bronzes recovered in a field at Aluara in 1947. Most of the twenty-nine bronzes, all of which are now in the collection of the Patna Museum, represent Jain subjects. This image has been published as a head of a Tirthankara (another name for a Jina),[35] but there are some unusual elements in its iconography, such as the *urna*-like mark on the forehead. It is actually cast in the form of a mask rather than a head.

It would appear to have been attached to a larger image originally, but there are no holes for rivets or any other device that may have secured it to another object.[36] The cross hatching depicting the hair is also unusual.

Aluara (also referred to as Machuatand Aluara) is a relatively minor site near Chandankiyari in the Dhanbad district, near the border of Bihar and West Bengal. This region was an important centre of Jainism in the medieval period.[37]

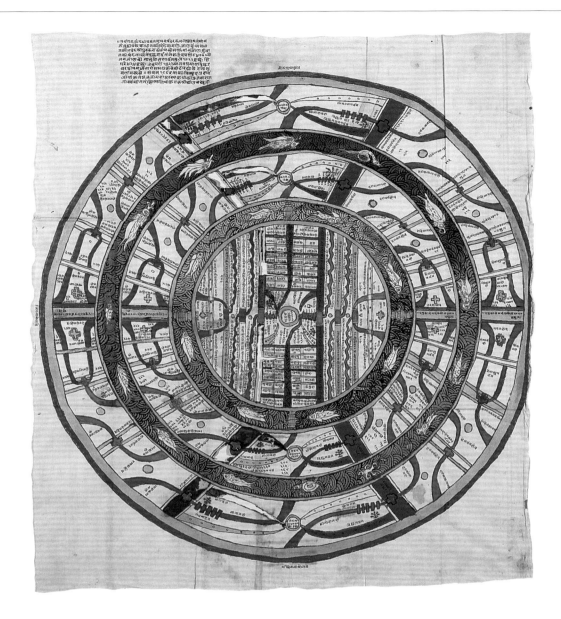

52 *The world of mortals (manushyaloka)*
western India (Gujarat or Rajasthan)
18th century
opaque watercolour on cotton; 72.5 x 84.0 cm
Collection of Michael and Mary Abbott, Adelaide

According to Jain cosmography, the universe is comprised of three ascending worlds. The lowest is the realm of the damned. The upper world (*urdhva-loka*) is the paradise of celestials, where Liberated Souls (*siddhas*) reside on its border with the non-world (*a-loka*). Lying in between is our world, the smallest of the three, known as *manushyaloka* (the world of mortals). It is into this world that the twenty-four Jinas were born, and it is only here that mortals may obtain liberation. Depicted as a flat disk in the form of a *mandala*, the world of mortals is comprised of continents and oceans surrounded by diamond ramparts and fences of jewels.

The circular land mass at the centre of the world of mortals is known as the Continent of the Wood-apple Tree (*jambudvipa*).

At its centre stands Mont Meru or Mandara, the *axis mundi* of the Indian universe, to which are joined two pairs of curved mountain ranges. The seven lands within this mighty continent are watered by great rivers, and divided by the mountain ranges running from east to west. Beyond lie two ring-like continents separated by circular oceans, the Sea of Salt (*lavanasamudra*) and the Black Sea (*kalodadhi*), here filled with fish and other aquatic animals. The two continents contain numerous streams and fragments of text. The outer Lotus Continent (*pushkaradvipa*) ends at a range of mountains known simply as 'Beyond Humankind' (*manushottara*), represented here by a simple yellow and red band.

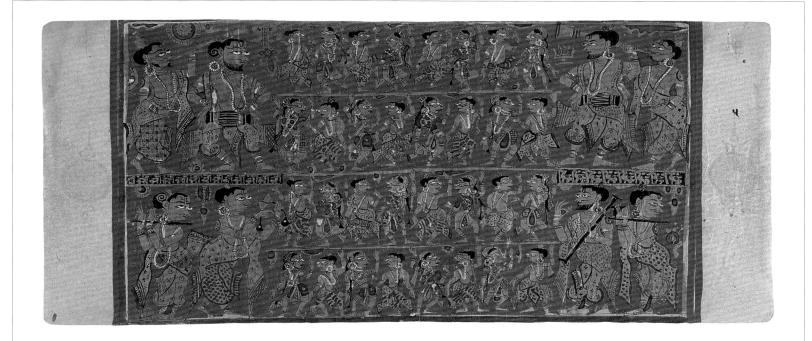

53 *Entertainment at Indra's Court*
western India (Gujarat or Rajasthan)
Sultanate period, 15th century
opaque watercolour and gold on paper; 11.5 x 27.0 cm
National Gallery of Australia, Canberra (1993.753)

Jain texts were produced in large numbers to ensure the preservation and dissemination of sacred knowledge; kings and wealthy laypersons commissioned manuscripts for temple libraries in order to gain religious merit. Sacred manuscripts also became objects of veneration in their own right. During ceremonial recitations from copies of the *Kalpasutra* (*The Book of Ritual*), pages with painted images were held up to the congregation for holy viewing or *darshana*.[38]

The earliest surviving Jain texts are on thin palm-leaf folios. When paper became the common medium in the mid-fourteenth century the horizontal format was retained. The most frequently illustrated Jain texts were the *Kalpasutra* and the *Kalakacharyakatha* (*The Story of the Monk Kalaka*), the latter text often added as an appendix to the former.

This comparatively rare full-page image presumably is from a combined manuscript of the *Kalpasutra* and *Kalakacharyakatha* (there are eight lines of text in large script on the verso alternating with lines in a smaller script). It is painted in the Western Indian style, distinguished by a linear treatment of forms (especially in depiction of clothes and textiles) with virtually no tonal modelling, and an almost universal preference for three-quarter profile. Most distinctively, the far eye is depicted as projecting beyond the face. This scene represents an entertainment at the celestial court of Indra, the Vedic and early Hindu king of the gods who also plays an important role in Jainism.[39] Two pairs of male musicians frame each side of the folio. Between them are four bands of smaller male and female dancers, their angular figures shimmering and vibrating against the opulent red background.

54a-b *Two Jinas*
two pages from a manuscript of the *Kalpasutra (The Book of Ritual)*
Jaunpur, Uttar Pradesh
Sultanate period, *c.*1465
paint, ink and gold on paper; 11.4 x 29.2 cm (each folio)
National Gallery of Australia, Canberra (1993.735 and 1993.736)

The first part of the *Kalpasutra* (*The Book of Ritual*) describes the lives of the twenty-four Jinas. Their biographies follow a similar pattern from birth to renunciation to final salvation as liberated souls. These two pages are from a manuscript of the *Kalpasutra* produced around 1465 in Jaunpur, the capital of an Islamic state of the same name just to the north of Varanasi.[40] Jaunpur became independent in the wake of Timur's conquest of Delhi in 1398, and was then ruled by the Sharqi (Eastern) sultans until about 1476. The text in this manuscript is written in gold ink on a crimson red ground with seven lines continuing on the verso of each page. The red circle in the centre of each page mimics the holes cut for the ties that bind palm-leaf manuscripts (pages of these paper manuscripts were still turned up and over rather than from side to side). The vegetal arabesques in the borders are related to contemporary Islamic manuscripts in India.

On the first page (top), a Jina is shown plucking out his hair as part of the process of renunciation. The four-armed god Indra sits on the right, ready to collect the hair in a golden vessel (only gods are shown with multiple arms in Jain art). The second page (bottom) depicts Parshvanatha, the twenty-third Jina, as a *siddha* (Liberated Soul) with his characteristic canopy of snakes. Parshvanatha was born a prince in the late ninth century BC; he took up the life of an ascetic at the age of thirty. In this illustration he is shown above a stylised representation of mountains, seated on the *siddhashila,* an open umbrella (seen sideways here) made of pure white gold that sits at the apex of the upper world (*urdhva-loka*) at the border of the non-world (*a-loka*).

55 *The monk Kalaka with the god Indra*
page from a manuscript of the *Kalakacharyakatha*
(*The Story of the Monk Kalaka*)
western India (Gujarat or Rajasthan)
Sultanate period, late 15th century
paint, ink and gold on paper; 29.9 x 11.0 cm
National Gallery of Australia, Canberra (1994.1453)

Among the many illustrated manuscripts produced for Jain patrons in fifteenth-century Gujarat, one of the most popular was the *Kalakacharyakatha*, the story of the Shvetambara monk, Kalaka. Gujarat flourished as an independent Islamic sultanate from 1401 until it was annexed by the Mughal emperor, Akbar, in 1572–73. Partly as a result of the flourishing trade passing through Gujarat, and the vast fortunes accumulated by Jain merchants, the conservative Western Indian style in which this manuscript is illustrated was energised by a burst of opulence in the mid-fifteenth century;[41] new pigments were added in painting, including ultramarine made from lapis lazuli, and there was an increased use of gold and silver.

This page displays the anonymous artist's highly innovative approach to the arrangement of text, illustration and borders (there are seven lines of text on the verso with rows of parrots in the borders). The main illustration, showing Kalaka enthroned under a jewelled canopy, is flanked by four female devotees in two vertical bands. Two Shvetambara monks are depicted in the right-hand border. The episode illustrated involves an encounter between Kalaka and the god Indra, classified as a *vyantaradevata* (peripatetic god) in the Jain tradition. Impersonating an old *brahman*, Indra had approached Kalaka to ask questions of a philosophical nature. When recognised by the monk, Indra manifested himself as the heavily-jewelled deity with a halo seen here to the right of Kalaka. The ornately decorated stand placed between them is a symbolic representation of Kalaka's absent guru.[42]

Auspicious Guardians

56 *Tree goddess (shalabhanjika)*
Karnataka
Hoysala period, *c.*1150–1200
stone (chloritic schist); 87.0 x 44.5 x 24.0 cm
National Gallery of Victoria, Melbourne, Felton Bequest 1963 (540/DS)

Artists in India have been called upon to give visual form to a vast array of demi-gods, guardians and nature spirits. Whether Hindu, Buddhist or Jain, almost all sacred places in India are protected and further sanctified by these auspicious guardians. In the Muslim sphere too, many palaces have their symbols of protection — the gateway of the palace built by the Mughal emperor Akbar at Fatehpur-Sikri in the 1570s, for example, was guarded by massive stone elephants.

Indian demi-gods are visualised in both human and animal form, or as hybrids of the human and animal worlds. They draw their power from the forces of nature, and frequently represent ancient beliefs — some Vedic, some aboriginal — that pre-date Hinduism, Buddhism and Jainism. Some are symbols of abundance and fertility, while others serve a more protective function. They all inhabit the plane between the human and the divine, between the earth and heaven. They also link the sacred spaces of man-made structures with the sacred power of natural sites.

Originally the focus of their own cults, the demi-gods of India were subsequently adopted, and their powers harnessed, to serve India's great religions. When their images were installed within sacred architecture they were not intended as the primary object of worship. Through the spontaneity of popular worship, however, their powers are still called upon, especially where matters of fertility are concerned.

Perhaps the most popular of the demi-gods is the *apsaras*, a celestial woman famed for the beauty of her dance. A descendent of the ancient *yakshi* (female nature spirit), she is frequently depicted in connection with a tree. In this form the *apsaras* is known as the tree goddess or *shalabhanjika* (literally, 'breaking a branch of a *shala* tree'). Representing both the power of nature and the Indian ideal of the sensual female form, this woman-and-tree motif is found on India's earliest Buddhist monuments as well as in later Jain and Hindu temples. The tree goddess combines earthly fertility and the generative powers of the divine. Never known by individual names, these figures stand midway between the divine and the human in the full bloom of eternal youth.

This twelfth-century stone image of a tree goddess displays all the characteristics traditionally associated with the allure of these figures. Originally from an unidentified Hindu temple in the area surrounding the city of Mysore in Karnataka, it is one of a group of four related *apsaras* images, each framed by a canopy of trees or creepers. This image is now in the collection of the National Gallery of Victoria, the other three sculptures are in the collection of the British Museum in London.[1]

The Melbourne image shows the semi-naked but heavily jewelled tree goddess standing in an accentuated *tribhanga* (triple-bend) pose. Beneath the curved canopy, and set deep within the bower, she appears to hold aside a flowering branch in order to look out. Further sculptural space is claimed with the help of the oscillating garlands that flip over her right hip and curve around her left arm and knee. Within the smooth contours of her face, the eyes and eyebrows are carved as sinuous outlines ('her eyebrow's arch is brother to Love's bow' wrote the poet Rajashekhara in another context, following a standard Indian metaphor[2]). The figure of an attendant on the lower right of the sculpture is given a more reserved pose but also stands on one foot with the heel of the other foot raised in the manner of the tree goddess.

The woman-and-tree motif is found in Indian art from at least the time of the Buddhist *stupas* at Bharhut (second century BC) and Sanchi (first century AD). It became a common theme in all Indian sacred architecture: usually installed at points of transition, these images bless the worshipper's journey to the sacred image or relic. The form of the tree goddess known as *shalabhanjika* refers to the theme of *dohada* (from the Sanskrit *daurhrida* — literally 'sickness of the heart' — referring to the longing of pregnant women for particular objects). Figuratively, *dohada* refers to the manner in which certain trees at the time of budding are thought to require the touch of a beautiful young woman's foot in order to burst into flower. In this example, the tree goddess touches the trunk of the tree with her heel as she grasps its flowering branch. Through these gestures flows a timeless transfer of fertility. In Buddhist art, the form of the tree goddess was modified in order to represent Mahamaya, the mother of the historical Buddha, holding onto a branch that lends her support at the miraculous birth of her son.

fig. 7: Keshava Temple, Somnathpur, Karnataka, 1268 (Photo: George Michell).

The Melbourne tree goddess belongs to the time of the Hoysala dynasty — their power lasted from about 1190 until 1310, when south India was invaded by the armies of the sultan of Delhi. The Hoysala kingdom was based in the area around present day Mysore; their capital, Dorasamudra, lies in ruins near the modern village of Halebid. One of the most important of the Hoysala kings was Bittideva (d.1141). Originally a Jain, he was converted to the worship of the Hindu god Vishnu in 1116 by the famous philosopher Ramanuja and was renamed Vishnudharma. He and his successors (and their queens and nobles) constructed numerous Hindu temples in the twelfth and thirteenth centuries; more than eighty survive in the Mysore region alone (fig. 7). The Hoysala temples are distinguished by the star-shape of the structure holding the sanctum and the extraordinarily elaborate carving of almost all surfaces. An unusually large amount of information survives about Hoysala sculptors and their techniques.[3] They revelled in the softness and fine texture of the chloritic schist in which the temples were constructed to produce work which has unparalleled surface detail; their practice of deep undercutting sets the main images 'afloat' above deep shadow, and smooth surfaces were often brought to a high polish. Many images bear the names of individual sculptors, although it is generally not possible to assign to them personal styles. Each temple, however, does seem to have its own style.

With its curved, three-dimensional tree canopy, the Melbourne image, for example, is quite different from the thirty-eight surviving figures at the highly ornate Chennakeshava Temple in Belur, dedicated to Vishnu by King Vishnudharma in 1117. In the Belur sculptures the foliage above the tree goddesses is more two dimensional, almost lacelike. The Hoysaleshvara Temple, built in honour of Shiva at the Hoysala capital between c.1121–1160, has three remaining tree goddess images that are closer in form but stylistically quite different.[4]

Hoysala images of tree goddesses were usually installed in temples as angled brackets at the tops of the massive lathe-turned stone columns that support the roof of the central hall, or outside the temple, under the eaves on the top of exterior pilasters (fig. 8). Images carved in chloritic schist, such as the Melbourne example, were usually installed outside (serpentinite was used for the interior bracket figures). Because the tree goddess brackets are set out at an angle of approximately forty-five degrees from the vertical, and up to four metres above the viewer, the torsos are frequently exaggerated and the legs foreshortened. These carved elements play no structural role in the temple; instead the tree goddess brackets act as a symbolic bridge between heaven and earth, the sacred and the profane.

fig. 8: Tree goddess *in situ*, Chennakeshvara Temple, Belur, Karnataka, 1117. Signed 'Dasoja'. (Photo: Kelleson Collyer).

The visualisation of demi-gods and nature spirits proceeded in tandem with the sentiments expressed in other art-forms. Sometimes the metaphors refer directly to music and dance; sometimes the poet appears to be describing a sculpture rather than a person. A verse in praise of a beautiful maiden quoted in an eleventh-century anthology of court poetry describes a 'pair of polished breasts . . . [that] seems to form a set of bellmetal cymbals raised for the holiday dance of Love, [and] trembling with bliss'.[6] In the presence of the gods in India, nothing is more auspicious than dance, music and poetry.

The sacred spaces of Hindu, Jain and Buddhist architecture are all strongly imbued with cosmic and natural symbolism. The hemispherical mound of the Buddhist *stupa*, for example, is viewed metaphorically as the dome of heaven, its surmounting mast as the universal axis, and the tiers of umbrellas (*chattras*) at the summit as the multiple layers of heaven. The tall tower of the Hindu temple, on the other hand, is regarded as the symbolic mountain at the centre of the cosmos, while the sanctum directly below functions metaphorically as a cave; the vertical axis is often described as the trunk of a gigantic tree. Where possible, these religious structures were constructed at sacred sites featuring water (whether a river, spring or artificial tank) and shade (sacred groves and related tree cults have always been a major feature of the Indian landscape).

The wide range of demi-gods depicted in the shrines and sanctuaries brings the auspicious power of nature right into the realm of the man-made. The most important are the original nature spirits, the male *yaksha* and the female *yakshi*, who date back to Vedic times. Among their many forms are the celestial *apsaras*, the fertile tree goddess, and the imposing door-guardian (*dvarapala*). The other figures of central importance are the snake-spirits, the male *naga* and female *nagini*. Usually depicted as half human and half serpentine, and belonging to a tradition that can be traced back to pre-Aryan snake cults, they journey between the subterranean world of the primal waters and the manifest world of creation. Many heavenly musicians are incorporated both within the sculptural programs of temples and as attendants in individual sculptures of major deities: they include the male *gandharvas* and their female counterparts the heavenly *apsarases*, the *kinnaras*, with their human heads and horses' bodies (like the centaurs of Greek mythology), and the *vidyadharas* (bearers of wisdom) who fly through the air carrying garlands of flowers. Legendary sages and seers are revered as transmitters of sacred lore, and animals can serve as the vehicle (*vahana*) of a god. The gargoyle-like *kirttimukha* (face of glory) is thought to ward off evil, while the crocodile-like *makara* invokes aquatic fertility.

Though seldom worshipped in their own right within the sacred spaces of India, these auspicious guardians play a vital role as mediators between nature, the human and the divine.

The concepts of female beauty embodied in Indian sculptures such as the Melbourne image of a tree goddess relate closely to those expressed in Indian literature. The work of Kalidasa, the greatest of India's writers in classical Sanskrit, provides numerous examples of related metaphors drawn from the natural world to describe canons of human beauty. In *The Cloud Messenger* (*Meghadutam*), Kalidasa's most famous lyric poem, a *yaksha* (male nature spirit) describes the beauty of his wife to the cloud that will carry his message to her Himalayan exile:

> There you will see her, in the springtime of youth, slender,
>
> her teeth jasmine-buds, her lips ripe bimba-fruit,
>
> slim-waisted with deep navel
>
> and the tremulous eyes of a startled doe,
>
> moving languidly from the weight of her hips,
>
> her body bowed down a little by her breasts . . . [5]

57 *Railing pillar with a nature spirit (yakshi)*
Mathura, Uttar Pradesh
Kushana period, 2nd century
sandstone; 103.0 x 23.5 cm
Indian Museum, Calcutta (M4/A20025)

Most religious architecture in India enforces some form of controlled ritual movement, and worshippers encounter many images during their journey to the sacred heart of the structure. Some images remind worshippers of nature's auspicious powers as they guard and sanctify the shrine. The pre-Vedic nature spirits known as *yakshis* (female) and *yakshas* (male) were originally worshipped among sacred trees and groves as part of fertility cults. Images of them, often closely related in form to the *shalabhanjika* tree goddess (see catalogue no. 56), were subsequently used in Buddhist, Jain and Hindu temples.

This image of a nude *yakshi* wearing heavy jewellery is carved on the front half of a railing pillar from an unidentified site in Mathura, one of the two main urban centres of the Kushana empire. Originally there may have been one or more narrative scenes carved on the rear surface. The pillar was once part of a railing enclosing the circumambulation (*pradakshina*) path around a Buddhist *stupa*. Carved in the pink sandstone favoured by Mathura sculptors, the pillar is now much darker due to surface grime. On each side are three sockets for the cross-beams. In most cases, *yakshis* are not depicted in the formal poses of classical Indian iconography. The significance of the dwarf-like figure on which this *yakshi* stands is uknown, and there may have been an image of an amorous couple (*maithuna*)[7] in the empty alcove above the *yakshi*.

58 *Serpent king and queen*
Nalanda, Bihar
Pala period, 9th–10th century
stone; 92.5 x 43.0 cm
Indian Museum, Calcutta (4216/A25170)

The snake (*naga*) has been worshipped in India since the beginning of recorded history. *Nagas* are believed to reside in a watery realm beneath the roots of trees; and in villages, stone images of snakes are placed under trees. Their intercession is sought for a multitude of reasons including the birth of children and protection against snake bites. Snake imagery was also incorporated early on within the major religions of India: the Buddha was offered shelter by the king of the *nagas* during a storm; the Jain saviour, Parshvanatha, is traditionally depicted with a protective hood of cobra heads (see catalogue no. 54b); and Vishnu sleeps on the serpent, Ananta, while he dreams the universe into creation.

Indian snake imagery is largely non-sectarian. This sculpture of a serpent king (*nagaraja*) with his queen could function in a wall niche of either a Hindu or Buddhist shrine. Depicted in half-human form, the king is sheltered by five cobra hoods and the queen by three. They are in the conventional guise of a loving couple (*maithuna*) — the king unites them within a garland, and the queen holds up a flower in her left hand. This sculpture was probably collected in Nalanda last century by the amateur archaeologist A.M. Broadley.[8] According to the Chinese Buddhist monk, Xuan Zang, who visited India between 627 and 645, a snake named Nalanda was the guardian deity of the city of the same name, whose famous monasteries attracted pilgrims from throughout the Buddhist world.[9]

59 *Nandi*
Tamil Nadu
Chola period, 10th–11th century
cast bronze; 51.4 x 52.1 cm
The Asia Society, New York:
Mr and Mrs John D. Rockefeller 3rd Collection (1979.30)

All major Hindu gods are provided with an animal vehicle (*vahana*). Shiva's vehicle is the humped bull, Nandi (the Happy One). Vishnu's vehicle is the mythical Garuda with the body of a man and the beak, talons and wings of a predatory bird, while the elephant-headed god Ganesha rides, somewhat improbably, upon a rat.

Images of Nandi are usually placed at the front of temples dedicated to Shiva on axis with the Shiva *linga* in the sanctum; sometimes, however, they have their own shrine as part of a larger temple complex. At Lepakshi in Andhra Pradesh, an eight-metre, sixteenth-century monolithic image of Nandi faces the Shiva temple, which is over a kilometre to the west. By approaching Nandi

at a Shiva temple, the worshipper commences a ritual journey along the temple's sacred axis towards the Shiva *linga*, which Nandi guards as its most faithful devotee. Nandi is also a symbol of Shiva's own strength and virility.

This Nandi was cast in bronze by the lost-wax method during the Chola period. Nandi licks his lips as he reclines on a stylised lotus base.[10] The saddle strap on his flank features an auspicious *kirttimukha* (face of glory). Nandi's form is treated with great sensitivity — his tail is tucked lightly over his rear right hoof, for example, and his hump ends in a graceful curl just in front of his saddle.

60 *Caparisoned bull*
Nathdvara, Rajasthan
*c.*1860
opaque watercolour and gold on paper; 32.0 x 41.5 cm
Courtesy of the Arthur M. Sackler Museum, Harvard University Art Museums,
Private Collection (570.1983)

The sanctity of the cow dates back more than two thousand years in India. Not only is the bull connected with Shiva (in the form of Nandi, his animal vehicle), but cow-imagery in general is especially prominent in the cult of Krishna (one of the ten incarnations of Vishnu) which grew to prominence among cattle-herding groups in northern India. This caparisoned bull was painted in Nathdvara, the small pilgrimage town near Udaipur in Rajasthan where a famous image of Krishna lifting Mount Govardhan is enshrined as Shri Nath-ji (see catalogue no. 18). Many painted hangings in the Shri Nath-ji temple feature cows, referring in part to Krishna's dalliances with the milkmaids of Braj, and to Krishna's protection of the Braj cattle-herders when he lifted Mount Govardhan during a furious storm.

This bull, decorated in a similar style to the earlier bronze image of Nandi (see catalogue no. 59), is dressed for a procession. This might be related to the Gopashtami festival in Nathdvara, when cattle are worshipped in honour of Krishna's promotion from a herder of calves to a cowherd. The painting could also be connected to the racing of bullock carts in Nathdvara.[11] It is a very sculptural painting — every curve and sag of the great beast is appreciated for its formal qualitites. The bull stands on a lightly washed 'ground', with the aniline-dye green background soaring up to the traditional high horizon of Indian painting.

61 *Celestial maiden (apsaras)*
Khajuraho, Madhya Pradesh
Chandella period, *c.*10th century
sandstone; 94.0 x 32.0 cm
Indian Museum, Calcutta (Br. 2/A25228)

The walls of Hindu temples are platforms for an extraordinarily rich array of imagery. This sculpture comes from an unidentified temple in Khajuraho, a major centre of the Chandella dynasty (from the tenth to the twelfth centuries) and one of the few surviving major Hindu temple sites in north India. It is a fine example of a popular type of sculpture depicting a celestial maiden (*apsaras*) gently removing her lower garment. *Apsarases* are not associated exclusively with any of the major religions; their images are thought to bring good luck to sacred monuments by providing entertainment for the deities enshrined within.

Although based on the model of the tree goddess (see catalogue no. 56), this *apsaras* standing under a mango tree neither kicks the tree nor grasps its branches. Instead, she stands coyly between two attendants, touching her left foot with the toes of her right foot. Two monkeys frolic in the tree above. The sculptor has even depicted the fine line of hair rising up to her navel, a sign of beauty much eulogised in Sanskrit poetry.[12] The exact function of this class of image is open to debate. One recent interpretation suggests that it represents an episode when women rushed to view Shiva's wedding procession, interrupting whatever they were doing: 'One woman was tying her waist girdle while another came out with her garments worn inside out.'[13]

62 *Elephant with riders*
Karnataka
Hoysala period, *c.*1250
stone; 37.9 x 38.5 x 15.0 cm
Private Collection

Rising above the sanctum, the superstructure of a Hindu temple carries few images of the major gods in their earthly manifestations. Exceptions to this are the towers of the Hoysala-period Hindu temples, in the modern state of Karnataka, which boast a profusion of small sculptures of an auspicious nature. This small stone plaque featuring a heavily-festooned elephant carrying a male and female rider was probably once included as part of such a tower.[14]

The god Indra, king of the heavens, is often depicted on Hindu temples riding his elephant vehicle, Airavata, while holding a *vajra* symbolising a thunderbolt or lightning. The elephant, depicted here with such a powerful sense of movement can be identified as Airavata due to its double tusks. The front rider, however, carries a large elephant goad rather than a *vajra*, thus possibly does not represent Indra. Although the smaller female figure behind, wearing a crown, appears to carry an elephant goad, she may well represent Indra's wife Indrani.

63 *Garuda attacking a female serpent (nagini)*
ancient Gandhara, Pakistan
Kushana period, 3rd century
stone (schist); height 40.6 cm
National Gallery of Australia, Canberra (1978.1032)

Temple columns were symbolic links between the earth and the celestial superstructure of a temple, and carried a wide variety of imagery to match their auspicious function. This small stone sculpture once might have functioned as the capital of the miniature column. Garuda, the mighty man-eagle of Indian mythology, is shown sinking his talons into the waist of a *nagini*, a female member of the *naga* or serpent clan.[15] In the Hindu context Garuda serves as Vishnu's vehicle, but he was also popular in Buddhist Gandhara — Jataka stories of the Buddha's previous lives tell of Garuda carrying off beautiful women.[16] An implacable enemy of the *nagas*, he is also depicted here devouring a snake, whose head and hood sits on top of his left wing.

Such images highlight the cosmopolitan nature of Gandharan art during the Kushana empire. Although the theme is typically Indian, Greco-Roman images representing the abduction by Zeus of the youth Ganymede appear to have influenced this composition. This sculpture also demonstrates how ancient Indian themes were merged into the new Buddhist iconography.

64 *Panel with grotesque relief*
Mathura, Uttar Pradesh
Gupta period, *c.*530
sandstone; 25.7 x 23.2 x 6.0 cm
On loan from the Board of Trustees of the Victoria and Albert Museum, London (IS 29-1987)

A grostesque, lion-like face with tendrils, and vapour or pearls issuing from its mouth, is a prominent feature on the superstucture of north Indian Hindu temples, above the entrance to the sanctum. Known as a *kirttimukha* (face of glory), it also appears on the doorways, pillars and ceilings of temples as well as in friezes running along walls. The original placement of this panel with half a grotesque face is unknown, but it does compare closely with a column capital in a ruined Hindu temple at Pipariya in Madhya Pradesh (although the latter shows a full face with fangs).[17]

The *kirttimukha* tradition began around the fourth or fifth century, during the Gupta period. Because there is no known Indian prototype for the *kirttimukha*, it may be related to Hellenistic heads of Gorgons (for example, Medusa, the most famous of the Gorgons, was depicted as a monster with bulging eyes and serpents for hair).[18] By the sixth century the *kirttimukha* had attained its standard form in India — usually a grotesque, jawless face, with prominent eyes and large fangs. The *kirttimukha* is often used as a crowning ornament at the top of carved stelas (see catalogue nos 15 and 45) and bronze throne backs (see catalogue no 29) above the image of the god or saviour. It is also used in representations of jewellery (see, for example, the belt worn by Shiva in catalogue no. 9).

65 *Double figure of a lion*
Gwalior, Madhya Pradesh
Vardhana period, 7th century
sandstone; 51.0 x 106.0 x 34.0 cm
National Museum, Delhi (51.95)

Lions are symbols of solar and royal power in India. Single stone lions often guard stairways; and the Hindu god Vishnu, the Buddha and the Jain saviours all sit on lion-thrones (*simhasana*). The lion is also the vehicle of the ferocious Hindu goddess Durga.

The original function of this magnificent sculpture of two superimposed lions is unknown. Although they share a common body, the lion on the right has a front and back paw while that on the left has just a front paw. Only the lion on the right has a tail. The composite creature, clinging to its stone slab perch,

was intended to be viewed from the front and sides only — the back is not fully carved. It might once have sat on the top of a pilaster, but does not have the form of a load-bearing capital.

This sculpture can be dated to the seventh century, to the reign of the Vardhanas who ruled parts of north India as one of the successor states to the more famous Guptas. Their two main urban centres were Thanesar and Kanauj, but this double lion is said to have been found in the narrow hill-top fort which rises one hundred metres above Gwalior in Madhya Pradesh.[19]

66 *Agni, the God of Fire*
central India
12th century
sandstone; height 70.7 cm
Collection of Michael and Mary Abbott, Adelaide

Hindu temples are built according to highly symmetrical plans. They are aligned on a cardinal axis, with the entrance usually facing towards the east. On the outside temple walls eight *dikpalas* guard the four cardinal directions and the four intermediate points of the compass. Agni, the God of Fire, is the *dikpala* of the south-east. The spatial roles of the *dikpalas* relate back to the original Vedic sacrifical altar at the earliest level of Hinduism. Like Agni, the seven other *dikpalas*[20] are Vedic gods of the elements who were eventually surpassed by newer gods such as Shiva and Vishnu, but retained their protective function.

Agni is the god of the sacrificial fire whose smoke carried offerings to heaven. He is one of the few Indian gods depicted as an older man rather than as an adolescent. Clockwise from the lower left, Agni's hands hold prayer beads; a sacrificial ladle in shape of the *yoni*; a sacred text in the form of a palm-leaf manuscript tied up with a string; and a vessel for ghee or water. In the lower part of the sculpture are representations of Agni's mount, the ram (the animal most often sacrificed in Vedic rituals), kneeling devotees and two larger standing figures that might represent Svaha and Svadha (the personifications of the ritual exclamation uttered while making the offering). In line with his guardian duties, this image of Agni would have been installed in a corner niche, at the eastern end of the south wall of the temple.

67 *Sage (rishi)*

Tadpatri, Anantapur district, Tamil Nadu
Vijayanagar period, 16th century
stone (granite); 88.0 x 32.0 x 18.0 cm
Government Museum, Madras (2546)

The cult of the ascetic is almost universal in India. Those who abandon worldly possessions in the search for liberation of the soul are widely revered. The Buddha and the Jain saviour, Mahavira, lived among numerous Hindu ascetics. Images of a wizened sage (*rishi*), often leaning on a staff, are frequently included in the sculptural programs of Hindu temples. *Rishis* are literally 'seers' (*rishi* is probably derived from an obsolete version of the root of the word *darshana*). They are regarded as sources of sacred lore and models of individual spiritual development. This *rishi*, wearing an animal skin around his waist, leans on a staff so massive that it resembles the battle maces wielded by door guardians (see catalogue no. 68).

This image was recovered from Tadpatri, a city with two temples built by governors of the Vijayanagar kings. One, the Ramalingeshvara temple, sits on the bank of the Penner River and is dedicated to Shiva. Its central *linga* stands in a pedestal perpetually filled by water from a spring, and its two unfinished gateways are covered with sculpture. The other, the Venkataramana temple, is dedicated to Vishnu. The exact source of this sculpture is not known.

68a-b *Pair of door guardians (dvarapalas)*
Tamil Nadu
Chola period, 10th century
stone; 178.0 x 61.0 x 37.0 and 177.0 x 61.0 x 38.0 cm
National Museum, Delhi (59.153/161 and 59.153/162)

The doorway into the sanctum of a Hindu temple is guarded by images of a number of deities and other auspicious creatures. In northern India these images include the river goddesses Ganges and Yamuna (representing the two main rivers of the northern plains). In the south, massive figures of *dvarapalas* (door guardians) are the most prominent, one on either side of the door. They are also found flanking the passage through the massive temple gateways of this region. The exact origin of these threatening creatures, with their bulging eyes and oversized weapons, is not known.

This pair of crowned, almost life-sized *dvarapalas* dates from the Chola period. They are depicted in a typical form, with fearsome faces and powerful bodies adorned with massive jewellery. Originally facing inwards towards the doorway, their bodies are complementary in pose but not symmetrical. Each guardian leans upon a huge war club intended to ward off evil. The guardian on the left has his right hand raised in the gesture of threat (*tarjani mudra*); the one on the right has his left hand in the gesture of wonder (*vismaya mudra*). The rough modelling of these guardians contrasts strongly with the refined lines of the images they guard, most particularly the sleek Chola bronzes.

69 *Image frame (parikara)*
probably eastern Rajasthan
mid-9th century
sandstone; 31.0 x 82.7 x 11.5 cm
National Museum of American Art, Smithsonian Institution, Gift of John Gellatly
(Courtesy of the Arthur M. Sackler Gallery, Smithsonian Institution), Washington D.C. (LTS 1985.1.592)

An image of a god is installed lavishly within the sanctum of a Hindu temple. Adorned with jewels and with clothes frequently changed, it is raised on a special base, often described as a throne — the temple is seen to be god's palace. If the image is carved on a stela, it is surrounded by smaller figures of auspicious demi-gods and surmounted by a *kirttimukha* (face of glory; see, for example, catalogue no. 15). With the exception of the Shiva *linga*, which stands free on a *yoni* base, the central image of a god is usually set within a stone or metal image frame (*parikara*).

This top portion of a stone image frame is from an unidentified temple dedicated to Vishnu. In its original state, there would have been side panels, giving the form of a doorway. At each end is the head of a *makara*, a mythical creature whose appearance is probably based on the freshwater crocodile of north India. At the top is a particularly fine example of a *kirttimukha*, from whose mouth spread tendrils of flower-buds. The three small columned niches hold images of the fifth, sixth and seventh of the ten *avataras* of Vishnu: from left to right, they are Vamana (the Dwarf), Parashurama (Rama with an Axe), and Rama' with a female attendant. The other *avataras* would have been depicted on the side panels. The rest of the frame is filled with groups of flower-laden *gandharvas* (male celestial musicians) and *apsarases* (female celestial dancers), providing entertainment for the god enshrined within.

70 *Water spout (pranala)*
Kaverippakkam, North Arcot district, Tamil Nadu
Pallava period, *c.*800
stone; 36.0 x 36.0 x 97.0 cm
Government Museum, Madras (71-16/37)

The journey to the image in a Hindu temple takes the devotee past animal vehicles, narrative scenes, goddesses, celestial dancers, nature spirits and guardians before the dark sanctum is entered. There, the worshipper 'takes' *darshana* of the god and makes an offering to it with the assistance of the attending priest. Along with the singing of hymns and the movement of oil lamps, other forms of worship include lustration of the image with water each morning. The remains of offerings, such as the lustral water, that have come into contact with the deity are offered to devotees as *prasada*, or divine 'grace'. The highly auspicious liquid offerings that have flowed over the image pass out of the sanctum (usually through the north wall) along a special spout called a *pranala* and fall into a stone basin. From there they are scooped up by devotees and sprinkled over the head.

The ends of most *pranalas* feature the face of a *makara* (the mythical aquatic creature), tiger or lion. This Pallava-period example belongs to a rarer group featuring the head of a *bhuta* (goblin) at the end of the unadorned rectangular water chute.[21] The *pranala* acts as a medium for dispersing divine grace. This *bhuta-pranala* with his fearsome face also protects the lustral water as it is transferred from deity to devotee.

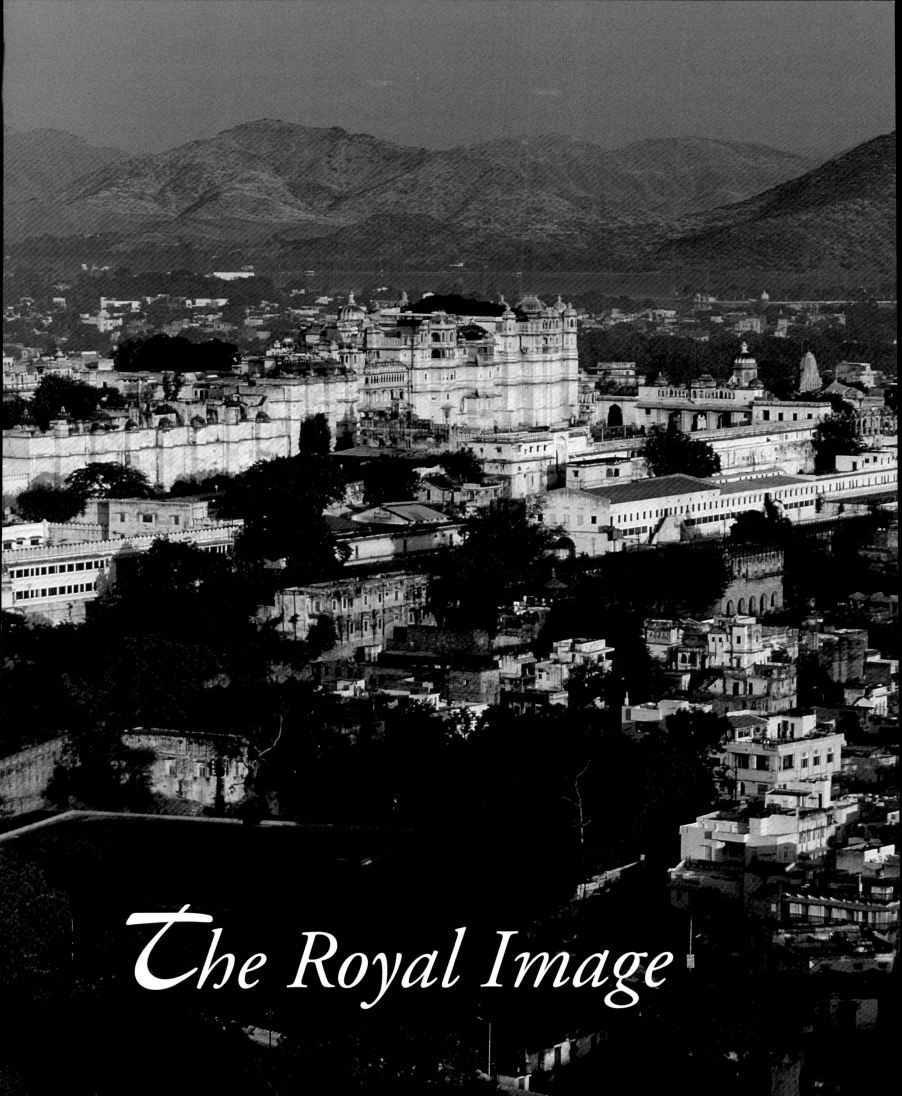

The Royal Image

71 attributed to GOVARDHAN (active *c*.1604–1640)
The Emperor Shah Jahan on the Peacock Throne
from an album of the Emperor Shah Jahan
north India (probably Agra)
Mughal dynasty, *c*.1635 (border *c*.1645)
opaque watercolour and gold on paper
37.3 x 26.2 cm (folio); 16.5 x 13.9 cm (painting)
Courtesy of the Arthur M. Sackler Museum, Harvard University Art Museums, Private Collection (651.1983)

The most dramatic change in the depiction of Indian kings occurred at the Mughal court of north India at the end of the sixteenth century. This change marked the first appearance of painted portraits in which the creation of an accurate likeness was of prime importance. Although earlier portraits often incorporated some individual traits, the aim had been to represent the power of the king rather than his personality. The Mughal emperor Akbar (r.1556–1605) not only sat for his own likeness, but also ordered portraits of his nobles in which, it was noted by his court historian Abul Fazl, 'those that have passed away have received a new life, and those who are still alive have immortality promised them'.[1] This new portraiture (usually small in scale and bound into imperial manuscripts or albums) was made for a restricted court audience, as part of an attempt to forge a new imperial image based upon Indian, Islamic and European visual models. Within the palace libraries, these historical portraits were juxtaposed with images of mythical and divine rulers, boosting the present ruler's legitimacy.

Since this moment at the end of the sixteenth century, numerous portraits have been painted for the Mughal emperors and the Rajput maharajas of north-west India. The Mughals were Muslims of central Asian origin who had conquered north India in 1526 (more than three hundred years after the first Muslim ruler had captured the throne of Delhi). The Rajputs, on the other hand, were Hindus whose ancestors had arrived in the region a thousand years earlier. At times these Mughal and Rajput rulers were implacable enemies, but on other occasions they entered into political alliances. Their cities, after all, were linked by a single road network used by warriors, ambassadors, traders and pilgrims of all persuasions. Most importantly, the Mughals and Rajputs inhabited the same north Indian landscape, with all its political and sacred associations. Outside the palace, the king presented himself to his subjects as he moved through his domains on military expeditions, hunting excursions or religious pilgrimages. Within the palace the king revealed himself to a more restricted audience using special architectural framing devices and carefully controlled axes of vision.[2] Mughal and Rajput portraits record these royal rituals being enacted within a shared geography of palace, countryside and garden.

The new importance of the accurate likeness in Mughal portraiture can be linked to the development of palace rituals involving the ceremonial appearance of the ruler.[3] It is also related to the growing interest in royal biography — two of the first four Mughal emperors (Babur and Jahangir) even wrote extensive memoirs. This is one of the greatest of all Mughal royal portraits; it shows the Emperor Shah Jahan (1592–1666) seated on the famous Peacock Throne. Framed by a brilliant border featuring gold-outlined flowers and miniature birds set within the graphic equivalent of a parterre, this composite page was originally mounted in one of the emperor's sumptuous albums.[4] Shah Jahan is depicted in strict profile, with a golden halo; he does not return the gaze of the viewer (nor does he actually look at the pink rose he holds in his right hand). The emperor's throne rests on a magnificent Mughal carpet on the terrace of a palace pavilion. Beyond a golden fence is a tangle of finely-painted plants. The golden surfaces of the throne, the sash tied around the emperor's waist and the fine arabesque on the maroon bolster cushion have all been pin-pricked, to capture and reflect more light. In this portrait, items of Shah Jahan's jewellery were originally set with real gems and pearls.

Parallel to the rise of Mughal court portraiture based on observation was the development of art historical connoisseurship and the subsequent change in the Mughal artist's status from anonymous craftsman to individual master. With the evolution of discernible personal styles (which were not necessarily linked to ideals of personal artistic expression), the Emperor Jahangir (r.1605–1627) was able to boast in his memoirs that he could recognise the hand of any artist living or dead.[5] This portrait of Jahangir's son and successor, Shah Jahan, can be attributed to Govardhan.[6] Little is known about this leading Mughal artist, except that his name indicates he was a Hindu, that his father (Bhavani Das) was a minor court painter for Akbar and that he signed his name with the title *khanazad* ('house-born'), signifying his birth at the imperial court.[7] Govardhan painted for three Mughal emperors (Akbar, Jahangir and Shah Jahan) during the first four decades of the seventeenth century, combining skilful modelling with a fine sense of psychological insight. Many of his paintings feature landscape backgrounds largely derived from European prints that had begun to arrive in India by the second half of the sixteenth century (see, for example, catalogue no. 94). This portrait of Shah Jahan ranks as one of Govardhan's most hieratic representations of Mughal royal power.

Shah Jahan was the fifth Mughal emperor of India, ruling from 1627–1658. Named Prince Khurram at birth, he was awarded the title Shah Jahan ('King of the World') ten years before he actually ascended the throne. At his accession, Shah Jahan adopted the additional title 'Second Lord of the [Auspicious Planetary] Conjunction', in direct imitation of his central Asian ancestor Timur (1336–1405), through whom the Mughals also claimed descent from the Mongol leader, Genghis Khan (1167–1227). Emulating Timur and his princely successors, Shah Jahan placed great importance on the patronage of both architecture and painting. In these works, the primary concern was presentation of the self, whether in paint or through ceremonial appearances.

It was Shah Jahan's grandfather, Akbar, who instigated the Mughal emperors' practice of giving *darshana* to their subjects. Just as a Hindu god is said to give *darshana* to worshippers who gaze at its image, Akbar would appear for the public each morning at a special palace window and later to assembled nobles within the palace audience hall. After Akbar's death in 1605, these rituals and their related architectural forms were refined considerably. One of the most original inventions of Mughal architecture in the early seventeenth century was the adoption of baluster columns to frame the ceremonial appearance of the emperor. The form of this four-part column (consisting of a base, a pot-like element, a shaft rising from among acanthus leaves and, finally, a capital) has a rich heritage. It can be traced back to the Hindu and Buddhist architecture of eastern India; to the wooden architecture of central Asia; and, most intriguingly, to European practices, reflected in the prints of Dürer and his circle, which were popular at the Mughal court from the second half of the sixteenth century.[8]

The most spectacular framing device used by Shah Jahan was the Peacock Throne. Originally known as the Jewelled Throne (*takht-i murassa'*), it took its popular name from the jewelled peacocks surmounting its four-sided canopy. The throne had been commissioned by Shah Jahan in 1628, soon after he came to power. Rubies, emeralds, garnets, diamonds and pearls from the state treasury were set in an elaborate gold structure which took seven years to complete. Work on the throne was supervised by a courtier known as Bibadal Khan ('the Khan without compare'), then superintendent of the imperial goldsmith's office (*zargar-khana*).[9] Govardhan's painting does not exactly match contemporary descriptions of the Peacock Throne — Mughal painting seldom attempted precise depictions of architecture. It incorporates, however, four slender baluster columns, which support the four-sided canopy in a manner reminiscent of earlier Mughal projecting windows used for the *darshana* ritual.

Judging by the emperor's age (he would appear to be in his early to mid-forties), this portrait must have been painted soon after the completion of the Peacock Throne in 1635. The throne was

originally placed in the Hall of Public Audience in the fortified Mughal palace in Agra (see fig. 12 for a plan of the fort). There it served as a focus for court ceremonies involving the appearance of the emperor and the dispensing of both justice and rewards. A description of one such event also highlights the growing use of solar symbolism at the Mughal court — while celebrating the tenth anniversary of his accession in 1637, Shah Jahan is described by an official historian as sitting on the Peacock Throne and distributing gold and jewels that 'fell upon his obedient subjects like auspicious rays from the all-powerful sun'.[10] In 1648 the Mughal capital was moved from Agra to the newly-constructed city of Shahjahanabad in Delhi (comprising what is now referred to as Old Delhi and the Red Fort). There too the Peacock Throne was placed in the middle of the Hall of Public Audience (fig. 9). In both Agra and Delhi, these audience halls were known as *chihil sutun* ('forty-pillared [hall]'). They were probably intended to be replicas of the great multi-columned hall built by the Achaemenid kings of Iran at Persepolis in the fifth century BC and later regarded as the mythical seat of King Solomon, the ideal king of the Islamic tradition.[11]

Unlike the Buddhist kings of ancient India, the Muslim emperors of Mughal India could not claim the distinctive characteristics (*lakshanas*) that would identify them as a *chakravartin*; unlike Hindu kings, they could not claim to be an incarnation of a god such as Vishnu. However, in the symbolically charged spaces of their palaces, the Mughal emperors claimed semi-divine status as the

fig. 9: Hall of Public Audience, Red Fort, Delhi, 1639–48 (Photo: Antonio Martinelli).

fig. 10: The Taj Mahal (1632–43) from the Red Fort, Agra, Uttar Pradesh (Photo: Antonio Martinelli).

'shadow of God on earth' (*al-zill Allah*). Bibadal Khan, who had supervised the construction of the Peacock Throne, clearly expressed the cosmic aspirations of Shah Jahan:

> That which was your throne as majestic as heaven
>
> Was the ornament of your justice over the world
>
> Thou wilt last as long as God exists
>
> For substance is ever accompanied by its shadow.[12]

Claims to divine status were boosted by the widespread use of solar symbolism, and a dynastic aura — the effulgence of a divine light that the Emperor Akbar traced back to a mythical Mongolian ancestress.[13] When Shah Jahan commissioned Govardhan to paint his portrait seated on the Peacock Throne it is not surprising that

he requested the inclusion of a golden halo. As his grandfather's historian had noted earlier, 'kings are fond of external splendour, because they consider it an image of the Divine glory'.[14]

Shah Jahan was deposed by his son, Aurangzeb, in 1658. Aurangzeb proclaimed himself 'Emperor of Hindustan' the following year, after ascending the Peacock Throne during his second coronation ceremony in Delhi. Shah Jahan spent the last eight years of his life imprisoned in his fort at Agra. After his death, he was buried alongside his wife, Mumtaz Mahall, further down the banks of the Yamuna river in the Taj Mahal (fig. 10), which he had constructed between 1632 and 1643. The Peacock Throne was captured by the Iranian king, Nadir Shah, during the looting of Delhi in 1739 and carried back to Teheran, where it was later dismantled.

72 attributed to MANAKU (*c.*1700–1760)
Vibhishana joins Rama's monkey and bear army
page from a manuscript of the *Ramayana*
Guler, Himachal Pradesh
*c.*1725
opaque watercolour and gold on paper; 60.3 x 83.2 cm
Courtesy of the Arthur M. Sackler Museum, Harvard University Art Museums, Private Collection (431.1983)

Indian royal images reside within an ancient tradition of kingship. Great kings of the past, both historical and mythical, served as models of behaviour and symbols of royal authority. Rama, an incarnation of the god Vishnu and heir to the throne of Ayodhya, is the hero of the vast *Ramayana* epic. After Rama and his wife Sita were exiled to the jungle for fourteen years, Sita was abducted by the evil king Ravana of Lanka. This unusually large *Ramayana* painting is from an unfinished manuscript commissioned by Raja Dalip Singh (r.1695–1741) of the Rajput state of Guler, in the Himalayan foothills where one of the so-called 'Pahari' or 'hill' schools of painting flourished from the late seventeenth to nineteenth centuries. Through his patronage the raja would have hoped to acquire some of Rama's timeless aura of royal virtue.

The event painted here by Manaku occurs while Rama lays seige to Lanka during his attempt to rescue Sita. At the left, the multi-headed Ravana sits atop his golden palace, below which animals and fish swim in the river's silver water (now oxydised). On the right, Ravana's brother, Vibhishana, has joined Rama's army of monkeys and bears (many painted with delightfully individual expressions). Facing the bearded Vibhishana is the exiled king Rama (with blue skin and holding a bow), behind him is his loyal brother Lakshman. Two monkey spies approach from Ravana's palace to survey the strength of Rama's forces. Manaku (active *c.*1700–1760) was the son of the artist Pandit Seu, and brother of Nainsukh, probably the most famous of all the Pahari artists (see catalogue no. 102).[15]

73 *The empty palace*
page from a manuscript of the *Ramayana*
Kangra, Himachal Pradesh
*c.*1775–80
opaque watercolour and gold on paper; 36.0 x 25.0 cm
National Gallery of Australia, Canberra (1990.1265)

This painting, from a manuscript of the *Ramayana* illustrated in the small Rajput state of Kangra in the foothills of the Himalayas, is possibly one of three illustrated manuscripts prepared for the 1781 wedding of the sixteen-year-old Raja Sansar Chand.[16] If so, it would have served as an excellent moral guide for the young king who ruled Kangra from 1775 to 1823. All three works were illustrated by artists who favoured looming architectural spaces viewed from high vantage points, and action that seldom focuses on the centre of the page.

In the *Ramayana*, Rama, the hero of the epic and true heir to the throne of Ayodhya, is exiled by his stepmother who wishes her son

(Rama's half-brother), Bharata, to rule instead. Bharata, however, does not support his mother's plot. In the episode illustrated here, Bharata has just returned from a jungle meeting during which Rama has convinced him to rule in his place for the prescribed fourteen years of his exile. Bharata is at the top centre, wearing Rama's sandals on his head as a mark of devotion to his exiled brother. Upon his return to Ayodhya, depicted on the right, he has found its citizens fleeing to the city of Nandigrama, on the left, where they will await Rama's return. Only one figure remains in the otherwise empty palace, leaning out from an upper level window to behold the arrival of Bharata.

74 *Rescue of the infant Iskandar (Alexander)*
folio from a series of the *Hamzanama* (*The Story of Hamza*)
north India
Mughal dynasty, *c.*1562–77
opaque watercolour and gold on cotton; 68.5 x 52.0 cm
Horace G. Tucker Memorial and Seth Augustus Fowle Funds. Courtesy Museum of Fine Art, Boston (24.129)

Muslim rulers in India looked to the mythical past for inspiration and legitimisation. For the Mughal emperors of north India, descendents of the Timurids (who ruled parts of central Asia, Persia and Afghanistan), this meant establishing connections with the heroes of the greater Islamic world. Of all Mughal projects inspired by these ambitions, none can compare in scale to the massive manuscript of the *Hamzanama* (*The Story of Hamza*), commissioned by the emperor Akbar (r.1556–1605) shortly after he ascended the throne of north India at the age of fourteen. Produced between about 1562 and 1577, this work originally consisted of 1400 paintings in fourteen volumes. The heavily modelled paintings on cotton, which break dramatically from the Timurid tradition of painting, chronicle the fictional adventures of Amir Hamza, an uncle of the Prophet Muhammad, as he sought converts to Islam.

Alexander the Great (Iskandar) conquered Iran in *c.*330 BC, entering north-west India in 327 BC. In Islamic Iran, this ancient conqueror eventually was transformed by legend into a model Iranian warrior, and then a universal prophet whose wisdom gained potency from his association with Aristotle. In this painting, the infant Alexander floats on a raft in windswept waters among fish, a snake, a turtle and a mythical crocodile. A fisherman wades out to his rescue, leaving his net and basket on the shore. The artist has given the action an Indian setting — in the background, sari-clad women balance terracotta water pots on their heads as they return to their walled town. The white building, above purple rocks painted according to Persian conventions, is probably intended to represent a Hindu temple.

75 attributed to MADHU KHANAZAD (active *c.*1582–1604)
from an unidentified manuscript, mounted as an album page
King Solomon's court
north India (probably Agra)
Mughal dynasty, *c.*1600–05
opaque watercolour on paper; 34.5 x 22.7 cm (folio); 27.3 x 15.4 cm (painting)
Collection Prince Sadruddin Aga Khan, Geneva (Ms. 116)

In the Muslim world Solomon (Suleyman) is regarded as the ideal king. He is credited with knowing all languages — human and animal. The two lines of Persian text on this page mention four Old and New Testament figures: 'In sympathy [he was like] Jacob, in beauty [like] Joseph; In piety [like] John, in sovereignty like Solomon.' Solomon was singled out for illustration in this painting attributed to Madhu.[17] Seated on a throne, he is attended by winged angels and monstrous *jinns*. Next to him is an attendant with flywhisk, the same symbol of royalty seen in Indian sculptures of deities. Animals and birds, many in pairs, crowd around Solomon's throne paying homage to his sovereignty. All of them are native to India except the mythical *simurgh*, the king of the birds, in the top

right corner. (The *simurgh* is of Chinese origin, coming to India via Persia.) A small hoopoe bird, Solomon's special messenger, sits alongside his left hand.

This painting was intended as a symbol of imperial justice, illustrating Solomon's ability to inspire peace among animals who are usually enemies. In India it might also be read as symbolising the king's ability to rule the multicultural community of the Indian subcontinent. There are similar angels and two *simurghs* in the central medallion of a painted ceiling, datable to *c.*1605–10, in the so-called Kala Burj (Black Tower) of the fortified Mughal palace in Lahore. When the emperor Jahangir gave *darshana* to his subjects from this room, he would assume the role of Solomon.[18]

76 *Shukadeva and the king*
Kishangarh, Rajasthan
*c.*1760
opaque watercolour on paper; 22.0 x 32.0 cm
On loan from the Board of Trustees of the Victoria and Albert Museum, London (IS 556-1952)

The kings of India sought to connect themselves with the spiritual power of important holy men. In this painting, the famous *rishi* (sage) Shukadeva is the central figure with a halo, seated on a throne, naked but for a garland of flowers. The figure seated on the grass in front of him is identified by a small inscription simply as a 'king' (*raja*). It is left open for interpretation whether he is an historical king or the mythical King Pariskshit, to whom Shukadeva recited the *Bhagavat Purana* scripture as he waited to die. The presumed patron of this painting was Maharaja Savant Singh (r.1748–1757; d.1764), a devotee of Krishna. Savant Singh's artists transposed the Krishna legends of Braj to the lakeside setting of Kishangarh in Rajasthan, and developed a unique style featuring large, dramatically exaggerated eyes.

The waterfront city at the top left is identified by inscription as Hastinapur (located on the banks of the Ganges between Delhi and the holy city of Haridvar, and a major site in the *Mahabharata* epic). The landscape in this painting, however, is similar to Kishangarh. In the wooded middle ground is an *ashram*, labelled as that of a *rishi* Shrang-ji, and tiny images of a king hunting. Shukadeva and the king are surrounded by a large group of holy men — small inscriptions give their names. Some, such as Narada (in the foreground with a stringed musical instrument over his shoulder), are well known in Hindu mythology; others are presumably local *rishis* favoured by Savant Singh.

77 *Prince Dara Shikoh with Mian Mir and Mulla Shah*
page from an imperial album
north India
Mughal dynasty, *c.*1635
opaque watercolour and ink on paper; 17.0 x 10.4 cm (painting)
Arthur M. Sackler Gallery, Smithsonian Institution, Washington D.C.
Purchase, Smithsonian Unrestricted Trust Funds, Smithsonian Collections Acquisition Program, and Dr Arthur M. Sackler (S86.0432)

The Mughal emperors often sought the intercession of holy men as sources of both spiritual authority and important boons. Of all the Mughal royal family, few were more closely connected with Muslim mystics than Prince Dara Shikoh (1615–1659), the eldest son of Shah Jahan. This broadminded prince was also keenly interested in Hinduism, translating fifty of the ancient Upanishads from Sanskrit into Persian under the title *Sirr-i Akbar* (*The Greatest Mystery*). Dara Shikoh linked kingship with spirituality, stating: 'In the prime of my youth a voice from the Unseen addressed me four times saying: "God will give you something that has not been conferred upon any emperor of the world."'[19]

In Mughal painting, usually only the emperor has a halo; however, as Shah Jahan's heir apparent, it is not surprising that Dara Shikoh (left, second from top) is depicted with a halo. However, it is an unusual sign of great respect for the two Muslim mystics seated to the right of Dara Shikoh to be granted halos. Labels identify them as Mian Mir (on the right) and his spiritual successor (*khalifa*) Mulla Shah Badakhshi (on the left).

Judging by Dara Shikoh's age, this painting must have been completed just before Mian Mir died in 1636. It might represent the occasion when Dara Shikoh first met Mulla Shah in 1635, while seeking solace with Mian Mir at his Lahore sanctuary following the death of the prince's first child.[20] Having offended orthodox Muslim clerics, Dara Shikoh was beheaded in 1659 by his younger brother Aurangzeb, who had usurped the throne from Shah Jahan the previous year. Mulla Shah died in 1661.

78a-b two pages from a manuscript of the *Kulliyat*
(*Collected Works*) of Sa'di
calligraphed by 'Abd al-Rahim of Herat
north India
Mughal dynasty, *c.*1600–05
opaque watercolour and gold on paper
Collection Prince Sadruddin Aga Khan, Geneva (Ms. 35)

a) attributed to AQA RIZA (active *c.*1580–1605)
The poet Sa'di with his patron (f. 91a)
41.7 x 26.4 cm (folio); 27.6 x 15.1 cm (painting)

Illustrating secular poetic texts written by the masters of Persian poetry allowed Mughal artists to visualise an idealised world. At times, such paintings reflect the Persianate world in which the poetry was originally created (it is surprising that verses by Indian poets were rarely illustrated at the Mughal court). On other occasions, these visions were transposed to Indian settings. This and the following painting (catalogue no. 78b) are among twenty-three included in a manuscript of the *Kulliyat* (*Collected Works*) of the Persian mystical poet Sa'di (d.1292), copied by one of the foremost Mughal calligraphers of the time, 'Abd al-Rahim of Herat also known as 'Amber Pen' ('*anbarim qalam*).

This page shows the poet Sa'di, on the left, wearing a black and white striped robe, seated in front of his patron, Abu Bakr, whom he eulogises as 'the axis of fortune's wheel, the successor of Solomon'.[21] In front of the poet are some of the tools of his trade: a book, a scroll, a pair of scissors, and a pen in a pot of ink. Between Sa'di and Abu Bakr is a tray of gold coins, symbolising the relationship between artist and patron. This painting has been attributed to Aqa Riza, who entered the service of the Mughal emperors when he arrived in India from Persia around 1580. The highly conventionalised portrayal of human figures (and their costumes) and the arrangement of the landscape demonstrate his Persian roots. Aqa Riza's two sons also worked as artists at the Mughal court.[22] One of them, Abu'l Hasan, rose to great heights of fame (see catalogue no. 91).

b) *A sinner's passionate plea to God* (f. 107b)
41.7 x 26.4 cm (folio); 27.6 x 15.3 cm (painting)

This painting illustrates an episode from the same manuscript of Sa'di's *Kulliyat* as the previous catalogue entry (no. 78a). It is set within an original vision of the Mughal landscape in India. In this story, a drunkard has been thrown out of a mosque after loudly demanding admission to paradise. He reminds God (Allah) of His promise to forgive those who repent their sins. The three lines of text in *nasta'liq* script in 'Abd al-Rahim's hand include part of his plea. Seated in the foreground with a flask of wine by his side, hands raised hopefully, the drunkard calls out, 'Oh Mighty! Forgive this wareless one; None's to be seen with a blacker record than mine . . . Oh God! Let me not cease to hope for pardon.'[23]

The key elements of the Mughal landscape depicted here commence with the walled city in the distance (influenced by pictorial devices of European prints, which arrived in India during the sixteenth century). Outside the city gate, amidst farming land, is a walled garden and, below that, a tree surrounded by a square platform on which travellers can rest. A grove of trees (near which two men debate a textual issue), a flowering shrub, a waterfall and a stream are the natural features most favoured as points of relaxation. The mountains in the middle distance are painted according to Persian conventions, with some of their peaks harbouring animal and semi-human faces.

79 attributed to MISKIN (active *c.*1580–1604)
Krishna lifting Mount Govardhan
page from a manuscript of the *Harivamsa* (*The Genealogy of Hari*)
north India
Mughal dynasty, *c.*1590
opaque watercolour and gold on paper; 28.9 x 20.0 cm
Lent by The Metropolitan Museum of Art, New York, Purchase, Edward C. Moore, Jr. Gift, 1928 (28.63.1)

Religious mythology has imbued many sites in India with special significance. The territory of the Mughal emperors, who were followers of Islam, included numerous Hindu and Buddhist sacred sites. The region of Braj, connected with the Hindu god Krishna (the Dark One), was situated between the two main Mughal capitals Agra and Delhi. Here Krishna is lifting up Mount Govardhan. The painting belongs to a manuscript of the *Harivamsa* (*The Genealogy of Hari* [another name for Vishnu]). This was one of a number of major Hindu texts the emperor Akbar had translated from Sanskrit to Persian during the late sixteenth century, to increase the understanding of Hindu India among his Muslim courtiers. By commissioning this painting, Akbar reaffirmed the sanctity of a Hindu site within his territory.

In the myth illustrated by this painting, Krishna had convinced the Braj cattle-herders to worship him instead of the Vedic god Indra, who unleashed a huge storm in revenge. Answering the cattle-herders's pleas for help, Krishna lifted up Mount Govardhan, the highest peak in Braj, sheltering them from Indra's storm. His skin painted blue to represent his darkness, Krishna is depicted accomplishing this feat with one hand, according to a standard iconographic type (see catalogue no. 18). The silver sky behind the storm-tossed trees is now oxydised. The painting has been attributed to the artist Miskin, who has added extra elements of visual interest, such as the woman in a green shawl to Krishna's right who looks out at the viewer while her husband sleeps.[24]

80 *Rishis worshipping a Shiva linga on Mount Kailasa*
page from a manuscript of the *Shiva Purana (The Ancient Story of Shiva)*
Kangra, Himachal Pradesh
*c.*1810
opaque watercolour and gold on paper; 28.5 x 43.5 cm
National Museum, Delhi (63.1155)

Mountains are important in Indian mythology. Their snow-covered peaks represent, among other things, the extreme opposite of the urban palace. Mount Kailasa (meaning 'crystalline' or 'icy') is a mythical peak that has also given its name to a section of the Himalayan range with many important pilgrimage sites. It is the abode of Shiva and the mythical source of the sacred Ganges river, whose waters are said to rise from the roots of a huge *jujube* tree there. It is an appropriate home for the ash-smeared Shiva, who is more closely connected to the raw power of nature than Vishnu, a deity usually depicted as a *chakravartin* with a crown and other emblems of royalty.

This painting is from Guler, in the Himalayan foothills not far from Kailasa's mythical location. Five *rishis* (literally, 'seers') worshipping a Shiva *linga* are depicted against a backdrop of snow-covered mountains. However, the setting is hardly one of untouched nature. The *linga*, and the *yoni* base into which it is set, are elevated within a dazzling golden terrace with hexagonal lotus ponds and flowering trees — more appropriate to a temperate climate. One *rishi*, wrapped in a tiger skin, pours an offering over the *linga* while the others, with rosaries held in their hands, worship it. Another five *rishis* pray beside the lotus-filled Ganges as it flows down to the plains of northern India. While the painting is clearly intended to recall Shiva's icy abode, it does not attempt to use the alpine landscape as a direct visual symbol of Shiva's primal powers.

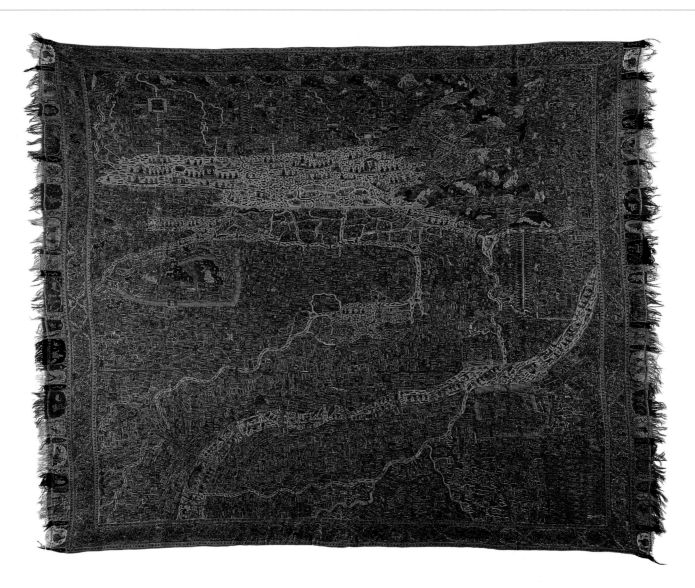

81 Workshop of SAYYID HUSSAIN SHAH and SAYYID MUHAMMAD MIR
Shawl with a map of the Kashmir Valley
Srinagar, Kashmir
*c.*1870
cashmere wool, natural dyes, twill weave, embroidery
National Gallery of Australia, Canberra
Gift of the Godfrey family 1992 (1992.281)

Depictions of Indian landscapes frequently emphasise the ownership of land. This celebrated shawl was embroidered with a bird's-eye view perspective of Srinagar and the vale of Kashmir. It is one of only four known Kashmiri map shawls,[25] and was commissioned by Maharaja Ranbir Singh in 1870, twelve years after India came under direct British rule. Combining cartography with some of the conventions of Indian painting, it highlights the landscape contributions of the Mughals (who annexed Kashmir in 1586) and the densely constructed city of Srinagar stretching along both banks of the Jhelum River. Two locations are especially prominent along the top of the shawl above Dal Lake: the famous Shalimar Garden, Shalimar laid out between 1620 and 1634 by Shah Jahan (p. 150), in the top left corner; and, to its right, Nishat Garden, built by

Shah Jahan's father-in-law, Asaf Khan. The Maharaja's interest in mapping his territory on a shawl may be related to the Grand Trigonometric Series of the Survey of India, which surveyed Kashmir between 1855 and 1864.

In 1896 the State Treasury sold this shawl to Major Stuart Godfrey, a British political officer in Kashmir. (Godfrey's descendents donated the shawl to the National Gallery of Australia in 1992.) The Godfrey shawl was exhibited in the Delhi Durbar loan exhibition of 1902–03, and in the 1911 Festival of the Empire exhibition at London's Crystal Palace. Its fame is well-founded — early reports claim that it took thirty weavers over a year to complete, at a time when the fine *pashmina* wool of which the shawl is made was sold in Kashmir for its weight in silver.[26]

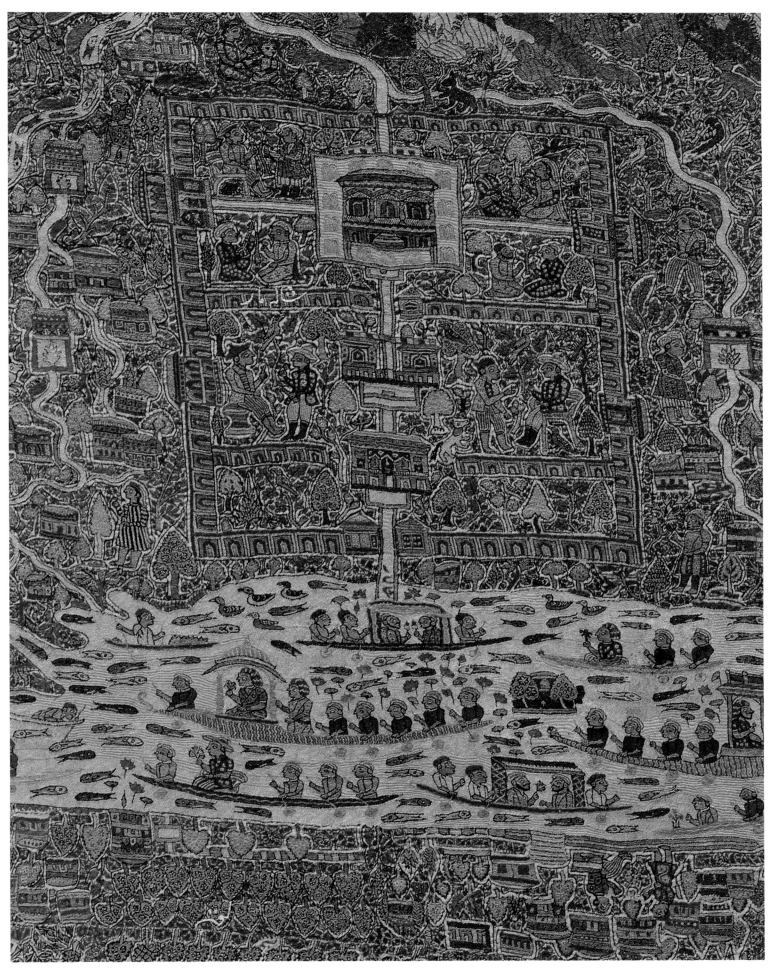

82 attributed to MANSUR (active *c*.1589–1625)
Peafowl in a landscape
north India (probably Agra)
Mughal dynasty, *c*.1610 (border *c*.1645)
opaque watercolour and gold on paper; 36.5 x 25.0 cm (folio); 19.1 x 10.8 cm (painting)
Courtesy of the Arthur M. Sackler Museum, Harvard University Art Museums, Private Collection (643.1983)

Possession of territory in India brought the Mughals face to face with the subcontinent's brilliant flora and fauna. Many Indian animals are attributed with multiple layers of religious and cultural symbolism. The bull, for example, is the vehicle of the god Shiva; the peacock is that of both Sarasvati, the Goddess of Learning, and Skanda, the God of War. In Indian poetry, the peacock also symbolises the monsoon — during that season, they dance noisily in their courtship rituals. Krishna, the divine lover, wears peacock feathers in his hair.

While the Mughal emperors were aware of these meanings, they also celebrated India's animal life as objects of great formal beauty.

Here the artist Mansur, upon whom the emperor Jahangir bestowed the title *nadir al-'asr* (Wonder of the Age), has painted a peacock and peahen from close observation.[27] The position of the peacock's right leg was changed during the painting process to better portray the sense of darting movement. Pigments made with expensive gold and lapis lazuli were lavished on the peacock's tail and throat — the latter is also highlighted with vermilion. Mansur became famous for his animal studies among which are depictions of exotic animals acquired by the Mughal emperors. These include a turkey brought from Goa in 1612, and a zebra brought from Abyssinia in 1621.

83 *The Emperor Muhammad Shah in his garden*
Delhi, Uttar Pradesh
Mughal dynasty, *c.*1730
black ink with colour washes; 53.0 x 86.5 cm
Francis Bartlett Fund and Special Contribution. Courtesy Museum of Fine Arts, Boston (14.686)

The Mughal emperors gave order to the universe in their formal gardens. These magnificent locations mediated the experiences of city and nature; here, the rulers executed the orders of government and pursued the pleasures of private leisure. As newcomers to the Indian subcontinent they also laid out gardens to revive memories of their ancestral homelands in central Asia where symmetrical walled gardens played a similar role in the regulation of urban spaces.[28]

In this lightly painted drawing, the Mughal emperor Muhammad Shah (r.1719–1748) halts on his ride through a Delhi garden among plane trees, plantains, cypress trees, flowering bushes and water canals with fountains and a miniature waterfall. Between his halo

and imperial parasol is a Persian inscription describing the emperor as possessed 'of radiant star-like glory'.[29] His furled imperial standard is carried by an attendant, depicted in the lower left corner. In front of the emperor stand his prime minister, holding a document, and an unidentified official. Outside the garden walls, to the left, the political reality of a military procession contrasts with the ordered symbolic world within. Delhi was sacked by the Shah of Persia in 1739, during Muhammad Shah's reign. In the wake of this disaster, many Mughal artists fled to the Rajput states in Rajasthan and to towns in the foothills of the Himalayas, such as Guler (compare the trees in this painting, with the grove of trees in catalogue no. 72 for example).

84 *The Emperor Muhammad Shah hunting*
Delhi, Uttar Pradesh
Mughal dynasty, *c.*1730
opaque watercolour and gold on paper; 30.7 x 43.8 cm (folio); 26.8 x 39.8 cm (painting)
National Gallery of Australia, Canberra (1992.1262)

In this painting Muhammad Shah (r.1719–1748) moves beyond the city and its gardens into the countryside, hunting with falcons (other paintings show him hunting with a rifle). He is attempting to create an image of himself as a ruler imbued with the power to control the forces of nature. Over the centuries, the symbolic intent of such action gradually overtook the reality of the king's actual political power. Here, Muhammad Shah hunts on horseback in a landscape infused with an atmosphere of poetic suggestion. On the left, across a river whose progress into the distance is suggested by the zig-zag line of its banks, a group of women have had their musical picnic disturbed by the emperor's approach, and have taken cover behind some trees.[30]

In the distance the rest of the imperial calvalcade proceeds slowly across the countryside under a dark monsoon sky.

When Muhammad Shah, known as *rangila* (the Pleasure Lover), ascended the throne the Mughal empire was in a state of political decline. In 1739 Delhi was sacked by the Persian ruler Nadir Shah. Camel-loads of loot from the Mughal imperial treasury, including the Peacock Throne, were carted back to Teheran. Nevertheless, Muhammad Shah's atelier was still capable of producing works of sublime beauty — the last great flowering of Mughal painting. There is no text on the verso of this painting; originally it would have been bound in an album, along with other paintings and calligraphies set within luxurious borders.

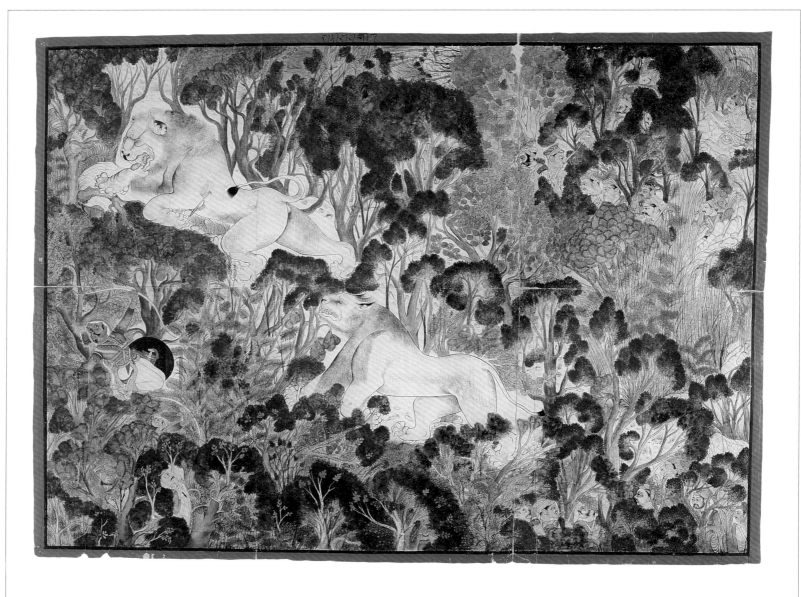

85 attributed to the KOTA MASTER
Rao Bhoj Singh hunting lion
Kota, Rajasthan
*c.*1720
opaque watercolour and gold on paper; 47.5 x 66.0 cm
Courtesy of the Arthur M. Sackler Museum, Harvard University Art Museums, Private Collection (547.1983)

In Rajasthan the royal image was created from an intricate web of relationships connecting religion, mythology, ancestral rights and the overriding Mughal power in Delhi. This is a posthumous hunting portrait of Rao Bhoj Singh of Bundi (r.1585–1607), a common ancestor of both the Bundi and Kota rulers of eastern Rajasthan. At the behest of the Mughal emperor Shah Jahan in 1631, Kota became semi-independent of Bundi. This watercolour was painted in the princely state of Kota, thirty-eight kilometres south-east of Bundi, a century after its subject's death. Bhoj Singh, identified by an inscription, launches an attack with a traditional bow and arrow on an impossibly massive lion (although guns were already in use in India by the time of his reign). This painting depicts the king as hero; a hunter worthy of the bow-wielding god Rama.

A member of the Hara clan, Bhoj Singh was an ally of the Mughal emperor Akbar, whom he served as a military commander in the contingent of another Rajput ruler. He achieved fame during the rule of Akbar's son, Jahangir, by objecting to the new emperor's desire to marry the granddaughter of Maharaja Man Singh of Jaipur; she was also Bhoj Singh's granddaughter on the maternal side. When Bhoj Singh died the next year, it was widely rumoured that he had committed suicide. Jahangir eventually married the princess; acknowledging the realities of the Mughal–Rajput alliance, Maharaja Man Singh sent a gift of sixty elephants.[31]

86 *Maharao Durjan Sal hunting with Krishna in the form of Shri Brijnath-ji*
Kota, Rajasthan
*c.*1725–50
opaque watercolour with gold on cotton; 102.4 x 191.3 cm
Howard Hodgkin Collection, London

In the princely states of Rajasthan, certain images of Hindu gods were regarded as possessing special charisma. Rulers looked to them for support while exercising the duties of kingship. Most famous were the nine peripatetic images of Krishna, passed down by the descendents of Vallabhacharya. These images include Shri Nath-ji in Nathdvara (see catalogue no. 18), which was the most renowned of all; and Shri Mathuranath-ji (The Lord of Mathura), which arrived in Kota in 1738. However, the tutelary deity of Kota is a small image of Krishna known as Shri Brijnath-ji which resides within the palace. It was brought to Kota by Maharao Bhim Singh I (r.1707–1720) in 1719 after a dual pilgrimage to Delhi (to pay his respects to the newly enthroned Mughal emperor Muhammad Shah) and Mathura (to take initiation into the Vallabha Sampradaya sect).[32] Upon his return to Kota, the king announced that he would henceforth rule only as Shri Brijnath-ji's chief minister.[33]

The Shri Brijnath-ji image was often installed on an elephant during battles; but this led to its loss in 1720, in the battle in which Bhim Singh was killed. Bhim Singh's son, Maharao Durjan Sal (r.1723–1757), recovered the image four years later. In this unusually long Rajput painting, probably made to decorate a royal tent, Durjan Sal is depicted on horseback at the upper right hunting rhinoceros. Accompanying him on the hunt, just to the left, is Shri Brijnath-ji himself, depicted as a blue-bodied Krishna in human form.

87 BAKHTA (active 1761–1811)
Rawat Gokul Das hunting
Deogarh, Rajasthan
1806
opaque watercolour with gold and silver on paper; 54.0 x 79.0 cm
Howard Hodgkin Collection, London

Some local chiefs under the Rajput kings cultivated the same symbolic powers as their overlords. The rawats of Deogarh, a small feudatory (*thikana*) 120 kilometres to the north of the Mewar capital at Udaipur, achieved a degree of independence based on special land grants in 1692. An inscription on the verso identifies the subject of this painting as Rawat Gokul Das of Deogarh (r.1786–1821). He is shown hunting on the banks of a lake named in the same inscription as the Singh Sagar (Lion Lake) near Deogarh. This painting is ascribed with the name of the artist Bakhta, who started his career in Udaipur (to whose maharaja the rawats of Deogarh owed allegiance) before moving to Deograh in the late 1760s.[34]

Gokul Das appears four times in a continuous narrative painted with multiple perspectives. The main image, at the bottom right, shows him hunting water fowl from an outcrop, painted with Bakhta's typical tightly-bunched rockforms. An elegant plume of smoke emerging from the rawat's matchlock suggests the blast of gun-fire echoing over the stillness of the lake. Gokul Das is not granted a halo, but wears his court finery, including a golden dagger and sword, a turban with jewelled ornaments and a feather. The ruler is also shown three times in the island pleasure pavilion: he takes another shot from a corner pavilion at the upper right, performs his toilet at the lower left, and generally enjoys the pleasures of his *zanana* (harem). Elsewhere, rocks swell into abstract forms in the foreground, and crocodiles bask on a distant island.

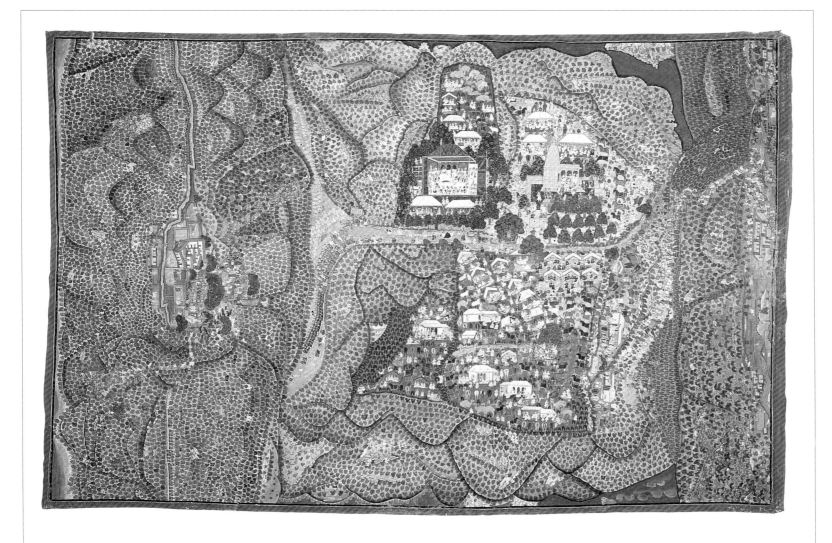

88 *Maharana Jawan Singh hunting*
Udaipur, Rajasthan
*c.*1830
opaque watercolour, gold and ink on cotton; 213.0 x 318.0 cm
National Gallery of Australia, Canberra (1993.734)

Mewar, ruled first from the mountaintop fortress of Chittorgarh, and then from the lakeside city of Udaipur, has always been regarded as the most senior Rajput state in western India. Claiming descent from the sun god, Mewar's Hindu rulers prided themselves on maintaining independence from the Muslim rulers of Delhi. Only in 1615 was a qualified submission made to the Mughal emperor Jahangir.

This unusually large painting on cotton was probably intended to be hung on the walls of one of the royal palaces or tents; it shows the ruler Maharana Jawan Singh (r.1828–1838) at nine stages during an imperial hunt outside Udaipur. On each occasion he is depicted with a golden halo; he also has an ornate royal parasol while in procession and actually hunting.[35] The combination of continuous narrative with a fractured perspective results in a highly

compelling work of art. Collisions between the planes are treated with nonchalant bravado by the artist — trees even hang upside down over one part of the procession.

The entire painting can also be read as an illustration of Rajput kingship, a *mandala* uniting the Maharana's political, religious and symbolic power. His political power is exercised in the red *darbar* tent, set alongside the temple, from which he derives his religious power. In the symbolic sphere, the king shows himself to his subjects as the supreme warrior hunting his way through the imperial realm. At the far left, an antelope is sacrificed to the king under a village tree. Painted so soon after the British gained suzerainty over Mewar in 1818, this great work must be seen as a brilliant attempt to recreate the symbolic aura of a golden past.

89 JAI RAM
Maharana Jagat Singh II attending a Rasalila performance
Udaipur, Rajasthan
1736
opaque watercolour and gold on paper; 59.8 x 44.8 cm
National Gallery of Victoria, Melbourne, Felton Bequest 1980 (AS130.1980)

The rulers of Rajasthan enhanced their spiritual status by their patronage of important religious performances conducted within their palaces. The *Rasalila* (*Play of Passion*) is the greatest of the dance dramas, revolving around Krishna's amorous exploits with the milkmaids of Braj. It incorporates the great circular dance of Krishna and the milkmaids (the *Rasamandala*), and enactments of many *lilas*, the divine 'sports' of Krishna's childhood in Braj. On the spiritual level, the *Rasalila* presents Krishna as the Supreme Soul (*paramatma*), his beloved milkmaids represent individual souls seeking union with the divine.

This painting records a *Rasalila* performed for Maharana Jagat Singh II of Mewar (b.1709; r.1734–1751) in a roof-top courtyard of his palace at Udaipur (see pp. 102–103 and fig. 13) on a full moon night in November 1736.[36] Jagat Singh commissioned

at least ten paintings of this one performance, but this work is the only one inscribed with the name of the artist Jai Ram,[37] and it is the first in the set.

Although they wear virtually identical costumes, the maharana can be distinguished from his companions (including brothers and nephews) by his gold-rimmed halo. He is also depicted in a larger scale, towering over all those in attendance. The maharana watches a woman performing the initial ritual invocation with a flaming lamp. At the top of the courtyard, one actor stands with his left arm raised as a living form (*svarup*) of Krishna lifting up Mount Govardhan (see also catalogue nos 18 and 79). In the lower right corner of the courtyard, below two sets of drums, is a miniature representation of Mount Govardhan.

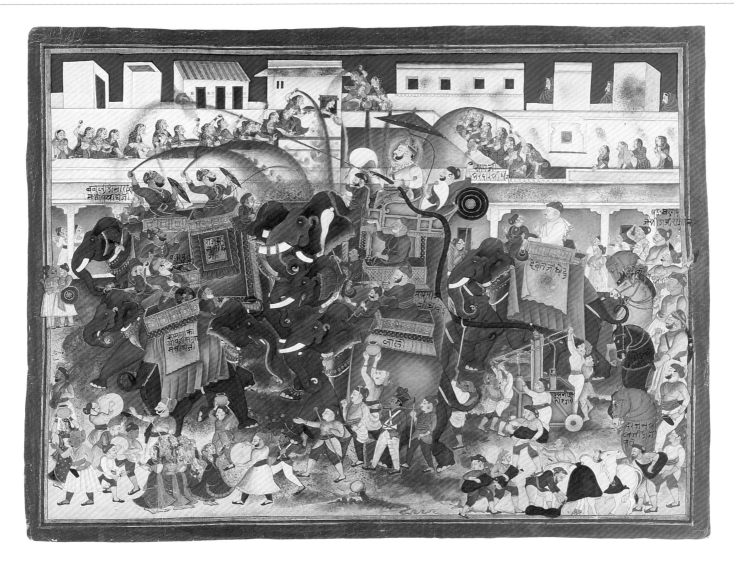

90 KISAN DAS
Maharao Ram Singh II celebrating Holi
Kota, Rajasthan
1844
opaque watercolour and gold on paper; 48.7 x 64.0 cm
National Gallery of Victoria, Melbourne, Felton Bequest, 1980 (AS511980)

Annual festivals provided Indian kings with opportunities to present themselves to their subjects during symbolically charged rituals. Maharao Ram Singh II (r.1827–1865), who ruled Kota under British suzerainty (note the presence of a soldier in a British-inspired uniform in the centre of this painting), devoted much of his time to ceremonial performances. Many of the surviving paintings from his reign depict him in state processions.

Based on ancient fertility rites, the spring Holi festival combines the celebration of Krishna's love-play in Braj with formal assemblies between the king and feudal subordinates. It sanctions the breaking of many social and class barriers: women can accost men, for example, and highly suggestive songs are sung. At the height of Holi, coloured liquids and powders are launched at friends and strangers alike. In this painting, Ram Singh rides through the streets of Kota on a massive elephant shooting jets of red liquid from a hose-pipe attached to what appears to be the palace fire-engine. Shaded by a red canopy of state (which also offered protection from showers of powder), he sits at the apex of a hierarchy rendered chaotic by the festivities. The artist Kisan Das took advantage of the Holi subject matter to push an intensely coloured painting style to its dramatic limits. Pools of red pigment are splattered on with the brush, rather than painted with the usual hard-edged precision of the later Kota manner.

91 ABU'L HASAN (born 1588–1589; active *c*.1600–1630)
The Emperor Jahangir at his audience window
page from a manuscript of the *Tuzuk-i Jahangiri* (*The Memoirs of Jahangir*)
north India (probably Agra)
Mughal dynasty, *c*.1620
opaque watercolour on paper; 55.7 x 35.0 cm (folio); 31.2 x 20.0 cm (painting)
Collection Prince Sadruddin Aga Khan, Geneva (M.141)

The central focus of Mughal court ritual was sighting the emperor. From the time of Akbar, the Mughal emperor presented himself to his subjects twice daily in the ritual of *darshana*. This intense interest in the person of the emperor helps explain the rise of true portraiture in Mughal India. For an illustrated version of the emporer's memoirs, the artist Abu'l Hasan, also known by the title of *nadir al-zaman* (the Wonder of the Time),[38] has painted Jahangir (r.1605–1627) giving *darshana* to his subjects from high up on the red sandstone ramparts of the Mughal fort in Agra (fig. 12). He appears, flanked by two princes, at a special balcony window which frames the emperor within white marble and gold. As though to emphasise the fact that *he* does not need to see his subjects, Jahangir is depicted in strict profile.

Standing on a platform gazing up at the emperor are grandees of the realm, including 'Itimad al-Dawla (the prime minister) and his son Asaf Khan (Jahangir's brother-in-law). An elderly holy man peeks out from a doorway beneath them. Further below, a multitude of other courtiers (almost all are true portraits) includes, on the right, the Persian envoy, an Abyssinian and a nobleman wearing eye-glasses. To the left, the golden chain of justice rises up to the palace. Even the humblest subject was able to rattle it to bring to the emperor's attention any injustice within the kingdom. Here, however, a complainant is chased away with a stick.

92 BISHAN DAS (active *c*.1589–1640)
Prince Babur arriving at Andijan
page from a manuscript of the *Baburnama* (*The Memoirs of Babur*)
north India
Mughal dynasty, *c*.1590
opaque watercolour, gold and ink on paper; 24.4 x 14.6 cm (painting)
National Gallery of Australia, Canberra (1989.348)

The Mughal emperor Akbar (r.1556–1605) created a new empire in India on the foundations laid by his grandfather, Babur, who had conquered Delhi in 1526. Akbar's fifty-year reign marks one of the most dynamic periods in Indian political and cultural history. He was deeply interested in the role of the king as an active agent in history, and illustrated manuscripts of royal histories were a cornerstone of his patronage of art. This painting belongs to an illustrated manuscript of his grandfather's autobiography (the *Baburnama*) from around the time when it was translated from Chaghatay Turki to Persian in 1590.[39]

This work by Bishan Das is one of the first paintings in a manuscript which originally consisted of nearly six hundred folios.

It records an occasion in 1449: riding into his ancestral fortress of Andijan in central Asia, the eleven-year old prince Babur (second from right) learns of his father's death;[40] he goes to the prayer platform (*namaz-gah*), at the left, to pray for the soul of his departed father. Although Bishan Das is renowned for his portraiture, here he resorted to a conventionalised figure in his depiction of the young prince (who looks older than eleven). The *Baburnama* was the first project in Bishan Das's long career working for the emperors Akbar, Jahangir and Shah Jahan over a period of at least fifty years. He also travelled to Persia (from 1613 to 1620) with the Mughal embassy.[41] Bishan Das painted this scene in the *nim qalam* (literally 'half-brush') style of muted colours and pale washes. It shows clearly his incipient talent for characterisation and gesture.

93 Designed by BASAWAN (active *c.*1560–1600);
right page painted by TARA THE ELDER (active *c.*1585–1590), left page painted by ASI (active *c.*1584–1596)
The Emperor Akbar watches a battle between two groups of holy men
double page from a manuscript of the *Akbarnama* (*The History of Akbar*)
north India
Mughal dynasty, *c.*1590
opaque watercolour on paper;
37.8 x 24.4 (right) and 37.9 x 25.1 cm (left)
On loan from the Board of Trustees of the Victoria and Albert Museum, London
(IS 2–1896–61/117 and IS 2–1896–62/117)

The *c.*1590 manuscript of the *Akbarnama* (*The History of Akbar*) is the first attempt in Muslim India to paint an emperor within actual contemporary events. The taste for painting history at Akbar's court had previously led to the production of an illustrated manuscript of the *Timurnama* (the history of the Mughal's fourteenth-century ancestor Timur) in *c.*1584. Akbar then opted for illustrated translations of the two great Hindu epics, the *Mahabharata* (1582–86) and the *Ramayana* (1584–89), before tackling his own history. Intriguingly, no formal individual portraits of Akbar are known from his reign. In paintings, he is almost always shown within an historical narrative played out in an Indian setting.

Mughal historical manuscripts include a significant number of double page illustrations. In this example, at the top of the right page, Akbar rides a horse. Because the Persian language is read from right to left, this page precedes the left hand page in the manuscript.

The subject is a dispute that took place in 1567 between the Puri and Kur groups of holy men, concerning the right to seek alms next to a sacred tank (depicted at the centre of the left page).[42] With the help of Akbar's army, the Puris drove the Kurs away. The Kur leader's horrific death by sword is shown in the lower section of the right page. The Puri leader is shown near the centre of the left border of this same page, wearing a crown of peacock feathers.

Akbar's artists usually worked in teams to produce historical manuscripts, with their names listed beneath each painting. An inscription running up the right hand border records the scene illustrated. This double page was designed by Basawan, one of Akbar's two most influential Indian painters.[43] Although the actual painting is credited to Tara the Elder and Asi, Basawan himself must have painted the death of the Kur leader, one of the most dramatic passages of painting in early Mughal art.

94 GOVARDHAN (active *c*.1604–1640)
The Emperor Akbar with a lion and calf
page from the so-called *Kevorkian Album*
north India (probably Agra)
Mughal dynasty, *c*.1630
opaque watercolour and gold on paper: 38.9 x 25.7 cm
Lent by The Metropolitan Museum of Art, New York,
Purchase, Rogers Fund and The Kervorkian Foundation Gift, 1955 (55.121.10.22v)

Shah Jahan (r.1627–1658) commissioned formal portraits of the earlier Mughal emperors as part of his interest in his dynastic past. This posthumous portrait removes his grandfather, the emperor Akbar (r.1556–1605), from the realm of historical narrative and presents him as a dynastic icon. Shah Jahan was especially fond of his grandfather (he died when Shah Jahan was thirteen), and his historians always referred to Akbar by his posthumous title *'arsh ashiyani* (Resting on the Divine Throne). Shah Jahan copied many of Akbar's policies, and his architecture often harks back to that of his grandfather's reign.

Painted early in Shah Jahan's reign, this three-quarter profile of Akbar is based on earlier contemporary likenesses. The artist Govardhan, whose name is inscribed beneath the painting, had worked for Akbar at the end of the sixteenth century and may have been painting from memory or with the aid of earlier sketches. Standing on a grassy knoll, Akbar carries the jewelled weapons of military might as well as a rosary signifying more spiritual pursuits. An angel holding a golden crown hovers over his head, while two other celestial figures play musical instruments. In a clear reference to the Solomonic ideal of kingship and justice (see catalogue no. 75), a lion and a cow repose on either side of the emperor. In the background — like the angels, clearly inspired by European prints — are two small rustic genre scenes, finely highlighted with white paint. The portrait of Shah Jahan on the Peacock Throne discussed earlier (see catalogue no. 71) is also attributed to Govardhan.

95 PAYAG (active *c.*1595–1655)
The Emperor Humayun seated in a landscape
page from the so-called *Late Shah Jahan Album*
north India (probably Delhi)
Mughal dynasty, *c.*1650
opaque watercolour and gold on paper; 44.4 x 33.0 cm (folio); 18.8 x 12.3 cm (painting)
Arthur M. Sackler Gallery, Smithsonian Institution, Washington D.C.
Purchase, Smithsonian Unrestricted Trust Funds, Smithsonian Collections Acquisition Program, and Dr Arthur M. Sackler (S86.0400)

This posthumous portrait of the second Mughal emperor, Humayun (r.1530–1540 and 1555–1556), was painted for an imperial album. It was made late in Shah Jahan's reign, roughly a decade before he was deposed by his son Aurangzeb in 1658. Within the album, this portrait faced a portrait of Babur, Humayun's father and the first Mughal emperor (now in the collection of the Musée Guimet in Paris[44]). Both paintings are set within opulent borders populated by celestial, human and animal figures. The portrait of Humayun has been extended slightly to fit the dimensions of its border.

Payag's signature is written in the base of the plane tree next to which the emperor is seated. Although he was painting shortly after Shah Jahan's extravagant new capital city in Delhi (Shahjahanabad) and the Taj Mahal in Agra were completed,

Payag chose not to employ a grand architectural setting (or even a throne). Instead, he placed Humayun in a modestly-scaled meadow with a meandering stream. Framed by a green halo emanating golden rays, Humayun examines a jewelled turban ornament in his left hand. Unlike his descendants who favoured Indian fashion (see, for example, catalogue no. 94), he wears a typically central Asian turban and gown. Within an otherwise barren landscape, tiny flowers emerge from a scattering of small rocks.

The borders amplify the painting's imperial message. Emerging from radiant clouds, two angels (based on European *putti*) hold a golden crown above Humayun's head, while three standing figures at the left of the page carry other symbolic objects, including a royal parasol.

96 CHITARMAN (active *c*.1625–1670)
The Emperor Shah Jahan nimbed in glory
north India (probably Agra)
Mughal dynasty, 1627–28
opaque watercolour and gold on paper; 38.9 x 25.7 cm
Lent by The Metropolitan Museum of Art, New York,
Purchase, Rogers Fund and The Kevorkian Foundation Gift, 1955 (55.121.10.24r)

In an age of exaggerated metaphors and panegyrics, Shah Jahan (r.1627–1658) referred to himself as the 'Shadow of God' and in direct imitation of his central Asian ancestor Timur, 'Second Lord of the [Auspicious Planetary] Conjunction' (*sahib-i qiran-i sani*). Although he termed himself a second Timur, this portrait of Shah Jahan could only have been painted in India. This fascinating work is open to more than one reading. It is unquestionably Chitarman's greatest masterpiece[45] and might, in fact, be interpreted as an attempt to claim for Shah Jahan the aura of the Hindu god, Vishnu. The painting is set in the Mughal palace in Agra, with the Yamuna River in the background and a walled garden on the opposite bank. The low dais, on which Shah Jahan is elevated against a rainbow-coloured halo (unique to Mughal painting), can be related to the black marble throne platform on a terrace at the Agra fort overlooking the Yamuna River.[46] If the artist Chitarman (a Hindu) wished to imply a link between Shah Jahan and Vishnu as the universal monarch (the Sanskrit word *chakravartin* carries the same meaning as the Persian *shah jahan*), then the 'European' angels above the emperor should be read as the Indian *gandharvas* (celestial musicians) or *vidyadharas* (knowledge-bearers) that appear so frequently on Hindu steles (compare, for example, catalogue no. 15). A newly created image of a Hindu god is often shown its reflection in a mirror immediately after the eye-opening ceremony; here, Shah Jahan admires a small, jewel-studded portrait of himself.

97 BICHITR (active *c*.1615–1650)
The Emperor Shah Jahan with Asaf Khan
page from an imperial album
north India (probably Delhi)
Mughal dynasty, *c*.1650
opaque watercolour and gold on paper
44.0 x 32.9 cm (folio); 26.3 x 18.7 cm (painting)
Arthur M. Sackler Gallery, Smithsonian Institution, Washington, D.C.
Purchase, Smithsonian Unrestricted Trust Funds, Smithsonian Collections Acquisition Program, and Dr Arthur M. Sackler (S86.0403)

In Mughal India, absolute power resided in the emperor; but Shah Jahan awarded his loyal Commander-in-Chief, Asaf Khan, the title *yamin al-dawla* (Right Hand of the State) with good reason. Asaf Khan had helped to secure Shah Jahan's succession to the throne after Jahangir died suddenly in 1627. He was also closely connected to both emperors by marriage. His father had served as Jahangir's prime minister, and his sister, known as Nur Jahan (the Light of the World), was Jahangir's wife. In addition, his daughter had married Shah Jahan in 1612. Known popularly as Mumtaz Mahall (the Chosen One of the Palace), she died in 1631 and lies buried with Shah Jahan (d.1666) in the white marble tomb in Agra that now carries a corrupted version of her name — the Taj Mahal.

This double portrait of Shah Jahan and Asaf Khan (who had died earlier, in 1641) was painted in about 1650 by Bichitr. The artist added the description 'slave of the court' to his signature between the two standing figures, in accordance with Mughal etiquette.[47] The barely articulated landscape in which the two figures stand is a standard feature of Mughal portraiture. As Shah Jahan faces the older Asaf Khan (on the right), a golden light emanating from a bearded patriarch in the heavens surges down into the emperor's halo. Could this be the same dynastic aura that, according to Akbar, had its origins when his semi–mythical ancestress, the Mongol queen Alanquwa, was impregnated by a miraculous beam of light?[48] Favoured as Asaf Khan might have been (Shah Jahan addressed him as *'ammu* [paternal uncle] in correspondence), he is never depicted with a halo.

98 *Rosette (shamsa) with the name and titles of the Emperor Shah Jahan*
opening page of the so-called *Kevorkian Album*
north India (probably Delhi)
Mughal dynasty, *c.*1645
opaque watercolour and gold on paper; 38.6 x 26.5 cm
Lent by The Metropolitan Museum of Art, New York, Purchase, Rogers Fund and The Kevorkian Foundation Gift, 1955 (55.121.10.39r)

'A flash from the world–pervading sun' read one of the chronograms composed to celebrate Shah Jahan's birth in 1592 (the year 1000 according to the Muslim calendar).[49] Solar symbolism would play a large role in the imperial imagery of Shah Jahan's reign. The *shamsa* is a solar device commonly used in the Islamic tradition of manuscript illumination. Derived from Timurid prototypes of central Asia, this magnificent Mughal *shamsa* is set within a field of golden birds; it is the opening page of an imperial album prepared for Shah Jahan. This miraculous combination of geometry and natural rhythms uses different tones of gold as well as other vibrant colours. In the central medallion, woven together in magnificently fluid Arabic lettering, are the emperor's name and titles: 'His Majesty, Shihab ad–Din Muhammad Shah Jahan, the King, Warrior of the Faith, may God perpetuate his kingdom and sovereignty.'[50]

Considering the presence of Shah Jahan's titles and the rampant solar symbolism of his reign, it may not be too far–fetched in the Indian context to consider this abstract device as a type of aniconic 'image' of the emperor. With a *simurgh* (the king of birds) in each corner, it could also be read as a *mandala* or cosmic diagram, with the Mughal imperial power emanating from Shah Jahan's name. As Akbar's official historian Abul Fazl had written half a century earlier, 'the *shamsa* of the arch of royalty is a divine light, which God directly transfers to kings, without the assistance of men'.[51] *Shamsa*-like halos were included above the heads of Mumtaz Mahall and Shah Jahan on their inlaid marble cenotaphs in the Taj Mahal.

99 *Portrait of the noble Iltifat Khan*
north India
Mughal dynasty, *c.*1640–50
opaque watercolour on paper; 43.0 x 31.6 cm
Howard Hodgkin Collection, London

The royal family was not the exclusive subject of Mughal portraiture. Important courtiers also had their likenesses painted, as did a smaller number of holy men, musicians and even artists themselves. This painted sketch is especially appealing for its revelations of the process of creating official images. The anonymous artist has clearly painted from life, but then corrected his line to strengthen the overall effect, especially in the profile of the face, the placement of the ear and the folds of the turban. Almost life-size, it was possibly a study for a wall painting.

The subject is identified by an inscription: 'Iltifat Khan, Shah Jahani noble'. Because it is written in *devanagari* script (used for Sanskrit and many later north Indian languages), as opposed to the Persian

script used in the Mughal court, it would appear that this drawing was once owned by a Rajput prince. Mirza Murad received the title Iltifat Khan from the emperor Jahangir in 1615. The son of one of the most powerful nobles of the early seventeenth century, he married the daughter of Abd al-Rahim Khan Khanan (1556–1627), the Commander-in-Chief of the Mughal armies and one of the very few officials to have kept a major atelier. This portrait dates from around the time Iltifat Khan retired from imperial service in 1642. An eighteenth-century compendium of biographies claims he resigned from service because 'he did not exert himself' and afterwards lived for a long time 'in tranquility and comfort in Patna . . . his days . . . spent in ease and freedom from care.[52]'

100 attributed to PAYAG (active *c*.1595–1655)
Prince and courtiers at camp
north India
Mughal dynasty, *c*.1650
opaque watercolour with gold on paper; 30.0 x 44.3 cm (folio); 14.2 x 19.5 cm (painting)
Terence McInerney, New York

Paintings intended for Mughal albums served diverse functions, and their subject matter can be difficult to identify. Here, an unidentified prince is shown carousing at night in a simple camp set up in the countryside. While food sits untouched on fine blue and white Chinese porcelain vessels, he leans against a bolster and drinks with a female companion. Despite her great elegance, she is unlikely to be his wife — a female member of the royal family would not generally be seen in the company of other men. The subject was perhaps intentionally generic, intended to function primarily as a vehicle for painterly virtuosity.

During the reigns of the emperors Akbar, Jahangir and Shah Jahan, from the mid-sixteenth to the mid-seventeenth century, Mughal artists received a level of patronage that encouraged the formation of individual styles. These styles gave rise to a strong tradition of connoisseurship at the Mughal court. Because numerous paintings are signed (or ascribed in the margins by palace librarians), it is possible to attribute through stylistic comparison unsigned works such as this (a rarity in the history of pre-modern Indian art). This painting has been attributed to the artist Payag, who worked for all three of the emperors mentioned here (who also painted the portrait of Humayun — see catalogue no. 95).[53] Few other Mughal artists attempted night scenes, but here Payag seems to relish the opportunity to paint such details as the reflection of the oil-lamp's flame on one of the glass wine flasks.

101 *A Mankot prince*
Mankot, Jammu and Kashmir
*c.*1700
opaque watercolour and gold on paper; 21.0 x 30.7 cm
National Gallery of Victoria, Melbourne
Felton Bequest 1976 (AS 131.1976)

Mughal imperial portraits combine the depiction of the observed features of the individual ruler with an overlay of imperial symbolism drawn from Timurid, Indian and European sources. Although they were officially tributaries of the Mughal emperors, the Hindu kings of the Rajput states (that now form parts of Rajasthan, the Panjab, Himachal Pradesh, and Jammu and Kashmir) displayed a different view of royal portraiture. The eternal was stressed over the empirical, and kingship itself over the individual king and his physiognomic traits. Although Rajput kings are often recognisable by their generalised facial features or the style of their beard or turban, their portraits seldom give any insight into character. More important are references to the *lakshanas* (characteristic or cognitive attributes) of the ideal

chakravartin (universal monarch).[54] Ironically, lesser mortals are often portrayed with more individuality because there were fewer conventions to be followed.

Mankot (modern Ramkot) is a tiny hill state only twenty-five kilometres long and fifteen kilometres wide. Following the standard composition used for Mankot royal portraits, this painting depicts a king seated on a carpet smoking hashish or opium through a *huqqa* — its hose traces a gentle loop against the typical flat yellow background before coming to halt just in front of his mouth. It is not possible to identify the ruler, although his royal status is beyond doubt — he is painted on a larger scale than the attendant carrying a peacock feather fan.

102 attributed to NAINSUKH (*c.*1710–1778)
Raja Balwant Singh on his palace roof
Jasrota, Jammu and Kashmir
1751
opaque watercolour, gold and ink on paper; 21.5 x 30.5 cm
Indian Museum, Calcutta (R.14 145/S.662)

In the history of painting from the Rajput hill states, no relationship between patron and artist can rival that between Prince Balwant Singh (1725–1763) and the painter Nainsukh (the Delight of the Eye); and no patron has left such a modest and melancholy image of himself. This prince from the minor state of Jasrota was a contemporary of both the Mughal emperor Muhammad Shah (see catalogue nos 83, 84) and Maharao Durjan Sal of Kota (see catalogue no. 86). Under Balwant Singh's enigmatic patronage, Nainsukh (brother of the artist Manaku, who painted the image at catalogue no. 72) produced more than fifty images showing the prince engaged in activities such as writing, having his beard trimmed, hunting ducks and listening to music. Other paintings show Balwant Singh in the setting of a grand palace.[55]

In this painting Balwant Singh sits alone on top of his palace, watching a monsoonal electrical storm while smoking a *huqqa*. Two inscriptions on the verso (the second one possibly written by Nainsukh) read: 'His Lordship is shown looking at the rains' and 'Raja Balwant Singhji — The year was [Samvat] 1808 [1751 AD]. The month was Sawan [July–August, during the monsoon] . . . The papiya bird.' The *papiha* bird often features in Indian mystical poetry because its rainy season song sounds like the words *piu kahan,* ('where is the beloved?') — separation from the beloved is a metaphor for separation from God. In the top right corner, however, two birds fly together. After Balwant Singh died in 1763, Nainsukh was a member of the party that took his ashes to the holy city of Haridvar on the Ganges.

103 *Maharaja Bhup Singh with his rani*
Guler, Himachal Pradesh
*c.*1795–1800
opaque watercolour on paper; 15.5 x 9.4 cm
On loan from the Board of Trustees of the Victoria and Albert Museum, London (IS 202–1949)

In the palaces of India there was strict control of access to the king by his subjects, and of men's visual access to the women of the royal family. The palaces of the Hindu Rajputs were divided into two main zones: that of men (the *mardana*) and that of women (the *zanana* or harem). Female dancers or musicians might perform before male audiences in the *mardana*, but queens and princesses would generally not be seen in any public or semi-public spaces. This segregation created a dilemma — how could a male artist paint the likeness of a royal consort without being able to see her? In most cases, the artists reverted to painting conventionalised images of women while honing their portrait skills on the male figures.

This small painting from the hill state of Guler shows Maharaja Bhup Singh (r.1790–1820 or 1826) relaxing under a quilt with a female companion, beneath suggestively voluptuous curtains. It is a rare example of such gentle intimacy in Indian art. Characteristically, however, the face of the maharaja is individualised, while his companion's is not — she may not, in fact, be his rani (queen). In typical Pahari fashion, the overall gentleness of the painting is suffused with touches of great boldness. The persimmon colour of the quilt, for example, contrasts boldly with the green of the bolster against which the couple recline. The maharaja is not seen in strict profile; the viewer can only guess what is capturing his focus beyond the borders of the painting.

104 *A woman on a terrace*
Bikaner, Rajasthan
late 17th century
opaque watercolour on paper; 18.4 x 12.6 cm
National Gallery of Victoria, Melbourne, Felton Bequest 1980 (AS34.1980)

The painting of women is the most private element of royal art in India. This subtle but brilliantly coloured painting from the Rajput state of Bikaner in the far desert west of Rajasthan does not have any political, narrative or geographical referents. The identity of the seated woman is not known, and it cannot even be determined whether she was meant to be identified. Perhaps she is an idealised lover, waiting for her beloved's return at the onset of the rainy season (when warfare ceases in Rajasthan and men return to their home seats). Although her eyes do not beckon, she sits alone in a setting made for two; the viewer must assume the role of her missing companion.

All the princely states of Rajasthan developed distinctive styles of painting within the predominant Rajput idiom. Painting at Bikaner was closest to the style of Mughal painting, but the treatment of landscape in the upper half of this painting remains defiantly idiosyncratic. Here, Mughal naturalism is used in the representation of an eccentrically tidy sense of nature. Lotus flowers and leaves alternate neatly in the pond, whose blue-grey waters are electrified by the coral-red fence. An orderly line of trees gives rhythm to the curved horizon, with the artist changing perspective halfway up the painting.

105 *A woman singing*
Kishangarh, Rajasthan
*c.*1740
opaque and transparent watercolour on paper; 37.0 x 25.5 cm
Howard Hodgkin Collection, London

In the Rajasthani state of Kishangarh, certain physical forms became remarkably stylised in the first half of the eighteenth century (see also catalogue no. 76). The two maharajas who ruled during this period, Raj Singh (r.1706–1748) and Savant Singh (r.1748–1764), were ardent devotees of Krishna in the form of Shri Nath-ji, as worshipped at Nathdvara in the neighbouring state of Mewar. Krishna and his beloved milkmaid, Radha, were the favourite subjects of Kishangarh court painting, a tradition revelling in the intoxication of divine love as described in mystical *bhakti* poetry. Savant Singh himself wrote devotional poetry under the nom-de-plume Nagari Das. The painting that flourished in this milieu created an image of the king as inspired mystic, rather than as the usurper of divine symbols. The image of

Radha was central in the Krishna-inspired poetry of the period — all beauty was measured against hers.

This Kishangarh painting depicts a female musician playing a stringed drone instrument known as the *tanpura*, and gesturing with her left hand while she sings. Her hair is covered by a translucent shawl. An inscription on the verso describes her as a *nayika*, one of the the eight ideal types of heroine classified in Sanskrit poetry. With her stylised, lotus-shaped eye, she is deliberately Radha-like in her beauty. Her eye is no longer merely an organ of vision; painted in tandem with an extravagantly arched eyebrow, it has been transformed into a symbol of beauty, an almost literal embodiment of the poetic epithet '*kamala-akshi*' (lotus-eyed).

106 *Maharaja Ram Singh II at worship*
Jaipur, Rajasthan
*c.*1870
opaque watercolour and gold on paper; 10.5 x 11.7 cm
Courtesy of the Arthur M. Sackler Museum, Harvard University Art Museums, Private Collection (507.1983)

Maharaja Ram Singh II ruled the Rajasthani state of Jaipur from 1851 to 1880, at the very moment when the modern began its eclipse of the traditional in the visual arts in India. Jaipur is just two hundred kilometres to the south of Delhi (the seat of the mighty Mughals and then a centre of British colonial power). Ram Singh 'ruled' under the watchful eyes of the British 'Resident'. With British support, his wealth increased as he monopolised the right to levy customs duties at the expense of his feudal lords.[56] While fulfilling his ritual duties as head of the Kachhwaha Rajput clan, he also learned how to dance and even partnered the wife of Lord Mayo at Viceregal balls.[57] Images of Ram Singh reflect this precarious balance between tradition and modernity.

A number of portraits show Ram Singh dressed in Anglicised Rajput court attire, wearing spectacles and polished black leather boots; however, in this small painting the maharaja presents himself as a Hindu devotee. The two crescent lines on his forehead, with a dot between the eyebrows, identify him as a *shakta*, a worshipper of the Great Goddess or *shakti*. Like King Narasimha sitting before his guru in the sculpture from Konarak (see catalogue no. 1a), here Ram Singh has divested himself of all royal symbols. He sits cross-legged in a yoga pose, with a simple cotton *dhoti* wrapped around his lower body and a heavy Shaivite rosary around his neck. His ascetic wooden sandals lie at the bottom right. Inconceivable in earlier Indian painting, Ram Singh stares straight out at the viewer. He was, in fact, intensely interested in new ways of looking; he learned the art of photography, and was photographed on a number of occasions.[58]

107 *Two Rajput princes*
Jodhpur, Rajasthan
*c.*1910
opaque watercolour on cotton with gold, silver and mica; 75.6 x 91.0 cm
National Gallery of Australia, Canberra (1992.1374)

During the nineteenth century the arrival of new image-making techniques in India was eagerly welcomed by the Rajput rulers of Rajasthan. Some court painters even took up photography, and the photographic vision radically changed the perspective of portraiture. This large, half-length double portrait, a format quite alien to Rajput painting, represents the last stage of traditional modes of royal patronage in north Indian painting.[59] Painted on cotton, the princes' jewellery and the gold ornament on their clothing is built up thickly and, in some areas, set with pieces of mica.

Partly surmised from the style of their turbans, it is likely that the two figures represent, Maharaja Sardar Singh (r.1895–1918) of the desert state of Jodhpur (on the left), and Thakur Mangal Singh of the Pokharan feudatory (*thikana*) within Jodhpur state.[60] It was Sardar Singh's son, Maharaja Umaid Singh (r.1918–1947), who built the huge Umaid Bhavan palace with its extraordinary art deco interiors in Jodhpur between 1929 and 1944. It would appear that this double portrait was painted from two separate photographs; the two princes are set in an impossible pose — there is simply no room for both pairs of legs. The swords they carry are the last symbols of Rajput power, which came to an end in 1948, the year after India gained independence from Britain. Here the swords compete with a symbol of modernism, the wristwatch, which was in use in Europe and North America by 1896, and among the maharajas of India not much later.

Appendices

Appendix 1
Architectural Plans

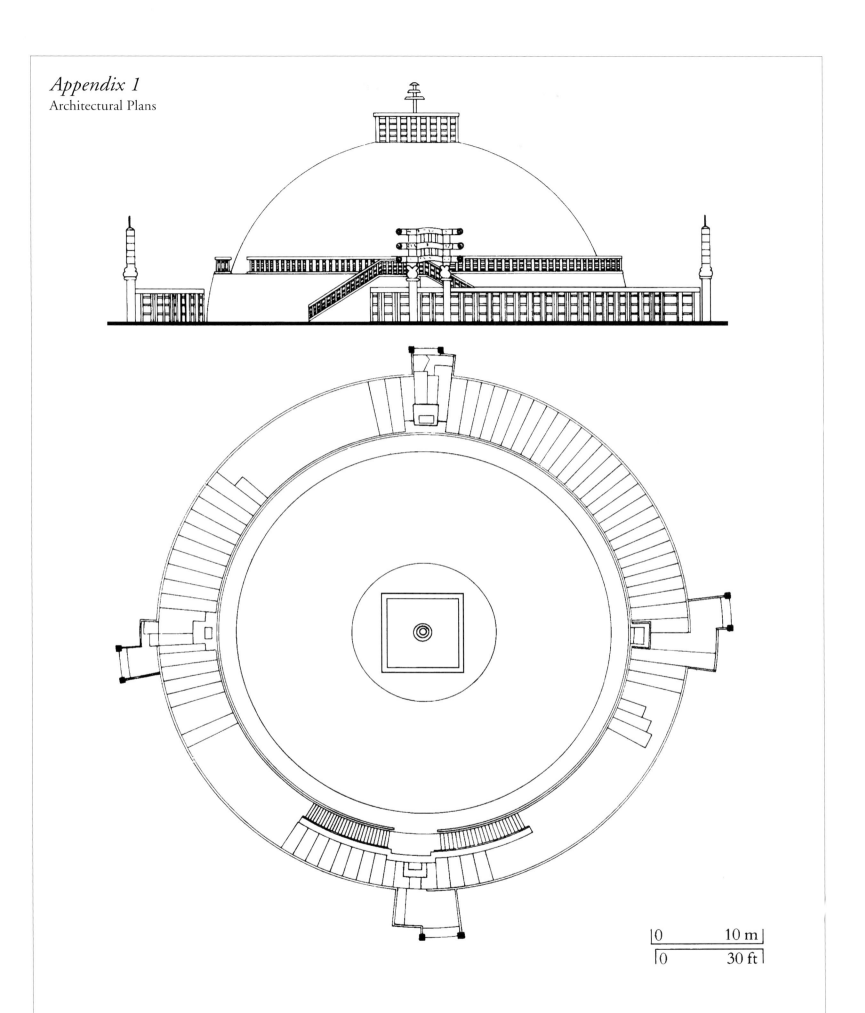

fig. 11: Plan, *stupa* 1, Sanchi, Madhya Pradesh, 3rd–1st century BC (after George Michell, *Monuments of India*, Vol. I).

151

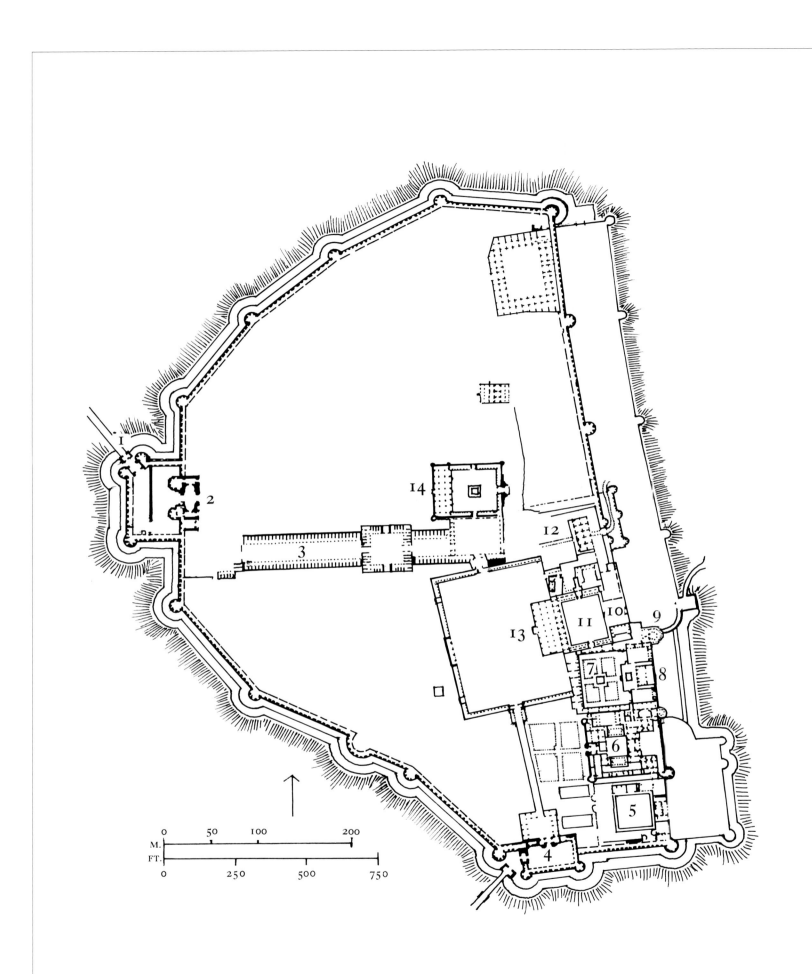

fig. 12: Plan, Red Fort, Agra, Uttar Pradesh, 1564 and later (after George Michell, *The Royal Palaces of India*).

(1) Delhi Gate; (2) Hathi Pol (Elephant Gate); (3) Bazaar street; (4) Amar Singh Gate and Akbari Gate; (5) Akbari Mahal; (6) Jahangiri Mahal; (7) Anguri Bagh (Grape Garden); (8) Khass Mahal; (9) Shah Burj; (10) Divan-i Khass (Hall of Private Audience); (11) Machchhi Bhavan; (12) Nagina Mosque; (13) Divan-i 'Amm (Hall of Public Audience); (14) Moti Masjid (Pearl Mosque).

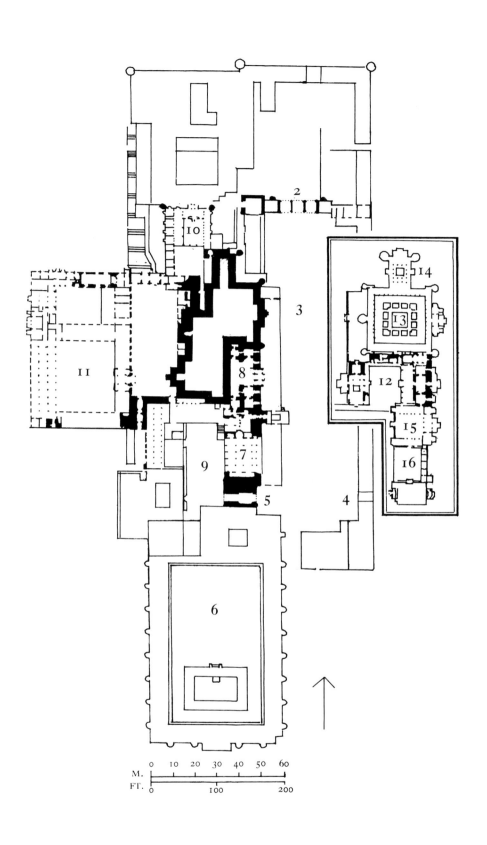

fig. 13: Plan, City Palace, Udaipur, Rajasthan, 1567 and later (after George Michell, *The Royal Palaces of India*).

(1) Badi Pol (Great Gate); (2) Tripolia (Triple Gate); (3) Manek Chowk; (4) Suraj Gate; (5) Toran Gate; (6) Lakshmi Chowk; (7) Sabha (Public Audience Hall); (8) Shila Khana; (9) Moti Chowk; (10) Mahendra Sabha; (11) Karan Nivas. On the upper levels (inset, right): (12) Rajya Angan Chowk; (13) Amar Vilas; (14) Badi Mahal; (15) Badi Chatur Chowk; (16) Mor (Peacock) Chowk.

Appendix 2

Objects in chronological order

Up to 300 AD

Self-born linga (svayambhu linga)
Narmada River, central India
age unknown
polished stone
catalogue no. 7

White dog barking at the Buddha
Jamalgarhi, ancient Gandhara
North West Frontier Province, Pakistan
Kushana period, c.2nd century
stone (schist)
catalogue no. 36

Great Decease of the Buddha
(mahaparinirvana)
ancient Gandhara, Pakistan
Kushana period, c.2nd century
stone (schist)
catalogue no. 37

Frieze with pipal leaves
Loriyan Tangai, ancient Gandhara
North West Frontier Province, Pakistan
Kushana period, c.2nd century
stone (schist)
catalogue no. 38

Figure of a bodhisattva
Mathura, Uttar Pradesh
Kushana period, 2nd century
sandstone
catalogue no. 41

Railing pillar with a nature spirit (yakshi)
Mathura, Uttar Pradesh
Kushana period, 2nd century
sandstone
catalogue no. 57

Women worshipping the footprints of the Buddha
Amaravati, Andhra Pradesh
Satavahana period, late 2nd century
limestone
catalogue no. 30

Bodhisattva
ancient Gandhara, Pakistan
Kushana period, late 2nd century
stone (schist)
catalogue no. 40

The Buddha with a statue
ancient Gandhara, Pakistan
Kushana period, 2nd–3rd century
stone (schist)
catalogue no. 3

Stupa gable
ancient Gandhara, Pakistan
Kushana period, 2nd–3rd century
stone (schist)
catalogue no. 35

Panel from a stupa with auspicious symbols
Nagarjunakonda, Andhra Pradesh
Ikshvaku period, 3rd century
limestone
catalogue no. 39

Garuda attacking a female serpent (nagini)
ancient Gandhara, Pakistan
Kushana period, 3rd century
stone (schist)
catalogue no. 63

300–700

Standing Buddha
Sarnath, Uttar Pradesh
Gupta period, c.430–50
sandstone
catalogue no. 32

Vishnu's discus (chakra purusha)
Pipariya, Satna district, Madhya Pradesh
Gupta period, c.510–20
sandstone
catalogue no. 16

Panel with grotesque relief
Mathura, Uttar Pradesh
Gupta period, c.530
sandstone
catalogue no. 64

Double figure of a lion
Gwalior, Madhya Pradesh
Vardhana period, 7th century
sandstone
catalogue no. 65

The bodhisattva Avalokiteshvara
north-west India
c.700
cast bronze inlaid with silver
catalogue no. 42

Water spout (pranala)
Kaverippakkam, North Arcot district, Tamil Nadu
Pallava period, c.800
stone
catalogue no. 70

The Hindu triad (trimurti)
North West Frontier Province (probably Swat), Pakistan
9th century
cast bronze inlaid with silver
catalogue no. 6

The Buddha 'calling the earth to witness'
his victory over Mara
Kurkihar, Bihar
Pala period, 9th century
cast bronze
catalogue no. 29

Tara, the Saviouress
Kurkihar, Bihar
Pala period, mid-9th century
cast bronze
catalogue no. 44

Image frame (parikara)
probably eastern Rajasthan
mid-9th century
sandstone
catalogue no. 69

Serpent king and queen
Nalanda, Bihar
Pala period, 9th – 10th century
stone
catalogue no. 58

Celestial maiden (apsaras)
Khajuraho, Madhya Pradesh
Chandella period, c.10th century
sandstone
catalogue no. 61

Pair of door guardians (dvarapalas)
Tamil Nadu
Chola period, 10th century
stone
catalogue nos. 68a–b

Seated Vishnu
Kongunadu, Coimbatore and Salem districts, Tamil Nadu
Chola period, c.950
cast bronze
catalogue no. 2

Shiva as Nataraja (the Lord of Dance)
Tamil Nadu
Chola period, c.950–1000
cast bronze
catalogue no.5

Sadashiva (Eternal Shiva)
Tamil Nadu
Chola period, late 10th century
stone (granulite)
catalogue no. 9

Vishnu as Shrinivasa with consorts
Sirupanaiyur, Thanjavur district, Tamil Nadu
Chola period, late 10th century
cast bronze
catalogue no. 17

Nandi
Tamil Nadu
Chola period, 10th – 11th century
cast bronze
catalogue no. 59

1000–1500

Votive stupa
eastern India (Bihar or Bengal)
Pala period, c.11th century
sandstone
catalogue no. 31

Mahakali, the Destroyer of Time
Tamil Nadu
Chola period, 11th century
cast bronze
catalogue no. 12

Standing Buddha
Nagapattinam, Tamil Nadu
Chola period, 11th century
cast bronze
catalogue no. 33

Marichi, the Goddess of Dawn
Bihar
Pala period, 11th century
stone
catalogue no. 46

Crowned Buddha
Kurkihar, Bihar
Pala period, 11th – 12th century
cast bronze with silver inlay
catalogue no. 34

Standing Jina
Karnataka
11th – 12th century
cast bronze
catalogue no. 48

Vishnu in the form of Trivikrama
Shialdi, Dhaka district, Bangladesh
Pala period, early 12th century
stone (phyllite)
catalogue no. 15

The saint Sambandar
Tamil Nadu
Chola period, 12th century
cast bronze
catalogue no. 10

The saint Manikkavachaka
Tamil Nadu
Chola period, 12th century
cast bronze
catalogue no. 11

Akshobhya Buddha in lotus mandala
eastern India (Bihar or Bengal)
Pala period, 12th century
cast bronze with silver and copper inlay and traces of gilding
catalogue no. 43

Prajnaparamita, the Goddess of Wisdom
Orissa
Eastern Ganga period, 12th century
stone
catalogue no. 45

Neminatha, the twenty-second Jina
Narhad, Pilani district, Rajasthan
Chahamana period, 12th century
stone (basalt)
catalogue no. 49

Head of a Jain image
Aluara, Dhanbad district, Bihar
Pala period, 12th century
cast bronze
catalogue no. 51

Agni, the God of Fire
central India
12th century
sandstone
catalogue no. 66

Tree goddess (shalabhanjika)
Karnataka
Hoysala period, c.1150-1200
stone (chloritic schist)
catalogue no. 56

Neminatha, the twenty-second Jina
Dilwara, Mount Abu, Rajasthan
Solanki period, 1160
stone (marble)
catalogue no. 50

Surya, the Sun God
Orissa
Eastern Ganga period, 13th century
stone (chloritic schist)
catalogue no. 22

Ganesha with Shakti
probably Konarak, Orissa
Eastern Ganga period, 13th century
stone (chloritic schist)
catalogue no. 23

King Narasimha I with his guru
Sun Temple, Konarak, Orissa
Eastern Ganga period, 1238–58
stone (chloritic schist)
catalogue no. 1a

King Narasimha I worshipping the Puri trinity
Sun Temple, Konarak, Orissa
Eastern Ganga period, 1238–58
stone (chloritic schist)
catalogue no. 1b

Elephant with riders
Karnataka
Hoysala period, c.1250
stone
catalogue no. 62

Altarpiece with the twenty-four Jinas (chaubisi)
Gujarat
Sultanate period, 15th century
cast bronze
catalogue no. 47

Entertainment at Indra's court
western India (Gujarat or Rajasthan)
Sultanate period, 15th century
opaque watercolour and gold on paper
catalogue no. 53

Two Jinas
two pages from a manuscript of the *Kalpasutra* (*The Book of Ritual*)
Jaunpur, Uttar Pradesh
Sultanate period, c.1465
paint, ink and gold on paper
catalogue nos. 54a–b

The monk Kalaka with the god Indra
page from a manuscript of the *Kalakacharyakatha* (*The Story of the Monk Kalaka*)
western India (Gujarat or Rajasthan)
Sultanate period, late 15th century
paint, ink and gold on paper
catalogue no. 55

Durga as the Slayer of the Buffalo Demon
(mahishasuramardini)
South Arcot district, Tamil Nadu
Vijayanagar period, 15th – 16th century
stone (granite)
catalogue no. 13

Sita
Karnataka
Vijayanagar period, 15th – 16th century
cast bronze
catalogue no. 14

Ganesha
Tamil Nadu
Vijayanagar period, 15th – 16th century
cast bronze
catalogue no. 24

1500 onwards

Five-faced linga (panchamukha linga)
Joti, Cuddapah district, Andhra Pradesh
Vijayanagar period, c.16th century
stone (granite)
catalogue no. 8

Aiyanar on an elephant
Thogur, Thanjavur district, Tamil Nadu
16th century
cast bronze
catalogue no. 28

Sage (rishi)
Tadpatri, Anantapur district, Tamil Nadu
Vijayanagar period, 16th century
stone (granite)
catalogue no. 67

Rescue of the infant Iskandar (Alexander)
folio from a series of the *Hamzanama*
(*The Story of Hamza*)
north India
Mughal dynasty, c.1562–77
opaque watercolour and gold on cotton
catalogue no. 74

Designed by BASAWAN (active c.1560–1600);
painting by NAND OF GWALIOR
(active c.1584–1596)
The Emperor Akbar on pilgrimage to Ajmer by foot
page from a manuscript of the *Akbarnama*
(*The History of Akbar*)
north India
Mughal dynasty, c.1590
opaque watercolour and gold on paper
catalogue no. 4

attributed to MISKIN (active c.1580–1604)
Krishna lifting Mount Govardhan
page from a manuscript of the *Harivamsa*
(*The Genealogy of Hari*)
north India
Mughal dynasty, c.1590
opaque watercolour and gold on paper
catalogue no. 79

BISHAN DAS (active c.1589–1640)
Prince Babur arriving at Andijan
page from a manuscript of the *Baburnama*
(*The Memoirs of Babur*)
north India
Mughal dynasty c.1590
opaque watercolour, gold and ink on paper
catalogue no. 92

Designed by BASAWAN (active c.1560–1600);
right page painted by TARA THE ELDER
(active c.1585–1590)
left page painted by ASI (active c.1584–1596)
*The Emperor Akbar watches a battle between
two groups of holy men*
double page from a manuscript of the
Akbarnama (*The History of Akbar*)
north India
Mughal dynasty, c.1590
opaque watercolour on paper
catalogue no. 93

attributed to MADHU KHANAZAD
(active c.1582–1604)
from an unidentified manuscript, mounted
as an album page
King Solomon's court
north India (probably Agra)
Mughal dynasty, c.1600–05
opaque watercolour on paper
catalogue no. 75

two pages from a manuscript of the *Kulliyat*
(*Collected Works*) of Sa'di
calligraphed by 'Abd al-Rahim of Herat
north India
Mughal dynasty, c.1600–05
opaque watercolour and gold on paper
a) attributed to AQA RIZA (active c.1580–
1605)
The poet Sa'di with his patron (f.91a)
b) *A sinner's passionate plea to God* (f.107b)
catalogue nos 78a–b

attributed to MANSUR (active c.1589–1625)
Peafowl in a landscape
north India (probably Agra)
Mughal dynasty, c.1610 (border c.1645)
opaque watercolour and gold on paper
catalogue no. 82

ABU'L HASAN (born 1588–1589; active
c.1600–1630)
The Emperor Jahangir at his audience window
page from a manuscript of the *Tuzuk-i Jahangiri*
(*The Memoirs of Jahangir*)
north India (probably Agra)
Mughal dynasty, c.1620
opaque watercolour on paper
catalogue no. 91

CHITARMAN (active c.1625–1670)
The Emperor Shah Jahan nimbed in glory
north India (probably Agra)
Mughal dynasty, 1627–28
opaque watercolour and gold on paper
catalogue no. 96

GOVARDHAN (c.1604–1640)
The Emperor Akbar with a lion and calf
page from the so-called *Kevorkian Album*
north India (probably Agra)
Mughal dynasty, c.1630
opaque watercolour and gold on paper
catalogue no. 94

*Prince Dara Shikoh with Mian Mir
and Mulla Shah*
page from an imperial album
north India
Mughal dynasty, c.1635
opaque watercolour and ink on paper
catalogue no. 77

attributed to GOVARDHAN
(active c.1604–1640)
The Emperor Shah Jahan on the Peacock Throne
from an album of the Emperor Shah Jahan
north India (probably Agra)
Mughal dynasty, c.1635 (border c.1645)
opaque watercolour and gold on paper
catalogue no. 71

Portrait of the noble Iltifat Khan
north India
Mughal dynasty, c.1640–50
opaque watercolour on paper
catalogue no. 99

*Rosette (shamsa) with the name and titles of the
Emperor Shah Jahan*
opening page of the so-called *Kevorkian Album*
north India (probably Delhi)
Mughal dynasty, c.1645
opaque watercolour and gold on paper
catalogue no. 98

PAYAG (active c.1595–1655)
The Emperor Humayun seated in a landscape
page from the so-called *Late Shah Jahan Album*
north India (probably Delhi)
Mughal dynasty, c.1650
opaque watercolour and gold on paper
catalogue no. 95

BICHITR (active c.1615–1650)
The Emperor Shah Jahan with Asaf Khan
page from an imperial album
north India (probably Delhi)
Mughal dynasty, c.1650
opaque watercolour and gold on paper
catalogue no. 97

attributed to PAYAG (active c.1595–1655)
Prince and courtiers at camp
north India
Mughal dynasty, c.1650
opaque watercolour with gold on paper
catalogue no. 100

A woman on a terrace
Bikaner, Rajasthan
late 17th century
opaque watercolour on paper
catalogue no. 104

The world of mortals (manushyaloka)
western India (Gujarat or Rajasthan)
18th century
opaque watercolour on cotton
catalogue no. 52

A Mankot prince
Mankot, Jammu and Kashmir
c.1700
opaque watercolour and gold on paper
catalogue no. 101

attributed to the KOTA MASTER
Rao Bhoj Singh hunting lion
Kota, Rajasthan
c.1720
opaque watercolour and gold on paper
catalogue no. 85

attributed to MANAKU (active c.1700–1760)
Vibhishana joins Rama's monkey and bear army
page from a manuscript of the *Ramayana*
Guler, Himachal Pradesh
c.1725
opaque watercolour and gold on paper
catalogue no. 72

*Maharao Durjan Sal hunting with Krishna
in the form of Shri Brijnath-ji*
Kota, Rajasthan
c.1725–50
opaque watercolour with gold on cotton
catalogue no. 86

The Emperor Muhammad Shah in his garden
Delhi, Uttar Pradesh
Mughal dynasty, c.1730
black ink with colour washes
catalogue no. 83

The Emperor Muhammad Shah hunting
Delhi, Uttar Pradesh
Mughal dynasty, c.1730
opaque watercolour and gold on paper
catalogue no. 84

JAI RAM
*Maharana Jagat Singh II attending a Rasalila
performance*
Udaipur, Rajasthan
1736
opaque watercolour and gold on paper
catalogue no. 89

A woman singing
Kishangarh, Rajasthan
c.1740
opaque and transparent watercolour on paper
catalogue no. 105

attributed to NAINSUKH (c.1710–1778)
Raja Balwant Singh on his palace roof
Jasrota, Jammu and Kashmir
1751
opaque watercolour, gold and ink on paper
catalogue no. 102

The musical mode Raga Megha-Malhara
from a manuscript of the *Ragamala* (*Garland of
Ragas*)
Bundi, Rajasthan
c.1760
opaque watercolour and gold on paper
catalogue no. 20

Shukadeva and the king
Kishangarh, Rajasthan
c.1760
opaque watercolour on paper
catalogue no. 76

The empty palace
page from a manuscript of the *Ramayana*
Kangra, Himachal Pradesh
c.1775–80
opaque watercolour and gold on paper
catalogue no. 73

Maharaja Bhup Singh with his rani
Guler, Himachal Pradesh
c.1795–1800
opaque watercolour on paper
catalogue no. 103

BAKHTA (active 1761–1811)
Rawat Gokul Das hunting
Deogarh, Rajasthan
1806
opaque watercolour with gold and silver on
paper
catalogue no. 87

*Rishis worshipping a Shiva linga on Mount
Kailasa*
page from a manuscript of the *Shiva Purana*
(*The Ancient Story of Shiva*)
Kangra, Himachal Pradesh
c.1810
opaque watercolour and gold on paper
catalogue no. 80

The wedding of Krishna and Rukmini
Garhwal or Kangra, Himachal Pradesh
c.1820
opaque watercolour and gold on paper
catalogue no. 21

Maharana Jawan Singh hunting
Udaipur, Rajasthan
c.1830
opaque watercolour, gold and ink on cotton
catalogue no. 88

Priests worshipping Krishna as Sri Nath-ji
Kota, Rajasthan
c.1840
opaque watercolour, ink, silver and gold on
cotton
catalogue no. 18

The infant Krishna floating on the cosmic ocean
Nathdvara, Rajasthan
c.1840
opaque watercolour, silver and gold on paper
catalogue no. 19

KISAN DAS
Maharao Ram Singh II celebrating Holi
Kota, Rajasthan
1844
opaque watercolour and gold on paper
catalogue no. 90

Caparisoned bull
Nathadvara, Rajasthan
c.1860
opaque watercolour and gold on paper
catalogue no. 60

Workshop of SAYYID HUSSAIN SHAH and
SAYYID MUHAMMAD MIR
Shawl with a map of the Kashmir Valley
Srinagar, Kashmir
c.1870
cashmere wool, natural dyes, twill weave,
embroidery
catalogue no. 81

Maharaja Ram Singh II at worship
Jaipur, Rajasthan
c.1870
opaque watercolour and gold on paper
catalogue no. 106

Ganesha
Kalighat, Calcutta, Bengal
c.1880
watercolour and silver paint on paper
catalogue no. 25

Kali
Kalighat, Calcutta, Bengal
c.1880
watercolour and silver paint on paper
catalogue no. 26

Bhairon Deo
Muria tribe, Bastar district, Madhya Pradesh
early 20th century
cast bell metal
catalogue no. 27

Two Rajput princes
Jodhpur, Rajasthan
c.1910
opaque watercolour on cotton with gold, silver
and mica
catalogue no. 107

Glossary

Apsaras: Minor female divinity, often depicted as a celestial dancer.

Asana: Literally 'seat' or 'throne', but also a description of the sitting position in which a deity or saviour is depicted. These include *padmasana* (lotus seat), with legs crossed and each foot resting on the opposite thigh, and *lalitasana*, with one leg folded up on the seat and the other hanging downwards. Yogic positions are also known as *asanas*.

Avalokiteshvara: 'The Lord who looks down (with compassion)', a **bodhisattva** embodying compassion.

Avatara: 'Descent', especially of a god from heaven to earth. The incarnation of a deity, especially the ten forms of the Hindu god **Vishnu**.

Bhakti: 'Devotion' to a deity, usually expressed as a form of mystical love.

Bodhi: Buddhist 'Enlightenment', achieved through the combination of compassion (*karuna*) and wisdom (*prajna*).

Bodhisattva: An 'Enlightenment being', capable of achieving **bodhi**, 'Enlightenment', who delays his own attainment of Buddhahood in order to help other living beings.

Brahma: The Hindu god of creation, and one of the three members of the Hindu triad, **trimurti**, along with **Shiva** and **Vishnu**.

Brahman (neuter): the Absolute in Hindu philosophy from which all existence is derived, and of which all Hindu gods are facets.

Brahman: Member of the Hindu priestly class. See also **kshatriya**.

Buddha: An 'enlightened one'; a title especially, but not exclusively, appplied to the historical **Shakyamuni Buddha** (*c.* 563–483 BC). See also **Jina Buddha**.

Chaitya hall: Buddhist hall, with a votive **stupa** set within an apsidal end; in western India many were in the form of caves cut into cliff-faces.

Chakra: A 'wheel' or 'discus', often imbued with solar symbolism, and one of the attributes of the Hindu god **Vishnu**. See also **dharmachakra** and **chakravartin**.

Chakravartin: Literally 'a turner of the wheel', but figuratively a universal monarch. In Hinduism, **Vishnu** is regarded as a *chakravartin* imposing order throughout the cosmos; in Buddhism, the Buddha is considered a *chakravartin* of the religious sphere.

Chattra: Circular parasol or canopy; a symbol of royalty.

Darshana: Literally 'seeing' or 'viewing'; sighting a revered person, sacred image or place, and taking into oneself their inherent religious power. In Hindu worship, the devotee 'takes' the *darshana* 'given' by the god. The term was later used by the Muslim Mughal emperors to describe the ritual of displaying themselves to their subjects.

Deva: A Hindu god.

Devi: A Hindu goddess.

Dharma: Moral or religious duty, law or custom; the Hindu term closest to the word 'religion', but much broader in scope. In Buddhism, it refers to the essence of the Buddha's teachings.

Dharmachakra: The 'wheel of the law', set into motion by **Shakyamuni Buddha** during his first sermon in the deer park at Sarnath; a symbol of the universality of the Buddha's teachings.

Dikpala: A guardian of one of the quarters of the universe. There are usually eight, each corresponding to the cardinal and intermediate points of the compass.

Dvarapala: Door guardian. Usually installed in pairs flanking the doorway to a shrine; their function is to ward off evil from the sanctum of a temple.

Garbha griha: Literally 'womb chamber', the dark sanctum of a Hindu temple.

Jataka: 'Birth story', detailing events in the previous lives of **Shakyamuni Buddha**.

Jina: 'Conqueror' or 'liberator', one of the twenty-four saviours of the Jain religion who have attained perfect knowledge; also known as **tirthankara** ('ford-finder'). See also **Mahavira**, **Neminatha** and **Parshvanatha**.

Jina Buddha: In **Vajrayana Buddhism**, one of the five 'conqueror Buddhas' emerging from the meditations of the Supreme Buddha Vajrasattva — they are Vairochana (the Resplendent), Akshobhya (the Imperturbable), Ratnasambhava (the Jewel-born), Amitabha (Boundless Light) and Amoghasiddhi (Infallible Success).

Kinnara: An auspicious sub-deity with a human head and the body of a horse or a bird.

Kirttimukha: 'Face of glory', a lion-like mask used to protect a temple or individual image from evil.

Krishna: The 'Dark One', the eighth **avatara** or incarnation of the Hindu god **Vishnu**.

Kshatriya: Member of the Hindu warrior and ruler class. See also **brahman**.

Lakshana: A 'mark', 'symbol' or 'sign', identifying the body of a **chakravartin**, **Buddha** or **bodhisattva**. The historical **Shakyamuni Buddha** is said to have been distinguished by thirty-two such *lakshanas*. See also **urna** and **ushnisha**.

Lakshmi: The Hindu goddess of good fortune and wealth, and the principal consort of the Hindu god **Vishnu**; also known as Shri.

Linga: A 'mark', 'symbol' or 'sign', especially of gender or sex. An aniconic form of the Hindu god **Shiva** in the shape of the male phallus.

Mahabharata: A vast Hindu epic, partly narrative and partly didactic, describing the struggle between two families (the Pandavas and the Kauravas) for the possession of northern India (Bharata).

Mahaparinirvana: The 'great final **nirvana**'; specifically the death of **Shakyamuni Buddha** at Kushinagara.

Maharaja/Maharana: King. See also **raja**.

Mahavira: The 'great hero', Vardhamana Mahavira (*c.* 599–527 BC), the twenty-fourth and last of the Jain saviours. See also **Jina**.

Mahayana Buddhism: The 'great vehicle' of Buddhism, a later development emphasising the role of **bodhisattvas** as compassionate saviours.

Maitreya: The 'friendly' or 'benevolent' one; a **bodhisattva** and the Buddha of the Future.

Makara: A mythical aquatic animal, originally inspired by the Indian freshwater crocodile; an auspicious guardian.

Mandala: A 'circle'; a circular diagram used as an aid for meditation. It can also serve as the ground plan for a temple.

Mantra: A mystical incantation that invokes the divinity being worshipped; the sound of a *mantra* is more important than its actual meaning.

Mara: 'Death'; the evil Destroyer in Buddhist mythology who attempted to dissuade the Buddha from his mission through the temptations of temporal power.

Meru: The mythical golden mountain at the centre of the Hindu universe.

Moksha: The 'release' or 'liberation' of the individual soul from the bonds of earthly existence, and the attainment of unity with the Absolute.

Mudra: A 'seal' or 'sign'; a conventional gesture in Indian art made by one or both hands to convey sacred meaning. These include: *abhaya* (fear-dispelling), *bhumisparsha* (earth-touching, symbolising the Buddha calling the earth to witness his victory over **Mara**), *chin* or *vyakhyana* (explanation or discourse), **dharmachakra** (preaching), *dhyana* (meditation), *kataka* (holding a flower), *varada* (charity), *vismaya* (wonderment or praise) and *vitarka* (discourse or discussion).

Mughal: Persian form of 'Mongol' (often also transliterated as 'Mogul'); a dynasty of Muslim kings of central Asian origin who ruled large parts of India from 1526–1857.

Mukha linga: A **linga** on which is depicted one or more human faces of the Hindu god **Shiva**. See also **linga**.

Mula murti: 'Root image'; the central, immovable image in the sanctum of a Hindu temple (almost always carved from stone). See also **murti** and **utsava murti**.

Murti: A 'form'; an image of a deity. In Hinduism, a manifestation more than a mere representation.

Naga: A snake, usually a cobra; a serpent deity.

Nayanmar: The sixty-three Shaivite saints of south India, including Sambandar and Manikkavachaka.

Neminatha: The twenty-second of the twenty-four Jain saviours. See also **Jina**.

Nirvana: The 'extinction' of the whole process of worldly existence and the cycle of rebirths; the ultimate goal of the Buddhist path.

Pahari painting: The so-called 'hill' schools of painting that flourished at the courts of the Hindu Rajput kings in the foothills of the Himalayas (north-west of Delhi) from the late-seventeenth century to the mid-nineteenth century.

Parshvanatha: The twenty-third of the twenty-four Jain saviours — a semi-historical figure born in the late ninth century BC. See also **Jina**.

Parvati: A Hindu goddess and consort, **shakti**, of the god **Shiva**. See also **shakti**.

Puja: Ritual acts of worship preformed in honour of a Hindu deity.

Puranas: Hindu scriptures containing 'tales of ancient times'; important sources for the mythologies of the Hindu deities.

Rao/Rawat: Title for a ruler (junior to a maharaja /maharana).

Raja: King.

Rajputs: Ethnic group whose Hindu kings ruled kingdoms that are now part of the modern Indian states of Rajasthan: in the desert west (including Mewar/Udaipur, Bikaner, Bundi, Jaipur, Jodhpur, Kishangarh and Kota); and Himachal Pradesh and Jammu and Kashmir in the Himalayan foothills to the north-west of Delhi (including Guler, Jasrota, Kangra and Mankot).

Ramayana: One of the two great Hindu epics of India. The story of Rama, the seventh **avatara** of the god **Vishnu**, and his faithful wife Sita.

Sanskrit: Along with Pali, one of the classical languages of India in which most of the canonical texts of Hinduism and Buddhism were composed.

Shakti: 'Energy', the female creative power; also the power of a male god personified as his consort in the form of a goddess. **Parvati** and **Lakshmi** are the *shaktis* of the Hindu gods **Shiva** and **Vishnu** respectively.

Shakyamuni: The historical Buddha who lived in north India from *c.* 563–483 BC. See also **Buddha**.

Shalabhanjika: A tree goddess; literally 'breaking a branch of the *shala* tree'.

Shamsa: Rosette; solar device commonly used in the Islamic tradition of manuscript illustration.

Shiva: The 'Auspicious', one of the three principal gods of Hinduism and a member of the Hindu triad, **trimurti**.

Shramanas: Ascetic wanderers such as **Shakyamuni Buddha** (the founder of Buddhism) and **Mahavira** (the founder of Jainism) who set out in the sixth century BC to find paths towards new spiritual goals.

Stupa: 'Crest' or 'summit', a sacred mound containing Buddhist relics and a focus for Buddhist worship; later, a symbol for the Buddha.

Tamil: One of the most important religious and literary languages of south India; still spoken in the state of Tamil Nadu.

Theravada Buddhism: 'Doctrine of the Elders', the traditional canon of early Buddhism considered by its followers to be the only authentic Buddhist doctrine; known pejoratively as Hinayana (the lesser vehicle) by adepts of Mahayana Buddhism. See also **Mahayana Buddhism**.

Tirthankara: 'Ford-finder', one of the twenty-four Jain saviours. See also **Jina**.

Tribhanga: The triple-bend pose used in Indian art.

Trimurti: The Hindu triad comprised of three manifestations of the Absolute: **Brahma** (the Creator), **Vishnu** (the Preserver) and **Shiva** (the Destroyer).

Urna: A tuft of hair between the eyebrows, and one of the thirty-two **lakshanas** by which the Buddha is recognised. See also **lakshana**.

Ushnisha: A knot of hair or turban, and, in the form of a cranial protrusion, one of the thirty-two **lakshanas** by which the Buddha is recognised; a symbol of the Buddha's great wisdom. See also **lakshana**.

Utsava murti: Portable Hindu images (almost always made of cast bronze) used during festival (*utsava*) worship. See also **murti** and **mula murti**.

Vahana: The bird or animal 'vehicle' on which a Hindu deity rides.

Vajrayana Buddhism: 'The Vehicle of the Thunderbolt'; a later form of Buddhism in which release, **moksha**, was sought through the acquisition of magical power (symbolised by the *vajra* or thunderbolt) during complex rituals and intensely-focused meditative practices.

Vedas: The early group of sacred texts, composed between about 1500 and 800 BC, that serve as the foundation of what is now known as Hinduism.

Vidyadharas: 'Knowledge bearers'; auspicious celestial beings often shown in flight carrying garlands of flowers.

Vishnu: The 'Pervader', one of the three principal gods of Hinduism and a member of the Hindu triad, **trimurti**. His ten **avataras**, or incarnations, include **Krishna** and **Rama**.

Yajña: The sacrificial rituals of early Vedic Hinduism.

Yaksha (female: yakshi): Ancient nature spirits, often incorporated in temples as auspicious guardians.

Yoga: One of the six orthodox systems of Indian philosophy. The word *yoga* is derived from the Sanskrit root *yuj*, 'to unite'. It teaches the way in which the individual soul (*jivatma*) and the universal soul (*paramatma*) can be united to achieve release, **moksha**, from suffering.

Yogi/Yogin: A practitioner of **yoga**.

Yoni: The female generative organ; when combined sculpturally with the **linga** they symbolise the power of divine procreation.

Notes

Full references for all texts cited in these notes appear in the Bibliography (pp. 163–68).

THE VISION OF KINGS — AN INTRODUCTION

1. Appar, *Tevaram*, Book VI, 301.1 (Civapuram), as translated in Indira Vishwanatham Peterson, *Poems to Siva: The Hymns of the Tamil Saints*, 1989, p. 112; see also pp. 69–72.

2. D.C. Sircar and S.R. Sarma, 'Kapilas inscriptions of Narasimhadeva', *Epigraphia Indica*, 1959, p. 43.

3. Alice Boner et al, *New Light on the Sun Temple at Konarka*, 1972, pp. xliii–xlv; and Thomas E. Donaldson, *Hindu Temple Art of Orissa*, 1987, vol. 3, pp. 592–95.

4. A variant of this ritual involves the painting of eyes on the image: see K.M. Varma, 'The Role of Polychromy in Indian Statuary', *Artibus Asiae*, vol. 24, 1961, pp. 122–25.

5. O.M. Starza-Majewski, 'King Narasimha I before his Spiritual Preceptor', *Journal of the Royal Asiatic Society*, 1971, p. 138.

6. *Baya Chakada*, as cited in Susan L. Huntington, *The Art of Ancient India*, 1985, p. 441 (where doubts about the authenticity of the text are noted).

7. Thomas E. Donaldson, *Hindu Temple Art of Orissa*, 1986, vol. 2, p. 613.

8. O.M. Starza-Majewski, 'King Narasimha I before his Spiritual Preceptor', *Journal of the Royal Asiatic Society*, 1971, p. 135.

9. For some other examples of Kongu bronzes, see R. Nagaswamy, 'Rare Bronzes from Kongu Country', *Lalit Kala*, 1961, pp. 7–10.

10. Diana L. Eck, *Darsan: Seeing the Divine Image in India*, 1981, pp. 5–6.

11. J. Auboyer, *Le trône et son symbolisme dans l'inde ancienne*, 1949, pp. 163–64.

12. Martin Lerner and Steven Kossak, *The Lotus Transcendent: Indian and Southeast Asian Art from the Samuel Eilenberg Collection*, 1991, pp. 86–87.

13. Abul Fazl, *Akbarnama* (*The History of Akbar*), H. Beveridge (transl.) vol. 2, pp. 510–11.

GODS AND GODDESSES

1. Vidya Dehejia, *Art of the Imperial Cholas*, 1990, pp. 39–42. This bronze image of Shiva Nataraja has been published previously in *Masterpieces of Asian Art in American Collections*, 1960; Shehbaz H. Sefrani, 'Samuel Eilenberg (1913–)', in Pratapaditya Pal (ed.), *American Coillectors of Asian Art*, 1986, pp. 149, 155–56; and *Palast der Gotter*, 1992, no. 158, pp. 226–28.

2. David Smith, 'Chidambaram', in George Michell (ed.), *Temple Towns of Tamil Nadu*, 1989, p. 330.

3. Appar, 'Koyil (Tillai)', *Tevaram*, IV.81.4, as translated in Indira Viswanathan Peterson, *Poems to Siva: The Hymns of the Tamil Saints*, 1989, p. 118.

4. Bettina Baumer, 'Unmanifest and manifest forms according to the Saivagamas', in Anna Libera Dallapiccola (ed.), *Shastric Traditions in Indian Arts*, 1989, vol. 1, p. 342.

5. According to documentation at the Government Museum in Madras, this *linga* was recovered from the Joti temple in the Siddhout *taluq* of Cuddapah district in the state of Andhra Pradesh, and presented to the museum in 1916.

6. The identification of this image raises certain problems. It could also represent what would be a rare image of the four-headed god Brahma, but this seems unlikely due to the presence of Shiva's third, vertical eye on all four faces; see *Asiatic Art in the Museum of Fine Arts Boston*, 1982, p. 168. There is also debate as to whether this type of Shiva image should be termed 'Sadashiva' or 'Mahesha'; see D.M. Srinivasan, 'Saiva Temple Forms: Loci of God's Unfolding Body', in Marianne Yaldiz and Wibke Lobo (eds) *Investigating Indian Art*, 1987, pp. 335–40.

7. *Kamikagama*, purvabhaga 4.362–65, as translated in Richard Davis, *Ritual in an Oscillating Universe: Worshiping Siva in Medieval India*, 1991, p. 116.

8. Richard Davis, *Ritual in an Oscillating Universe: Worshiping Siva in Medieval India*, 1991, pp. 112–22.

9. This sculpture has been published previously in Stella Kramrisch, *Manifestations of Shiva*, 1981, no. 124, p. 150; and Michael Brand (ed.), *Traditions of Asian Art: Traced through the Collection of the National Gallery of Australia*, 1995, p. 58.

10. Vidya Dehejia, 'Sambandar: a Child–Saint of South India', *South Asian Studies*, vol. 3, 1987, pp. 53–61.

11. Manikkavachaka, *Thiruvachagam*, hymn 6, verses 49 and 46, as translated in G.U. Pope (ed.), *The Tiruvacagam*, 1900, p. 100–01.

12. *Gli Dei dell'India: 4,000 Anni di Statue in Bronzo*, 1993, no. 23, p. 40 (exhibition catalogue, Museo degli Argenti, Palazzo Pitti, Florence).

13. George Michell (ed.), *In the Image of Man: The Indian Perception of the Universe through 2000 Years of Painting and Sculpture*, 1982, p. 219.

14. *Markandeya Purana*, as translated in Wendy Doniger O'Flaherty, *Hindu Myths*, 1975, p. 248.

15. I am indebted to Dr Valerie J. Roebuck in Manchester for help in confirming the identification of this image as Sita. It has previously been published as a 'Female deity, probably Çiva-Kâmasundarî' (H.F.E. Visser, *Asiatic Art*, 1948, no. 332, p. 76 and pl. 194). An illustration published in 1935 (*Exposition de Sculptures et Bronzes Anciens de l'Inde*, 1935, pl. XIX, no. 30) shows the sculpture before it was cleaned. I have previously dated the sculpture to the fifteenth century (Michael Brand (ed.), *Traditions of Asian Art*, 1995, p. 59), but more recently George Michell has argued for a sixteenth–century date (*The New Cambridge History of India* I: 6, *Architecture and Art of Southern India: Vijayanagar and the Successor States*, 1995, fig. 146, pp. 198–201).

16. For a mid–tenth century set of images of Rama, Lakshman and Sita, see Pramod Chandra, *The Sculpture of India*, no. 94, 1985, pp. 194–95.

17. Trivikrama (literally 'three strides') is one of the twenty-four forms of the four-armed standing Vishnu known as the *chaturvimshatimurti*; see Jitendra Nath Banerjea, *The Development of Hindu Iconography*, 3rd edn, 1974, pp. 410–11. This sculpture has been published previously in N.K. Bhattasali, *Iconography of Buddhist and Brahmanical Sculptures in the Dacca Museum*, 1929, pl. xxxi, p. 86; and Jane Casey (ed.), *Medieval Sculpture from Eastern India: Selections from the Nalin Collection*, 1985, no. 57, pp. 84–85.

18. For a discussion of the ruined temple at Pipariya from which this image was recovered, see Joanna Gottfried Williams, *The Art of Gupta India: Empire and Province*, 1982, pp. 116–17 (this image is illustrated in fig. 178, the remains of the larger Vishnu as fig. 177). For an image of the Man-Lion incarnation of Vishnu holding personifications of the discus and club, see Pratapaditya Pal, *Indian Sculpture*, 1986, vol. 1, no. S129, pp. 252–53, colour plate p. 59.

19. Douglas Barrett, 'A Bronze Srinivasa Group', in Douglas Barrett, *Studies in Indian Sculpture and Painting*, 1990, p. 268.

20. V.N. Srinivasa Desikan, *Guide to the Bronze Gallery*, (1972) rpt 1994, p. 4.

21. For an early nineteenth-century account of the Nathdvara temple, see James Tod, *Annals and Antiquities of Rajasthan, or, the Central and Western Rajpoot States of India*, (1829) rpt 1972, vol. 1, pp. 415–22.

22. Robert Skelton, *Rajasthani Temple Hangings of the Krishna Cult*, 1973, nos 11–15 and p. 93.

23. B.N. Goswamy, *Essence of Indian Art*, 1986, p. 224.

24. The National Museum in Delhi holds another twenty-four pages from the same manuscript. For a brief description of this manuscript and its contents, see Klaus Ebeling, *Ragamala Painting*, 1973, p. 221 (where it is dated Bundi/Kota c.1775); see also, Milo Beach, *Rajput Painting at Bundi and Kota*, 1974, p. 21 and fig. 41.

25. As quoted in Klaus Ebeling, *Ragamala Painting*, 1973, p. 128.

26.   I am grateful to Robert Skelton for additional information concerning the subject matter and origin of this painting. For similar paintings attributed to Garhwal, see W.C. Archer, *Paintings from the Punjab Hills*, 1973, vol. 1, p. 118, nos. 24i–ii (illustrated in vol. 2, p. 87). For similar paintings attributed to Kangra, see *ibid.*, vol. 1, pp. 304–05, no. 61 (illustrated in vol. 2, p. 225); and B.N. Goswamy and Eberhard Fischer, *Pahari Masters*, 1992, p. 382. A painting from a private collection of 'Krishna's marriage', attributed to Garhwal, *c.* 1810, (illustrated in George Michell (ed.), *In the Image of Man*, no. 304, p. 182) may be from the same manuscript, but has not been sighted by the author. Its dimensions are listed as '37.0 x 51.0 cm'.

27.   Susan L. Huntington, *The Art of Ancient India*, 1985, fig. 19.33, p. 439.

28.   The ten images come from two sets and include two Suryas: see Thomas E. Donaldson, *Hindu Temple Art of Orissa*, vol. 2, p. 609. A Brihaspati, Rahu and Ketu come from the same set as the Surya published here. This Surya comes from a series acquired in India by 'Hindoo' Stewart in the late eighteenth–early nineteenth century. The other series is said to have come from the Sun Temple in Konarak.

29.   Y. Krishna, 'Evolution of the Iconography of Ganesha', *Lalit Kala*, no. 27, 1993, p. 11.

30.   Thomas E. Donaldson, *Hindu Temple Art of Orissa*, 1986, vol. 2, p. 614, and vol. 3, p. 1244 (Donaldson connects it with three other images at the British Museum showing Shiva Nataraja, Durga Mahishamardini and Surya); Alice Boner et al, *New Light on the Sun Temple of Konarka*, 1972, pp. 117–18.

31.   For more information about the Kalighat tradition of painting, see W.G. Archer, *Kalighat Paintings*, 1971; and Tapati Guha-Thakurta, *The Making of a New 'Indian' Art: Artists, Aesthetics and Nationalism in Bengal, c.1850–1920*, 1992, pp. 18–27.

32.   Jaidev Baghel (as told to Roshan Kalapesi), 'Of "Devis" and "Devas"', in Carmen Kagal (ed.), *Shilpakar*, 1982, p. 48.

33.   For a brief discussion of this headdress, see Wilfrid Grigson, *The Maria Gonds of Bastar*, 1938, pp. 79–81 and plates VIII and IX.

34.   This work continues today, but often for new patrons such as state handicraft emporia and private art dealers. The National Gallery of Australia possesses a contemporary sculpture of Krishna with a cow by Jaidev Baghel (b. 1949) who won India's national master-craftsmen award in 1977 (this sculpture was purchased through the Elaine and Jim Wolfensohn Gift).

35.   For more information on the terracotta horses, see Stephen P. Huyler, 'Gifts of Earth: Votive Terracottas of India', *Asian Art*, pp. 6–37. See also, Stella Kramrisch, *Unknown India: Ritual Art in Tribe and Village*, 1968, pl. I, II and VI/VII, pp. 56–57. For some stone images of Aiyanar dating from the eighth to twelfth centuries, see M.E. Adiceam, 'De Quelques Images d'Aiyanar-Sasta', *Arts Asiatiques*, 1978, pp. 87–104.

36.   Louis Dumont, 'Définition structurale d'un dieu populaire tamoul: Aiyanar, le Maître', *Journal Asiatique*, 1953, pp. 263–69.

37.   V.N. Srinivasa Desikan (*Guide to the Bronze Gallery*, (1972) rpt 1994, pp. 51–52, 67 and pl. XXXII) dates this example to the second quarter of the seventeenth century. Another bronze image of Aiyanar from Thogur has been published as twelfth century (C. Sivaramamurti, *South Indian Bronzes*, 1981). Pratapaditya Pal dates a third Thogur Aiyanar, in the collection of the Los Angeles County Museum of Art, as twelfth–thirteenth century (*Indian Sculpture*, 1988, vol. 2, no. 149, pp. 281–82).

ENLIGHTENED SAVIOURS

1.   *Majjhima Nikaya* 26.21, as cited in H.W. Schumann, *The Historical Buddha: The Times, Life and Teachings of the Founder of Buddhism*, 1989, p. 56.

2.   John S. Strong, *The Legend of King Asoka: A Study and Translation of the Asokavadana*, 1983, pp. 105-09.

3.   Asanga, *Mahayanasutralankara* (Ornament of Mahayana Sutras), as cited in Wm. Theodore de Bary (ed.), *Sources of Indian Tradition*, 1958, vol. 1, p. 172.

4.   Janice Leoshko, 'The Vajrasana Buddha', in Janice Leoshko (ed.), *Bodhgaya: The Site of Enlightenment*, 1988, p. 30 ff.

5.   Parameshvari Lal Gupta, *Patna Museum Catalogue of Antiquities*, 1965, p. 129, pl. XXIX.

6.   As translated in John S. Strong, *The Legend of King Asoka*, 1983, p. 244.

7.   Edward Conze, *Buddhism: Its Essence and Development*, 1959, pp. 80–81.

8.   The large group of Amaravati sculptures removed to the British Museum in 1880 was re-installed in 1992. For a detailed study of those sculptures and the stupa itself, see Robert Knox, *Amaravati: Buddhist Sculpture from the Great Stupa*, 1992 (for a reconstruction of the stupa, see fig. 9). For other Amaravati sculptures now in the Government Museum in Madras, see C. Sivaramamurti, *Amaravati Sculptures in the Madras Government Museum*, 1956.

9.   F.H. Gravely and C. Sivaramamurti, *Guide to the Archaeological Galleries* (1939) rpt 1992, p. 7.

10.   Simon Lawson, 'Votive Objects from Bodhgaya', in Janice Leoshko (ed.), *Bodhgaya*, 1988, pp. 61–72.

11.   Joanna Gottfried Williams, *The Art of Gupta India*, 1982, pp. 15, 76 and fig. 85.

12.   T.N. Ramachandran, *The Nagapattinam and other Buddhist Bronzes in the Madras Museum*, (1954) rpt 1992, p. 39.

13.   Paul Mus, 'Le Buddha Paré. Son Origine Indienne', *Bulletin de l'école Française d'Extrême-Orient*, vol. 27, 1928, p. 147–278; Jane Anne Casey (ed.), *Medieval Sculpture from Eastern India*, 1985, p. 24.

14.   Susan L. Huntington (*The 'Pala-Sena' Schools of Sculpture*, 1983, fig. 185 and p. 147) has argued that for stylistic reasons the sculpture exhibited here should be given a slightly later date than the three inscribed ones (*ibid.*, figs 69–71).

15.   N.G. Majumdar, *A Guide to the Sculptures in the Indian Museum*, (1936) 1987, part 2, pp. 58–59 and pl. VIb. For another example of this episode, see Humera Alam, *Gandhara Sculptures in Lahore Museum*, 1988, no. 23a, p. 20 and fig. 51.

16.   For a plan of the site, see James Fergusson, *History of Indian and Eastern Architecture*, (1876) revised edition of 1910 rpt 1972, vol. 1, woodcut no. 119, p. 212. A major collection of sculptures from Jamalgarhi belonging to E. Clive Bayley was destroyed in the fire at the Crystal Palace in London in 1866.

17.   This relief was previously published in connection with an exhibition held in 1993 at the Fine Arts Museum in Ulaanbaatar in Mongolia: *The Way of the Buddha: an Exhibition of Buddhist Art from the Collection of the Indian Museum*, 1993, no. 39, p. 36.

18.   For the identification of a similar (though forward-facing) figure in a relief in the collection of the Victoria and Albert Museum, see Zwalf, *Buddhism: Art and Faith*, 1985, no. 26, p. 38. For a similar figure seen from the rear, see Hans Christoph Ackerman, *Narrative Stone Reliefs from Gandhara in the Victoria and Albert Museum in London*, 1975, p. 71, pl. XVa.

19.   These friezes are represented in depictions of *stupas* from Amaravati: see Robert Knox, *Amaravati*, 1992, nos. 68 and 71, pp. 130–37.

20.   For more details concerning the idenitfication and dating of this sculpture, see John Guy, 'A Kushan Bodhisattva and Early Indian Sculpture', *Art Bulletin of Victoria*, no. 24 (1983), pp. 33–46 (for a hypothetical reconstruction, see fig. 2, p. 35).

21.   Pramod Chandra, *The Sculpture of India*, 1985, p. 87.

22.   Previously published in Piriya Krairiksh, 'The Arts of Asia and Southeast Asia', in James Mollison, and Laura Murray (eds), *Australian National Gallery. An Introduction*, 1982, pp. 154–55; and Michael Brand (ed.), *Traditions of Asian Art*, 1995, pp. 52–53.

23.   W. Zwalf, *Buddhism: Art and Faith*, 1985, p. 115.

24.   Joanna Gottfried Williams, *The Art of Gupta India*, 1982, p. 79.

25.   Alexander Piatigorsky, 'The Visual World of Vajrayana Philosophy', in Deborah Ashencaen and Gennady Leonov, *The Mirror of Mind: Art of Vajrayana Buddhism*, 1995, p. 4.

26.   *Ashtasahasrika Prajnaparamita* (The Eight Thousand Perfection of Wisdom), 7.170–71, as translated in Wm. Theodore de Bary (ed.), *Sources of Indian Tradition*, 1958, vol. 1, p. 180.

27.   Previously published in Pramod Chandra, *Indian Sculpture from the Collection of Mr and Mrs Earl Morse*, 1963, no. 20, p. 19; and Michael Brand, (ed.) *Traditions of Asian Art*, 1995, pp. 50–51.

28.   For a discussion related to a tenth century Pala stone image of Marichi, see Susan L. Huntington and John C. Huntington, *Leaves from the Bodhi Tree*, 1989, pp. 135–36.

29.   Anusua Sengupta, *Buddhist Art of Bengal (From the Third Century B.C. to the Thirteenth Century A.D.)*, 1993, p. 148.

30.   Benoytosh Bhattacharyya, *The Indian Buddhist Iconography*, (1958) 2nd edition 1968, p. 211 (this image of Marichi is illustrated as an example, fig. 152).

31.   *Gli Dei dell'India*, 1993, no. 58, pp. 76–77. Another *chaubisi* in the collection of the Los Angeles County Museum of Art (dated 1464) with virtually identical iconography carries an inscription identifying the central Jina as Shantinatha (Pratapaditya Pal, *Indian Sculpture*, 1988, vol. II, pp. 146–47).

32.   This image has been published previously with varying attributions: George Michell (ed.), *In the Image of Man*, 1982, no. 342, p. 194; and U.P. Shah, 'Jaina Bronzes — A Brief Survey', in U.P. Shah and M.A. Dhaky (eds), *Aspects of Jaina Art and Architecture*, 1975, fig. 43.

33.   John E. Cort, 'Following the Jina, Worshipping the Jina: An Essay on Jain Rituals', in Pratapaditya Pal, *The Peaceful Liberators*, 1994, pp. 46–48.

34.   I am grateful to Vidya Dehejia for providing this information.

35.   P.L. Gupta, *Patna Museum Catalogue of Antiquities*, 1965, p. 161, pl. XXXVII.

36.   For an almost contemporary head of a Buddha in a similar format from Orissa, see Nihar Ranjan Ray et al, *Eastern Indian Bronzes*, 1986, no. 285, p. 166.

37.   Kamini Sinha, *The Early Bronzes of Bihar*, 1983, pp. 19–21.

38.   John Guy, 'Jain Manuscript Painting', in Pratapaditya Pal, *The Peaceful Liberators*, 1994, p. 91.

39.   For a similar page that actually shows a four-armed Indra presiding over the entertainment, see Pratapaditya Pal (ed.), *The Peaceful Liberators*, 1994, no. 87, p. 210 and illustrated as fig. 62 on p. 96. See also a page from an earlier *Kalpasutra* manuscript (dated 1292) in the National Museum in Delhi (48.29), and another in the collection of the Jain Bhandar in Jaisalmer (illustrated in Saryu Doshi, *Masterpieces of Jain Painting*, 1985, fig. 9, pp. 50–51).

40.   For illustrations of other pages from this same manuscript, see Pramod Chandra and Daniel J. Ehnbohm, *The Cleveland Tuti-nama Manuscript and the Origins of Mughal Painting*, 1976, nos. 9 and 10, p. 24 and pl. 4; Karl Khandalavala and Saryu Doshi, *A Collector's Dream: Indian Art in the Collections of Basant Kumar and Saraladevi Birla and the Birla Academy of Art and Culture*, 1987, fig. 4.6, p. 61; and Pratapaditya Pal (ed.), *The Peaceful Liberators*, 1994, no. 86a–d, p. 92 and 209. The maunscript to which these pages once belonged is closely related to another *Kalpasutra* dated 1465 (Samvat 1522) now in the Narasinhajini Polno Jnana Bhandara in Baroda (see Moti Chandra and Karl Khandalavala, 'An Illustrated *Kalpasutra* painted at Jaunpur in A.D. 1465', *Lalit Kala*, no. 12 (1962), pp. 8–15).

41.   For other paintings in the 'opulent' style, see Saryu Doshi, *Masterpieces of Jain Painting*, 1985, pp. 12–13, 50–51 and 110–11; and B.N. Goswamy and Eberhard Fischer, *Wonders of a Golden Age: Painting at the Court of the Great Mughals*, 1987, no. 3, p. 29.

42.   W.N. Brown, *The Story of Kalaka*, 1933, pp. 85–86 and plate 8, fig. 20. I am grateful to Terence McInerney for additional research on this page.

AUSPICIOUS GUARDIANS

1.   Douglas Barrett, Four Hoysala Sculptures, *Annual Bulletin of the National Gallery of Victoria*, vol. 6, (1964), pp. 8–10. The tree goddess in the three related British Museum sculptures is shown dancing flanked by two small drummers; adjusting her hair in a mirror; and playing a drum while flanked by two more small drummers. All four images appear to have once belonged to the collection of Lord Dalhousie, the last British Governor–General of India (1848–56).

2.   Rajashekhara, in Vidyakara, *Subhasñitaratnakosha* (*Treasury of Well–turned Verse*), as translated in Daniel H.H. Ingalls, *Sanskrit Poetry: from Vidyakara's 'Treasury'*, 1965, no. 419, p. 133.

3.   S. Settar, *The Hoysala Temples*, 1992, vol. 1, pp. 130–43.

4.   I am indebted to Dr Kelleson Collyer in Melbourne for this information.

5.   Kalidasa, *Meghadutam*, 81 in Kalidasa, *The Loom of Time: A Selection of His Plays and Poems*, transl. Chandra Rajan, 1989, p. 156.

6.   Vasukalpa, in Vidyakara, *Subhashitaratnakosha* (*Treasury of Well–turned Verse*), as translated in Ingalls, *Sanskrit Poetry*, 1965, no. 399, p. 131.

7.   For a set of three similar pillars with cross-beams intact from Bhuteshvara near Mathura (also from 2nd century and now too in the Indian Museum), see Susan L. Huntington, *The Art of Ancient India*, 1985, fig. 8.35, p. 156.

8.   The collection put together by A.M. Broadley during a period of administrative service in southern Patna district was at first installed in the Bihar Museum in Bihar Sharif, before being moved to the Indian Museum, Calcutta, in 1891. An early photograph of the Bihar Museum appears to show this image (Frederick M. Asher, 'The Former Broadley Collection, Bihar Sharif', *Artibus Asiae*, vol. 32, nc. 2/3, 1970, plate VIII, second from left). The original caption states that the sculpture was discovered in Nalanda.

9.   Thomas Watters, *On Yuan Chwang's Travels in India*, 1904–05, vol. II, p. 165. Yuan Chwang is another transliteration of the name Xuan Zang.

10.   The base could have been made later than the image of Nandi (there is a thin line visible where the two are joined); see Denise Patry Leidy, *Treasures of Asian Art*, 1994, pp. 50–51.

11.   Stuart Cary Welch, *Room for Wonder: Indian Painting During the British Period 1760–1880*, 1978, no. 63, p. 143.

12.   See, for example, Kalidasa's description in praise of the form of Shiva's *shakti*, Parvati: 'a delicate line of young hair crossing the knot of her skirt and entering her deep navel seemed a streak of dark light from the blue gem centering her belt' (quoted in Vishakha N. Desai and Darielle Mason (eds), *Gods, Guardians and Lovers*, 1993, no. 46, p. 217).

13.   *Shiva Purana, Parvatikhand*, 45:29, as quoted in Shobita Punja, *Divine Ecstacy: the Story of Khajuraho*, 1992, p. 162; see also pp. 254–56. For a different interpretation of the erotic sculptures at Khajuraho, see Devangana Desai, 'Placement and Significance of Erotic Sculptures at Khajuraho', in Michael W. Meister (ed.), *Discourses on Siva*, 1984, pp. 143–55.

14.   I am indebted to Dr Kelleson Collyer for information about this object and its relationship to Hoysala temples.

15.   This sculpture was previously published in Isao Kurita, *Gandharan Buddhist Art*, 1990, vol. 2, no. 511, p. 177. For another example, in the collection of the Metropolitan Museum of Art in New York, see Stanislaw Czuma, *Kushan Sculpture*, 1985, no. 95, p. 182. For an image identified as 'Garuda abducting Queen Kakati', in the collection of the Victoria and Albert Museum in London (IS 5–1973), see Isao Kurita, *op. cit.*, no. 510, p. 176.

16.   Albert Grünwedel, *Buddhist Art in India*, rpt 1985, pp. 109–10. For a more extensive and speculative discussion of the subject, see Ananda K. Coomaraswamy, 'The Rape of a Nagi: An Indian Gupta Seal', *The Bulletin of the Museum of Fine Arts* (Boston), vol. 35, no. 209, (1937), pp. 38–41 and vol. 35, no. 210 (1937), pp. 56–57.

17.   For the Pipariya column, see Joanna Gottfried Williams, *The Art of Gupta India*, 1982, p. 117 and pl. 176.

18.   For a discussion of the history of the *kirttimukha*, see M.K. Dhavalikar, 'Kirttimukha', in N S. Nagaraja Rao (ed.), *Kusumanjali: New Interpretation of Indian Art and Culture*, 1987, pp. 349–54.

19.   Sir Leigh Ashton (ed.), *The Art of India and Pakistan*, 1947, no. 236, p. 54, pl. 30.

20.   The other seven *dikpalas* are Indra, the king of the gods (east); Yama, ruler of the dead (south); Nirriti, the god of elves and night–wanderers (south–west); Varuna, the god of water and the ocean (west) Vayu, the god of wind (north–west); Kubera, the god of wealth (north); and Ishana, the embodiment of air (north–east).

21. M.A. Dhaky, 'The "Pranala" in Indian, South-Asian and South-East Asian Sacred Architecture', in Bettina Baumer (ed.), *Rupa Pratirupa: Alice Boner Commemoration Volume*, 1982, pp. 141–42 (this *bhuta–pranala* is illustrated as fig. 8c). For a *pranala* in the form of a complete *bhuta* on the north exterior wall of the sanctum of the early Chola Jalanatheshvara Temple at Takkolam near Kanchipuram, see Douglas Barrett, *Early Chola Architecture and Sculpture*, 1974, fig. 7.

THE ROYAL IMAGE

1. Abul Fazl, *A'in-i Akbari* (*The Institutes of Akbar*), H. Blockmann et al (transl.), 1977, vol. 1, p. 115.

2. Gülru Necipoglu, 'Framing the Gaze in Ottoman, Safavid and Mughal Palaces', *Ars Orientalis*, vol. 23 (1993), pp. 303–42.

3. Michael Brand, 'Mughal Ritual in Non-Mughal Cities: the Case of Jahangir in Mandu', *Environmental Design*, nos 1–2 (1991), pp. 16–17.

4. The border has been attributed to the so-called 'Master of the Borders': Stuart Cary Welch, *India: Art and Culture 1300–1900*, 1985, p. 234.

5. Nur al-Din Muhammad Jahangir, *Tuzuk-i Jahangiri* (*The Memoirs of Jahangir*), A. Rogers (transl.), 1968, vol. 2, p. 20.

6. Stuart Cary Welch, *India: Art and Culture 1300–1900*, 1985, p. 234.

7. For more information on Govardhan, see Milo Beach, *The Grand Mogul: Imperial Painting in India 1600-1660*, 1978, pp. 118–125, and Amina Okada, *Imperial Painters: Indian Miniatures from the Sixteenth and Seventeenth Centuries*, 1992, pp. 185–205.

8. Ebba Koch, 'The Baluster Column — A European Motif in Mughal Architecture and its Meaning', *Journal of the Warburg and Courtauld Institutes*, vol. 4, 1982, pp. 251–62.

9. 'Abd al-Hamid Lahawri, *Badshah Namah*, (*History of the Emperor*), Mawlawis Kabir al-din Ahman and Abd al-Rahim (eds), vol. 2, p. 79.

10. 'Inayat Khan, *Shahjahannama* (*The History of Shah Jahan*), A.R. Fuller (transl.), 1990, p. 219.

11. Ebba Koch, 'Diwan-i 'Amm and Chihil Sutun: the Audience Halls of Shah Jahan', *Muqarnas*, vol. 11, 1994, pp. 143–65.

12. Shah Nawaz Khan, *Maathir-ul-Umara* (*Biographies of the Nobles*), H. Beveridge (transl.), 1888–91, 1979, vol. 1, pp. 398–99.

13. Michael Brand and Glenn D. Lowry, *Akbar's India: Art from the Mughal City of Victory*, 1985, pp. 14–17.

14. Abul Fazl, *A'in-i Akbari* (*The Institutes of Akbar*), H. Blockmann et al (transl.), 1977, vol. 1, p. 52.

15. For a detailed discussion of all evidence relating to Manaku and his work, see B.N. Goswamy and Eberhard Fischer, *Pahari Masters*, 1992, pp. 240–65.

16. W.G. Archer, *Visions of Courtly India*, 1976, p. 72 (other folios from the *c.*1775 *Ramayana* are illustrated at catalogue nos. 40–42).

17. Stuart Cary Welch and Anthony Welch, *Arts of the Islamic Book*, 1982, p. 190.

18. Ebba Koch, 'Jahangir and the Angels: Recently Discovered Wall Paintings under European Influence in the Fort of Lahore', in Joachim Deppert (ed.), *India and the West*, 1983, pp. 173–95. For a related discussion, see also Ebba Koch, *Shah Jahan and Orpheus: the Pietre Dure Decoration and the Programme of the Throne in the Hall of Public Audiences in the Red Fort of Delhi*, 1988, especially pp. 23–28 and 31–32.

19. As quoted in Annemarie Schimmel, *Islam in the Indian Subcontinent*, 1980, p. 98.

20. Glenn D. Lowry with Susan Nemazee, *A Jeweller's Eye: Islamic Arts of the Book from the Vever Collection*, 1988, no. 72, p. 208.

21. B.N. Goswamy and Eberhard Fischer, *Wonders of a Golden Age*, 1987, no. 12, p. 44.

22. For more information on the life and works of Aqa Riza, see Milo Beach, *The Grand Mogul*, 1978, pp. 24–25 and 92–95; and Amina Okada, *Imperial Mughal Painters*, 1992, pp. 105–11.

23. B.N. Goswamy and Eberhard Fischer, *Wonders of a Golden Age*, 1987, no. 77, p. 158.

24. For more information on the life and work of Miskin, see Milo Beach, *The Imperial Image*, 1981, pp. 124–26 and Amina Okada, *Imperial Mughal Painters*, 1992, pp. 125–36.

25. Two of the others are currently held at the Victoria and Albert Museum in London, one in the permanent collection (IS31–1970) and one on loan from the Royal Collection (royal loan no. 743). The fourth is in the collection of the Sri Pratap Singh Museum in Srinagar.

26. Anon., 'An Extinct Art', *Magazine of Art*, vol. 25 (1901), pp. 452–53. For more information about the making of the shawl, see Robyn Maxwell's catalogue essay in Michael Brand (ed.), *Traditions of Asian Art*, 1995, p. 70.

27. For more information on the life and work of Mansur, see Milo Beach, *The Grand Mogul*, 1978, pp. 137–43 and *The Imperial Image*, 1981, pp. 81–82; Asok Kumar Das, 'Mansur', in Pratapaditya Pal (ed.), *Master Artists of the Imperial Mughal Court*, 1991, pp. 39–52; and Amina Okada, *Imperial Mughal Painters*, 1992, pp. 216–25.

28. For a discussion on the relationship between city and garden in early Mughal India, see James L. Wescoat, Jr, 'Gardens versus Citadels: the Territorial Context of Early Mughal Gardens', in John Dixon Hunt (ed.), *Garden History: Issues, Approaches, Methods*, 1992, pp. 331–58.

29. Vishakha N. Desai, *Life at Court*, 1985, no. 17, p. 20.

30. Another Muhammad Shah period painting, apparently based on a European print, exhibits the same treatment of the receding river (see Stuart Cary Welch and Anthony Welch, *Arts of the Islamic Book*, 1982, no. 78, pp. 231–32). See also a painting from about 1760, attributed to the school of the artist Mihr Chand in Lucknow, with a similar composition (Basil Gray (ed.), *The Arts of India*, 1981, fig. 166).

31. Shah Nawaz Khan, *Maathir-ul-Umara* (*Biographies of the Nobles*), H. Beveridge (transl.), (1888–91) rept 1979, vol. 1, pp. 408–09; and Nur al-Din Muhammad Jahangir, *Tuzuk-i Jahangiri* (*The Memoirs of Jahangir*), A. Rogers (transl.), 1968, vol. 1, pp. 144–45.

32. For the story of Shri Brijnath-ji's travels, including translated excerpts from a *c.*1858 Kota royal chronicle, see Norbert Peabody, 'In Whose Turban does the Lord Reside?', *Comparative Studies in Society and History*, vol. 33, no. 4 (1991), pp. 733–739. A *c.*1826 painting of Shri Brijnath-ji is illustrated there as fig. 4.

33. Andrew Topsfied and Milo Beach, *Indian Paintings and Drawings from the Collection of Howard Hodgkin*, 1991, no. 37, p. 94.

34. Andrew Topsfield and Milo Beach, *Indian Paintings and Drawings from the Collection of Howard Hodgkin*, 1991, pp. 102–105.

35. Seven other large Mewar paintings on cloth are known: two each are in the Udaipur Palace collection and the Victoria and Albert Museum in London, and one each in the collections of Ralph Benkaim in Los Angeles, the Rijksmuseum in Amsterdam and another private collection. For two smaller Mewar hunting scenes with Maharana Jawan Singh painted on paper (both approximately 148.0 x 95.0 cm), see Andrew Topsfield, *The City Palace Museum Udaipur: Painting of Mewar Court Life*, 1990, nos. 26–27.

36. Andrew Topsfield, *Paintings from Rajasthan*, 1980, p. 94.

37. Andrew Topsfield, 'Udaipur Paintings of the *Rasalila*', Art Bulletin of Victoria, 1987, pp. 54–70.

38. For more information about the life and work of Abu'l Hasan, the son of the immigrant Persian artist Aqa Riza (who painted the work in catalogue no. 78a), see Milo Beach, *The Grand Mogul*, 1978, pp. 86–92; Jeremiah P. Losty, 'Abu'l Hasan', in Pratapaditya Pal, *Master Artists of the Imperial Mughal Court*, 1991, pp. 69–86; and Amina Okada, *Imperial Mughal Painters*, 1992, pp. 170–84.

39. A new translation is about to be published: *The Baburnama: Memoirs of Babur, Prince and Emperor*, translated, edited and annotated by Wheeler M. Thackston, New York: Oxford University Press, forthcoming 1995.

40. For the passage illustrated, see Zahir al-Din Muhammad Babur, *Baburnama*, Annette Beveridge (transl.), (1922) p. 29.

41. For more information on Bishan Das and his work, see Milo Beach, *The Grand Mogul*, 1978, pp. 107–11 and Amina Okada, *Imperial Mughal Painters*, 1992, pp. 154–63.

42. For the passage illustrated, see Abul Fazl, *Akbarnama*, H. Beveridge (transl.), 1973, vol. II, pp. 422–24.

43. For more information on Basawan and his work, see Milo Beach, *The Imperial Image*, 1981, pp. 89–91; Amina Okada, 'Basawan', in Pratapaditya Pal (ed.), *Master Artists of the Imperial Mughal Court*, 1991, pp. 1–16; and Amina Okada, *Imperial Mughal Painters*, 1992, pp. 77–94.

44. *A la cour du Grand Moghol*, 1986, p. 28. The album to which both paintings once belonged (now known as the *Late Shah Jahan Album*) was taken to Persia by Nadir Shah after he sacked Delhi in 1739. It eventually reached the Parisian art dealer Georges Demotte via Russia.

45. For some of the little information known about Chitarman and his work, see Milo Beach, *The Grand Mogul*, 1978, pp. 111–13.

46. A standing portrait of the Mughal noble I'tibar Khan from c.1623–25 appears to show the same building and garden across the river in the background: see *A la cour du Grand Moghol*, 1986, no. 17, p.46.

47. For more information on the life and work of Bichitr, see Milo Beach, *The Grand Mogul*, 1978, pp. 101–07; and Amina Okada, *Imperial Mughal Painters*, 1992, pp. 164–70.

48. Michael Brand and Glenn D. Lowry, *Akbar's India*, 1985, pp. 14–17.

49. 'Inayat Khan, *Shah Jahan Nama*, A.R. Fuller (transl.), 1990, p. 5. Each letter of the Arabic alphabet in which the Persian language is written has been assigned a numerical value — the challenge in composing a chronogram is to make the letters in the statement add up to the date being celebrated.

50. Stuart Cary Welch et al, *The Emperor's Album*, 1987, p. 81.

51. Abul Fazl, *A'in-i Akbari* (*The Institutes of Akbar*), H. Blockmann et al (transl.), 1977, vol. 1, p. 52.

52. Shah Nawaz Khan, *Maathir-ul-Umara* (*Biographies of the Nobles*), H. Beveridge (transl.), 1888–91, vol. 2, p. 247.

53. For more information on Payag and his work, see Milo Beach, *The Grand Mogul*, 1978, pp. 151–54; Joseph M. Dye III, 'Payag', in Pratapaditya Pal (ed.), *Master Artists of the Imperial Mughal Court*, 1991, pp. 119–34 (with this painting illustrated as fig. 14 and dust-jacket); and Amina Okada, *Imperial Moghul Painters*, 1992, pp. 207–15.

54. For extended discussions on this subject, see Vishakha N. Desai, 'Timeless Symbols: Royal Portraits from Rajasthan 17th–19th Centuries', in Karine Schomer et al (eds.), *The Idea of Rajasthan*, 1994, pp. 316–19; and B.N. Goswamy, 'Essence and appearance: some notes on Indian portraiture', 1986, pp. 193–96.

55. For more information on the life and work of Nainsukh, see B.N. Goswamy, 'The Painter Nainsukh and his Patron Balwant Singh', in Barbara Stoler Miller (ed.), *The Powers of Art: Patronage and Indian Culture*, 1992, pp. 235–44 and B.N. Goswamy and Eberhard Fischer, *Pahari Masters*, 1992, pp. 268–305.

56. Robert W. Stern, *The Cat and the Lion: Jaipur State in the British Raj*, 1988, p. 115.

57. Stuart Cary Welch, *Room for Wonder*, no. 64, 1978, p. 144.

58. At least one photograph of Ram Singh was taken by Bourne and Shepherd for their *History of the Imperial Assemblage at Delhi* in 1877 (Christies auction catalogue, *19th and 20th Century Photographs*, London: 19 October 1994, lot 58, p. 21).

59. For a half length photograph of Maharaja Jaswanth Singh (r.1873–95) from the early 1880s, see Clark Worswick and Ainslee Embree, *The Last Empire: Photography in British India, 1855-1911*, 1976, p. 117.

60. I am grateful to Aman Nath in Delhi for his help in trying to identify these two princes. For a photograph of Sardar Singh taken between about 1880 and 1900 and later included as part of a Jodhpur family tree compiled in c.1910, see Judith Mara Gutman, *Through Indian Eyes: 19th and Early 20th Century Photography from India*, 1982, p. 116. This painting was first published as 'Jaipur, circa 1920', in the Sotheby Parke Bernet auction catalogue, *Fine Oriental Miniatures, Manuscripts and Islamic Works of Art*, New York: 21 May 1981, lot 83.

Bibliography

A la cour du Grand Moghol. Paris: Bibliothèque Nationale, 1986.

Abul Fazl, *Akbarnama,* 3 vols. Translated by H. Beveridge. Delhi: Ess Ess Publications, 1973.

Abul Fazl. *Ain-i Akbari,* 3 vols. Translated by H. Blockmann et al. New Delhi: Munshiram Manoharlal, 1977.

Ackermann, Hans Christoph. *Narrative Stone Reliefs from Gandhara in the Victoria and Albert Museum in London.* Rome: IsMEO, 1975.

Adiceam, M.E. 'De quelques images d'Aiyanar-Sasta'. *Arts Asiatiques,* 34, (1978), pp. 87–104.

Alam, Humera. *Gandhara Sculptures in Lahore Museum.* Lahore: Lahore Museum, 1988.

Alamkara: 5,000 Years of Indian Art. Singapore: National Heritage Board, 1994. Ahmedabad: Mapin, 1994.

Allchin, Bridgit and Allchin, Raymond. *The Rise of Civilisation in India and Pakistan.* Cambridge: Cambridge University Press, 1982.

Ambalal, Amit. *Krishna as Shrinathji.* Ahmedabad: Mapin, 1987.

Anand, Mulk Raj. 'In Praise of Hoysala Art'. *Marg,* vol. 31 (1), December 1977.

Anon. 'An Extinct Art'. *Magazine of Art,* vol. 25, (1901), pp. 452–53.

Appadurai, Arjun. 'Introduction', in Appadurai, A. (ed.). *The Social Life of Things: Commodities in Cultural Perspective.* Philadelphia, PA. Symposium on the Relationship between Commodities and Culture. 1984. Cambridge: Cambridge University Press, 1986, pp. 3–63.

Archer, W.G. *The Loves of Krishna in Indian Painting and Literature.* London: Allen and Unwin, 1957.

Archer, W.G. *Indian Painting in Bundi and Kotah.* London: HMSO/Victoria and Albert Museum, 1959.

Archer, W.G. *Kalighat Paintings.* London: HMSO, 1971.

Archer, W.G. *Indian Paintings from the Punjab Hills: A Survey and History of Pahari Miniature Painting,* 2 vols. London; New York: Sotheby Parke Bernet, 1973.

Archer, W.G. *Visions of Courtly India: The Archer Collection of Pahari Miniatures.* Washington DC: The Foundation, 1976.

Ashencaen, Deborah and Leonov, Gennady. *The Mirror of Mind: Art of Vajrayana Buddhism.* London: Spink, 1995.

Asher, Catherine B. *Architecture of Mughal India.* Cambridge: Cambridge University Press, 1992.

Asher, Catherine B. 'Sub-Imperial Palaces: Power and Authority in Mughal India'. *Ars Orientalis* [Special Issue on Pre-Modern Islamic Palaces], vol. 23 (1993), pp. 281–302.

Asher, Frederick M. 'The Former Broadley Collection, Bihar Sharif'. *Artibus Asiae,* vol. 32:2/3, (1970), pp. 105–24.

Asher, Frederick M. *The Art of Eastern India, 300–800.* Minneapolis: University of Minnesota Press, 1980.

Ashton, Sir Leigh (ed.). *The Art of India and Pakistan: A Commemorative Catalogue of the Exhibition Held at the Royal Academy of Arts, London, 1947–48.* London: Faber & Faber, 1950.

Asia Society. *Handbook of the Mr and Mrs John D. Rockefeller 3rd Collection.* New York: Asia Society, [1981].

Asiatic Art in the Museum of Fine Arts Boston. Boston: Museum of Fine Arts, 1982.

Association pour l'Étude de la Documentation des Textiles d'Asie. *Quelques aspects du châle cachemire.* Paris: A.E.D.T.A., 1987.

Auboyer, J. *Le trône et son symbolisme dans l'Inde ancienne.* Paris: Presses universitaires de France, 1949.

Jaidev Baghel (as told to Roshan Kalapesi). 'Of "Devis" and "Devas"', in Carmen Kagal (ed.). *Shilpakar,* Bombay: Crafts Council of Western India, 1982.

Bakker, Hans (ed.). *The History of Sacred Places in India as Reflected in Traditional Literature: Papers on Pilgrimage in South Asia. Panels of the VIIth World Sanskrit Conference,* vol. 3. Leiden: Brill, 1990.

Balasubrahmanyam, S.R. *Early Chola Temples: Parantaka I to Rajaraja I, AD 907–985.* Delhi: Orient Longmans, 1971.

Balasubrahmanyam, S.R. *Middle Chola Temples: Rajaraja I to Kulottunga, AD 985–1070.* Faridabad: Thomson Press, 1975.

Banerjea, Jitendra Nath. *The Development of Hindu Iconography.* New Delhi: Munshiram Manoharlal, 1974.

Barrett, Douglas. 'Bronzes of Northwest India and Western Pakistan'. *Lalit Kala* 11, (1962), pp. 35–44.

Barrett, Douglas. 'Four Hoysala Sculptures'. *Annual Bulletin of the National Gallery of Victoria,* vol. 6, (1964), pp. 8–10.

Barrett, Douglas. *Early Chola Architecture and Sculpture; 866–1014 AD.* London: Faber, 1974.

Barrett, Douglas. *Studies in Indian Sculpture and Painting.* London: Pindar Press, 1990.

Basham, A.L. 'The Evolution of the Concept of the Bodhisattva', in Kawamura, L.S. (ed.). *The Bodhisattva Doctrine in Buddhism.* Calgary Buddhism Conference, 1978. Waterloo, Ont.: Wilfred Laurier University Press, 1981.

Barz, R.K. *The Bhakti Sect of Vallabhacarya.* Faridabad, Haryana: Thompson Press, 1976.

Bettina Baumer (ed.). *Rupa Pratirupa: Alice Bonner Commemoration Volume.* New Delhi: Biblia Impex, 1982.

Beach, Milo Cleveland. *Rajput Painting at Bundi and Kota.* Ascona: Artibus Asiae, 1974.

Beach, Milo Cleveland. 'The Context of Rajput Painting'. *Ars Orientalis* 10, (1975), pp. 11–17.

Beach, Milo Cleveland. *The Grand Mogul: Imperial Painting in India, 1600–1660.* With contributions by Stuart Cary Welch and Glenn D. Lowry. Williamstown, MA: Sterling and Francine Clark Art Institute, 1978.

Beach, Milo Cleveland. *The Imperial Image: Paintings for the Mughal Court.* Washington, DC: Freer Gallery of Art, 1981.

Beach, Milo Cleveland. 'The Mughal Artist', in Meister, Michael W. (ed.). *Making Things in South Asia: The Role of Artist and Craftsman: Proceedings of the South Asia Seminar, IV: 1985–86.* Philadelphia: Department of South Asia Regional Studies, 1988, pp. 78–85.

Beach, Milo Cleveland. *Mughal and Rajput Painting.* Cambridge: Cambridge University Press, 1992.

Bhardwaj, Surinder Mohan. *India: A Study in Cultural Geography.* Berkeley: University of California Press, 1973.

Bhattacharyya, Benoytosh. *The Indian Buddhist Iconography: Mainly Based on the Sadhanamala and Cognate Tantric Texts of Rituals.* 2nd edn, rev. Calcutta: K.L. Mukhopadhyay, 1968.

Bhattacharyya, B.C. *The Jaina Iconography.* 2nd edn, rev. Delhi: Motilal Banarsidass, 1974.

Bhattacharya, Sabyasachi and Thapar, Romila (eds). *Situating Indian History for Sarvepalli Gopal.* Delhi: Oxford University Press, 1986.

Bhattasali, Nalina Kanta. *Iconography of Buddhist and Brahmanical Sculptures in the Dacca Museum.* Dacca: Rai S.N. Bhadra Bahadur, 1929.

Blurton, T. Richard. *Hindu Art.* London: British Museum, 1992.

Boner, Alice et al. *New Light on the Sun Temple of Konarka.* Varanasi: Chowkhamba Sanskrit Series Office, 1972.

Boner, Alice. *Principles of Composition in Hindu Sculpture Cave Temple Period.* Delhi: IGNCA/Banarsidass, 1990.

Brand, Michael. 'Mughal Ritual in non-Mughal Cities: The Case of Jahangir in Mandu'. *Environmental Design,* nos 1–2, (1991), pp. 16–17.

Brand, Michael (ed.) *Traditions of Asian Art: Traced through the Collection of the National Gallery of Australia*. Canberra: National Gallery of Australia, 1995.

Brand, Michael and Lowry, Glenn D. *Akbar's India: Art from the Mughal City of Victory*. New York: Asia Society Galleries, 1985.

Brown, W.N. *The Story of Kalaka: Texts, History, Legends, and Miniature Paintings of the Svetambara Jain hagiographical Work 'The Kalakacaryakatha'*. Washington, DC: Smithsonian Institution, 1933.

Brown, W.S. *A Descriptive and Illustrated Catalogue of Miniature Paintings of the Jaina Kalpasutra as Executed in the Early Western Indian Style*. Washington DC: Smithsonian Institution, 1934.

Bunce, Fredrick W. *An Encyclopaedia of Buddhist Deities, Demigods, Godlings, Saints and Demons with a Special Focus on Iconographic Attributes*. 2 vols. New Delhi: D.K. Printworld, 1994.

Caillat, Colette and Ravi Kumar. *The Jain Cosmology* Basel: R.Kumar; Bombay: Exclusively distributed in India by Jaico Pub. House, 1981.

Canby, Sheila (ed.) *Humayun's Garden Party: Princes of the House of Timur and Early Mughal Painting*. Bombay: Marg Publications, 1994.

Casey, Jane Anne (ed.) *Medieval Sculpture from Eastern India: Selections from the Nalin Collection*. Livingston, N.J.: Nalini International Publications, 1985.

Chandra, Lokesh (ed.) *Dimensions of Indian Art: Pupil Jayakar Seventy*, 2 vols. Delhi: Agam Kala Prakashan, 1986.

Chandra, Moti. *Jain Miniature Paintings from Western India*. Ahmedabad: S.M. Nawab, 1949.

Chandra, Moti and Khandalavala, Karl. 'An Illustrated *Kalpasutra*, Painted in Jaunpur in A.D. 1465'. *Lalit Kala*, no. 12, (1962), pp. 8–15.

Chandra, Moti and Shah, Umakant P. *New Documents of Jaina Painting*. Bombay: Shri Mahavira Jaina Vidyalaya, 1975.

Chandra, Pramod. *Indian Sculpture from the Collection of Mr and Mrs Earl Morse*. Cambridge, MA: Fogg Art Museum, Harvard University, 1963.

Chandra, Pramod. *Studies in Indian Temple Architecture: Papers Presented at a Seminar held in Varanasi, 1967*. New Delhi: American Institute of Indian Studies, 1975.

Chandra, Pramod. *The Cleveland Tuti-nama Manuscript and the Origins of Mughal Painting*. Cleveland: Cleveland Museum of Art, 1976.

Chandra, Pramod. 'Hindu Ascetics in Mughal Painting' in Meister, Michael W. (ed.) *Discourses on Siva: Proceedings of a Symposium on the Nature of Religious Imagery*. Philadelphia: University of Pennsylvania Press, 1984, pp. 312–16.

Chandra, Pramod (ed.) *The Sculpture of India, 3000 BC – 1300 AD*. Washington: National Gallery of Art, 1985.

Chandra, Ramaprasad. *Medieval Indian Sculpture in the British Museum*. London: K.Paul, Trench, Trubner, 1936.

Chattopadhaya, Brajadulal. 'The Emergence of the Rajputs as Historical Process in Early Medieval Rajasthan' in Karine Schomer et al. (eds) *The Idea of Rajasthan: Explorations in Regional Identity*, vol. 2, New Delhi: Manohar/ American Institute of Indian Studies, 1994, pp. 161–91.

Chattopadhyaya, Brajadulal. *The Making of Early Medieval India*. Delhi: Oxford University Press, 1994.

Chaudhuri, K.N. *Asia Before Europe: Economy and Civilisation of the Indian Ocean from the Rise of Islam to 1750*. Cambridge: Cambridge University Press, 1990.

Conze, Edward. *Buddhism: Its Essence and Development*. New York: Harper, 1959.

Conze, E. *The Prajnaparamita Literature*. 2nd edn, rev. Tokyo: Reiyukai, 1978.

Coomaraswamy, Ananda K. *Catalogue of the Indian Collections in the Museum of Fine Arts, Boston*, 5 vols. Boston: MFA, 1923–30.

Coomaraswamy, Ananda. *The Dance of Siva: Fourteen Indian Essays*. New York: Sunwise Turn, 1924.

Coomaraswamy, Ananda K. 'The Origin of the Buddha Image'. *Art Bulletin*, 9, (1927), pp. 287–317.

Coomaraswamy, Ananda K. 'The Rape of a Nagi: An Indian Gupta Seal', *The Bulletin of the Museum of Fine Arts* (Boston), vol. 35, no. 209 (1937); vol. 35, no. 210 (1937).

Coomaraswamy, Ananda K. *Yaksas*. Washington: Smithsonian Institution, 1928-31. Reprint. New Delhi: Munshiram Manoharlal, 197-.

Coomaraswamy, Ananda K. *Rajput Painting: Being an Account of the Hindu Paintings of Rajasthan and the Panjab Himalayas from the Sixteenth to the Nineteenth Century*, 2 vols. Reprint. New York: Hacker Art Books, 1975.

Coomaraswamy, Ananda K. *Coomaraswamy*. 3 vols. Edited by Roger Lipsey. Princeton: Princeton University Press, 1977.

Coomaraswamy, Ananda K. *Spiritual Authority and Temporal Power in the Indian Theory of Government*. Reprint. New Haven: American Oriental Society, 1942. Kraus Reprint 1976. Delhi: IGNCA/Oxford University Press, 1993.

Courtright, Paul B. *Ganesha: Lord of Obstacles, Lord of Beginnings*. New York/Oxford: Oxford University Press, 1985.

Cribb, Joe. 'The Origin of the Buddha Image', in Bridget Allchin (ed.). *South Asian Archaeology 1981: Proceedings of the Sixth International Conference of South Asian Archaeologists in Western Europe*. Cambridge: Cambridge University Press, 1984, pp. 231–44.

Czuma, Stanislaw J. *Kushan Sculpture: Images from Early India*. Cleveland, Ohio: Cleveland Museum of Art/Indiana University Press, 1985.

Dallapiccola, Anna L. *The Ramachandra Temple at Vijayanagara*. New Delhi: Manohar/ American Institute of Indian Studies, 1992.

Dallapiccola, Anna Libera (ed.). *Shastric Traditions in Indian Arts*, 2 vols. Stuttgart: Franz Steiner Verlag Wiesbaden GMBH, 1989, 1990.

Dallapiccola, Anna Libera and Lallement, Stephanie Zingel-Avé (eds). *The Stupa: Its Religious, Historical and Architectural Significance*. Wiesbaden: Franz Steiner Verlag, 1980.

Das, Asok Kumar. 'Mansur', in Pal, Pratapaditya (ed.). *Master Artists of the Imperial Mughal Court*. Bombay: Marg Publications, 1991.

Dasgupta, S.B. *An Introduction to Tantric Buddhism*. 3rd edn. Calcutta: University of Calcutta, 1974.

Davies, Philip. *The Penguin Guide to the Monuments of India, Vol. II: Islamic, Rajput, European*. London: Penguin, 1989.

Davis, Richard. *Ritual in an Oscillating Universe: Worshipping Siva in Medieval India*. Princeton NJ: Princeton University Press, 1991.

Dayal, Har. *The Bodhisattva Doctrine in Buddhist Sanskrit Literature*. Delhi: Motilal Banarsidass, 1975.

de Bary, Wm. Theodore (ed.). *Sources of Indian Tradition*. New York: Columbia University Press, 1958.

Dehejia, Vidya. 'Sambandar: A Child-Saint of South India'. *South Asian Studies*, vol. 3, (1987), pp. 53–61.

Dehejia, Vidya. *Slaves of the Lord: The Path of the Tamil Saints*. New Delhi: Munshiram Manoharlal, 1988.

Dehijia, Vidya. *Art of the Imperial Cholas*. New York: Columbia University Press, 1990

Dehejia, Vidya (ed.). *Royal Patrons and Great Temple Art*. Bombay: Marg Publications, 1988.

Derrett, John Duncan Martin. *The Hoysalas: A Medieval Indian Royal Family*. Madras: Oxford University Press, 1957.

Desai, Devangana. *Erotic Sculpture of India: A Socio-Cultural Study*. New Delhi: Tata McGrath-Hill, 1975.

Desai, Devangana. 'Placement and Significance of Erotic Sculptures at Khajuraho', in Meister, Michael W. (ed.). *Discourses on Siva: Proceedings of a Symposium on the Nature of Religious Imagery*. Philadelphia: University of Pennsylvania Press, 1984, pp. 143–55.

Desai, Vishakha N. *Life at Court: Art for India's Rulers, 16th – 19th Centuries*. Boston: Museum of Fine Arts, 1985.

Desai, Vishakha N. 'Timeless Symbols: Royal Portraits from Rajasthan 17th – 19th Centuries', in Karine Schomer et al (eds). *The Idea of Rajasthan: Explorations in Regional Identity*, vol. 1. New Delhi: Manohar/American Institute of Indian Studies, 1994, pp. 313–42.

Desai, Vishakha N. and Leidy, Denise Patry. *Faces of Asia: Portraits from the Permanent Collection*. Boston: Museum of Fine Arts, 1989.

Desai, Vishakha and Mason, Darielle (eds). *Gods, Guardians and Lovers: Temple Sculptures from North India AD 700–1200*. New York: Asia Society Galleries/Mapin Publishing, 1993.

Deva, Krishna. *Temples of North India*. 2nd edn, rev. New Delhi: National Book Trust, 1977.

Deva, Krishna. *Temples of Khajuraho*. New Delhi: Archaeological Survey of India, 1990.

Dhaky, M.A. 'The "Pranala" in Indian, South Asian and South-east Asian Sacred Architecture', in Bettina Baumer (ed.). *Rupa Pratirupa: Alice Boner Commemoration Volume*. New Delhi: Biblia Impex, 1982, pp. 119–66.

Digby, Simon. 'The Sufi *shaykh* and the Sultan: A Conflict of Claims to Authority in Medieval India'. *Iran*, 28, (1990), pp. 71–81.

Diksht, R.K. *The Chandellas of Jejakabhukti*. Delhi: Motilal Banarsidass, 1977.

Donaldson, Thomas E. *Hindu Temple Art of Orissa*, 3 vols. Leiden: Brill, 1985–87.

Doniger, Wendy. *Siva: The Erotic Ascetic*. London: Oxford University Press, 1981.

Doshi, Saryu. *Masterpieces of Jain Painting*. Bombay: Marg Publications, 1985.

Doshi, Saryu (ed.). *Tribal India: Ancestors, Gods, and Spirits*. Bombay: Marg Publications, 1992.

Dumont, L. 'Définition structurale d'un dieu populaire tamoul: Aiyanar, le Maître'. *Journal Asiatique*, 241, (1953), pp. 255–70.

Dutt, Sukumar. *Buddhist Monks and Monasteries of India: Their History and Their Contribution to Indian Culture*. London: George Allen and Unwin, 1962.

Ebeling, Klaus. *Ragamala Painting*. Basel: Ravi Kumar, 1973.

Eck, Diana L. *Darsan: Seeing the Divine Image in India*. 2nd edn. Chambersburg, Pa.: Anima Books, 1985.

Eschmann, Anncharlott; Kulke, Hermann and Tripathi, Gaye C. (eds). *The Cult of Jagannath and the Regional Tradition of Orissa*. Delhi: Manohar, 1978.

Fabri, C.L. 'Mathura of the Gods'. *Marg*, 7:2, (March 1954), pp. 8–22.

Fergusson, James. *History of Indian and Eastern Architecture*. 2 vols. 2nd edn, rev. New Delhi: Munshiram Manoharlal, 1972.

Fisher, Robert E. *Buddhist Art and Architecture*. London: Thames and Hudson, 1993.

Fuller, C.J. *The Camphor Flame: Popular Hinduism and Society in India*. Princeton, NJ: Princeton University Press, 1992.

Getty, Alice. *The Gods of Northern Buddhism: Their History and Iconography*. Oxford: Clarendon Press, 1928. Reprint. New York: Dover, 1988.

Ghosh, A. *Jaina Art and Architecture*, 3 vols. New Delhi: Bharatiya Jnanpith, 1974.

Ghosh, A. (ed.) *An Encyclopaedia of Indian Archaeology*. New Delhi: Munshiram Manoharlal, 1989.

Gli Dei dell'India: 4,000 Anni di Statue in Bronzo: Cento Capolavori dal Museo Nazionale di Nouva Delhi. [Catalogue of an exhibition held at the Museo degli Argenti, Palazzo Pitti, Florence]. Livorno: Sillabe, 1993.

Gombrich, Richard F. *The World of Buddhism: Buddhist Monks and Nuns in Society and Culture*. New York: Thames and Hudson, 1991.

Gonda, J. *Ancient Indian Kingship from the Religious Point of View*. Leiden: E.J. Brill, 1966.

Gonda, J. *Eye and Gaze in the Veda*. Akademie avn Wetenschappen. Amsterdam. Afdeeling letterkunde. Verhandelingen, nieuwe reeks, deel 75; no. 1. n.d.

Goswamy, B.N. 'Of Patronage and Pahari Painting', in Pratapaditya Pal (ed.). *Aspects of Indian Art: Papers Presented in a Symposium at the Los Angeles County Museum of Art, October 1970*. Leiden: E.J. Brill, 1972, pp. 130–38.

Goswamy, B.N. *Essence of Indian Art*. San Francisco: Asian Art Museum of San Francisco, 1986.

Goswamy, B.N. 'Essence and Appearance: Some Notes on Indian Portraiture', in Skelton, Robert et al (eds). *Facets of Indian Art*. London: Victoria and Albert Museum, 1986.

Goswamy B.N. 'The Painter Nainsukh and his Patron Balwant Singh', in Miller, Barbara Stoler (ed.). *The Powers of Art: Patronage and Indian Culture*. Delhi: Oxford University Press, 1992.

Goswamy, B.N. and Eberhard Fischer. *Wonders of a Golden Age: Painting at the Court of the Great Mughals, Indian Art of the 16th – 17th Centuries from Collections in Switzerland*. Zurich: Museum Rietberg, 1987.

Goswamy, B.N. and Eberhard Fischer. *Pahari Masters: Court Painters of Northern India*. (*Artibus Asiae Supplementum*, 38). Zurich: Artibus Asiae Publishers and Museum Rietberg, 1992.

Gravely, F.H. and Ramachandran, T.N. *Catalogue of the South Indian Hindu Metal Images*. Madras: Superintendent, Government Press, 1932. *Bulletin of the Madras Government Museum*, n.s., vol. 1, pt. 2.

Gravely, F.H. and Sivaramamurti, C. *Guide to the Archaeological Galleries*, 1939. Reprint. Madras: Director of Museums, 1992.

Gravely, F.H. and Sivaramamurti, C. *Illustrations of Indian Sculpture: For Use with the Guide to the Archaeological Galleries*. 1939. Reprint. Madras: Director of Museums, 1992.

Gravely, F.H., Sivaramamurti, C. et al. *An Introduction to South Indian Temple Architecture and Sculpture*. 3rd edn. 1939. Reprint. Madras: Director of Museums, 1992.

Gray, Basil (ed.). *The Arts of India*. Ithaca, New York: Cornell University Press, 1981.

Grigson, Wilfred V. *The Maria Gonds of Bastar*. Oxford: Oxford University Press, 1938.

Grünwedel, Albert. *Buddhist Art in India: Translated from the "Handbuch" of Prof. Albert Grünwedel by Alice C. Gibson; Revised and Enlarged by Jas. Burgess*. 1901. Reprint. New Delhi: Cosmo Publications, 1985.

Guha-Thakurta, Tapati. *The Making of a New 'Indian' Art: Artists, Aesthetics and Nationalism in Bengal, c.1850–1920*. Cambridge: Cambridge University Press, 1992.

Gupta, P.L. (ed.). *Catalogue of Antiquities*. Patna: Patna Museum, 1965.

Gupta, S.P. (ed.). *Masterpieces from the National Museum Collection*. New Delhi: National Museum, 1985.

Gutman, Judith Mara. *Through Indian Eyes: 19th and early 20th Century Photography from India*. New York, New York: International Center of Photography, 1982.

Guy, John. 'A Kushan Bodhisattva and Early Indian Sculpture'. *Art Bulletin of Victoria*, no. 24 (1983), pp. 33–46.

Guy, John and Swallow, Deborah (eds). *Arts of India: 1500–1900*. London: Victoria and Albert Museum, 1990.

Haque, Enamul. *Bengal Sculptures: Hindu Iconography up to c.1250*. Dhaka: Bangladesh National Museum, 1992.

Harle, J.C. 'Durga, Goddess of Victory'. *Artibus Asiae*, 26:3/4, (1963), pp. 237–46.

Harle, James C. *Gupta Sculpture: Indian Sculpture of the Fourth to the Sixth Centuries A.D.* Oxford: Clarendon Press, 1974.

Harle, James C. *The Art and Architecture of the Indian Subcontinent*. Harmondsworth: Penguin, 1986.

Hawley, Jack. 'A Feast for Mount Govardham', in Eck, Diana and Mallison, Françoise, (eds). *Devotion Divine: Bhakti Traditions from the Regions of India*. Groningen/Paris: Egbert Forsten/ Ecole Française d'Extrême Orient, 1991, pp. 155–79.

Hiltebeitel, Alf. 'Krsna at Mathura', in Srinivasan, Doris Meth (ed.) *Mathura: The Cultural Heritage*. New Delhi: American Institute of Indian Studies, 1989, pp. 93–102.

Hsuan-tsang, *c*.596–664. *Si-yu-ki: Buddhist Records of the Western World*. Translated by Samuel Beal. Reprint. New York: Paragon Reprint, 1968.

Huntington, Susan L. *The "Pala-Sena" Schools of Sculpture*. Leiden: E.J. Brill, 1984.

Huntington, Susan L. *The Art of Ancient India: Buddhist, Hindu, Jain*. New York: Weatherhill, 1985.

Huntington, Susan L. and John C. *Leaves from the Bodhi Tree: The Art of Pala India (8th – 12th Centuries) and Its International Legacy*. Dayton, Ohio: Dayton Art Institute in association with University of Washington Press, 1989.

Huyler, Stephen P. 'Gifts of Earth: Votive Terracottas of India'. *Asian Art*, vol. 1:3, (Summer 1988), pp. 6–37.

Inden, Ronald B. *Imagining India*. Oxford: Basil Blackwell, 1990.

Indian Bronze Masterpieces: The Great Tradition. New Delhi: Brijbasi for the Festival of India, 1988.

The Indian Heritage: Court Life and Arts Under Mughal Rule. London: Victoria and Albert Museum, 1982.

Indian Museum. *A Guide to the Sculptures in the Indian Museum*. Contents: Majumdar, N.G. *Part 1: Early Indian schools; Part 2: The Graeco-Buddhist school of Gandhara*. Bloch, Theodor. *Supplementary Catalogue of the Archaeological Collection of the Indian Museum*, 3 vols in 1. 1911–36. Reprint. Patna: Eastern Book House, 1987.

The Indian Museum 1814–1914. Calcutta: Trustees of the Indian Museum, 1914.

Ingalls, Daniel H.H. *Sanskrit Poetry: From Vidyakara's "Treasury"*. Translated by Daniel H.H. Ingalls. Cambridge, MA: Belknap Press of Harvard University Press, 1965.

Jahangir, Nur al-Din Muhammad, 1569–1627. *The Tuzuk-i-Jahangiri: or, Memoirs of Jahangir*, 2 vols in 1. Translated by A. Rogers. H. Beveridge (ed). 2nd edn. Delhi: Munshiram Manoharlal, 1968.

Jain, Jyotindra and Fisher, Eberhard. *Jaina Iconography*, 2 parts. Leiden: E.J. Brill, 1971.

Jayasmal, K.P. 'Metal Images from Kurkihar Monastery'. *Journal of the Indian Society of Oriental Art*, 2:2, (1934), pp. 70–82.

Joshi, N.P. *Mathura Sculptures: A Handbook to Appreciate Sculptures in the Archaeological Museum, Mathura*. Mathura: Archaeological Museum, 1966.

Jouveau-Dubreuil, G. *Iconography of Southern India*. Translated by A.C. Martin. Paris: Guenther, 1937.

Kalidasa. *The Loom of Time: A Selection of His Plays and Poems*. Translated by Chandra Rajan. New Delhi: Penguin; New York: Viking Penguin, 1989.

Kausar, Sajjad, Brand, Michael and Wescoat, James L. Jr. *Shalamar Garden, Lahore: Landscape, Form and Meaning*. Pakistan: Department of Archaeology and Museums, Ministry of Culture, 1990.

Khan, 'Inayat. *Shah Jahan Nama of Inayat Khan: An Abridged History of the Mughal Emperor Shah Jahan*. Translated by A.R. Fuller. W.E. Begley and Z.A.Desai (eds). Delhi; Oxford: Oxford University Press, 1990.

Khan, Shah Nawaz. *Maathir-ul-Umara*, 2 vols. Translated by H. Beveridge. Calcutta: Asiatic Society, 1888–91. Reprint. Patna: Janaki Prakashan, 1979.

Khandalavala, Karl and Doshi, Saryu. *A Collector's Dream: Indian Art in the Collections of Basant Kumar and Saraladevi Birla and the Birla Academy of Art and Culture*. Bombay: Marg Publications, 1987.

Knox, Robert. *Amaravati: Buddhist Sculpture from the Great Stupa*. London: British Museum Press, 1992.

Koch, Ebba. 'The Baluster Column — A European Motif in Mughal Architecture and its Meaning'. *Journal of the Warburg and Courtauld Institutes*, vol. 45, (1982), pp. 251–62.

Koch, Ebba. 'Jahangir and the Angels: Recently Discovered Wall Paintings under European Influence in the Fort of Lahore', in Joachim Deppert (ed.). *India and the West: Proceedings of a Seminar Dedicated to the Memory of Herman Goetz. (South Asian Studies; 15)*. New Delhi: Manohar Publications, 1983.

Koch, Ebba. *Shah Jahan and Orpheus: The 'pitre dure' Decoration and the Program of the Throne in the Hall of Public Audiences at the Red Fort of Delhi*. Graz: Akademische Druck-u. Verlagsanstalt, 1988.

Koch, Ebba. *Mughal Architecture: An Outline of its History and Development, 1526–1858*. Munich: Prestel, 1991.

Koch, Ebba. 'Diwan-i `Amm and Chihil Sutun: The Audience Halls of Shah Jehan'. *Muqarnas*, vol. 11 (1994), pp. 143–65.

Kramrisch, Stella. *Unknown India: Ritual Art in Tribe and Village*. Philadelphia: Philadelphia Museum of Art, 1968.

Kramrisch, Stella. *Manifestations of Shiva*. Philadelphia: Philadelphia Museum of Art, 1981.

Kramrisch, Stella. *The Hindu Temple*, 2 vols. Reprint. Delhi: Motilal Banarsidass, 1986.

Krishna, Y. 'Evolution of the Iconography of Ganesha'. *Lalit Kala*, no. 27, (1993), pp. 9–19.

Krishna Sastri, H. *South Indian Images of Gods and Goddesses*. Madras: Madras Government Press, 1916.

Kurin, Richard. 'Making Exhibitions Indian: "Aditi" and "Mela" at the Smithsonian Institution', in Meister, Michael W. (ed.). *Making Things in South Asia: The Role of Artist and Craftsman: Proceedings of the South Asia Seminar, IV: 1985–6*. Philadelphia: Department of South Asia Regional Studies, 1988, pp. 196–210

Kurita, Isao. *Gandharan Buddhist Art*, vol. 2. Tokyo: Nigensha Publishing Co., 1990.

Lahawri, 'Abd al-Hamid. *Badshah Namah*, Mawlawis Kabir al-din Ahman and Abd al-Rahim (eds). Calcutta: Asiatic Society, 1867.

Lannoy, Richard. *The Speaking Tree: A Study of Indian Culture and Society*. London: Oxford University Press, 1971.

Leidy, Denise Patry. *Treasure of Asian Art: The Asia Society's Mr and Mrs John D. Rockefeller 3rd Collection*. New York: Asia Society Galleries; Abbeville Press, 1994.

Leoshko, Janice (ed.). *Bodhgaya: The Site of Enlightenment*. Bombay: Marg Publications, 1988.

Lerner, Martin and Kossak, Steven. *The Lotus Transcendent: Indian and Southeast Asian Art from the Samuel Eilenberg Collection*. New York: Metropolitan Museum of Art, 1991.

Liebert, Gösta. *Iconographic Dictionary of the Indian Religions: Hinduism, Buddhism, Jainism. (Studies in South Asian Culture*, vol.5). Leiden: Brill, 1976.

Lohuizen-de Leeuw, J.E. van. 'Gandhara and Mathura: Their Cultural Relationship', in Pratapaditya Pal (ed.). *Aspects of Indian Art: Papers Presented in a Symposium at the Los Angeles County Museum of Art*, October, 1970, pp. 27–43.

Lohuizen-de Leeuw, J.E. van. 'New Evidence with regard to the Origin of the Buddha Image', in Hartel, Harbert (ed.). *South Asian Archaeology 1979: Papers from the Fifth International Conference of the Association of South Asian Archaeologists in Western Europe*. Berlin: D.Reimer Verlag, 1981, pp. 377–400.

Losty, Jeremiah P. 'Abu'l Hasan', in Pal, Pratapaditya (ed.). *Master Artists of the Imperial Mughal Court*. Bombay: Marg Publications, 1991.

Lowry, Glenn D. with Susan Nemazee. *A Jeweller's Eye: Islamic Arts of the Book from the Vever Collection*. Washington DC: Arthur M. Sackler Gallery, 1988.

Mahapatra, Sitakant (ed.). *Realm of the Sacred: Verbal Symbolism and Ritual Structures*. Calcutta/New York: Oxford University Press, 1992.

Mallmann, Marie-Thérèse de. *Les enseignements iconographiques de l'Agni-Purana. (Musée Guimet. Annales. Bibliothèque d'études*, 67). Paris: Presses Universitaires de France, 1963.

Mallmann, Marie-Thérèse de. *Introduction à l'étude d'Avalokitesvara. (Museé Guimet. Annales. Bibliothèque d'études*, 57). Paris: Presses Universitaires de France, 1967.

Mallmann, Marie-Thérèse de. *Introduction à l'iconographie du tântrisme bouddhique*. Paris: Librarie Adrien-Maisonneuve, 1975.

Manasara. *Architecture of Manasara*. Translated from the original Sanskrit by Prasanna Kumar Acharya. 2nd edn. New Delhi: Oriental Books Reprint Corporation, 1980.

Maxwell, T.S. *Visvarupa*. Delhi: Oxford University Press, 1988.

Meister, Michael W. 'The Hindu Temple: Axis of Access', in Kapila Vatsyayan (ed.) *Concepts of Space Ancient and Modern*. New Delhi: Indira Gandhi National Centre for the Arts and Abhinav Publications, 1991, pp. 269–80.

Meister, Michael W. (ed.). *Discourses on Siva: Proceedings of a Symposium on the Nature of Religious Imagery*. Bombay: Vakils, Feffer & Simons Ltd, 1984; Philadelphia: University of Pennsylvania Press, 1984.

Meister, Michael W. (ed.) *Making Things in South Asia: The Role of Artist and Craftsman: Proceedings of the South Asia Seminar, IV: 1985–6*. Philadelphia: Department of South Asia Regional Studies, 1988.

Michell, George. 'The Regents of the Directions in Space: A Set of Sculptural Panels from Alampur'. *Art and Archaeological Research Papers* IV, (1973), pp. 297–308.

Michell, George. *The Hindu Temple: An Introduction to its Meaning and Forms*. Chicago: University of Chicago Press, 1988.

Michell, George. *The Penguin Guide to the Monuments of India, Vol 1: Buddhist, Jain, Hindu*. London: Penguin, 1990.

Michell, George. *The Royal Palaces of India*. London: Thames and Hudson, 1994.

Michell, George. *Architecture and Art of Southern India: Vijayanagara and the Successor States*. Cambridge: Cambridge University Press, 1995. (*The New Cambridge History of India*, I:6.)

Michell, George (ed.). *In the Image of Man: The Indian Perception of the Universe through 2000 Years of Painting and Sculpture: Hayward Gallery, London 25 March – 13 June 1982*. London: Arts Council of Great Britain/Weidenfield and Nicolson, 1982.

Michell, George (ed.). *Temple Towns of Tamil Nadu*. Bombay: Marg Publications, 1993.

Miller, Barbara Stoler (ed.). *The Powers of Art: Patronage in Indian Culture*. Delhi: Oxford University Press, 1992.

Mishra, Vibhuti Bhushan. *Religious Beliefs and Practices of North India During the Early Medieval Period*. Leiden: E.J. Brill, 1973

Mitra, Debala. *Buddhist Monuments*. Calcutta: Sahitya Samsad, 1971.

Mitra, Rajendralala Raja. *The Antiquities of Orissa*, 2 vols. Reprint. Calcutta: R.K. Maitra, 1961–63.

Mollison, James and Murray, Laura (eds). *Australian National Gallery, An Introduction*. Canberra: Australian National Gallery, 1982.

Mosteller, John F. *The Measure of Form: A New Approach for the Study of Indian sculpture*. New Delhi: Abhinav, 1990.

Mus, Paul. 'Le Buddha Paré: Son Origine Indienne'. *Bulletin de l'Ecole Française d'Extrème-Orient*, vol. 27, (1928), pp. 147–278.

Nagaswamy, R. 'Rare Bronzes from Kongu Country'. *Lalit Kala*, no. 11, (1961), pp. 7–10.

Nagaswamy, R. *Masterpieces of Early South Indian Bronzes*. New Delhi: National Museum, 1983.

Necipoglu, Gulru. 'Framing the Gaze in Ottoman, Safavid and Mughal Palaces'. *Ars Orientalis* [Special Issue on Pre-Modern Islamic Palaces], vol. 23, (1993), pp. 303–42.

Nehru, Lolita. *Origins of the Gandharan Style: A Study in Contributory Influences*. Delhi: Oxford University Press, 1989.

O'Flaherty, Wendy Doniger. *Hindu Myths: A Source Book*. Translated from the Sanskrit with an Introduction by Wendy Doniger O'Flaherty. Harmondsworth, Middlesex: Penguin, 1975.

Okada, Amina. 'Basawan', in Pal, Pratapaditya (ed.). *Master Artists of the Imperial Mughal Court*. Bombay: Marg Publications, 1991.

Okada, Amina. *Imperial Mughal Painters: Indian Miniatures from the Sixteenth and Seventeenth Centuries*. Translated by Deke Dusinberre. Paris: Flammarion, 1992.

Pal, Pratapaditya. *Indian Sculpture: A Catalogue of the Los Angeles County Museum of Art Collection*, 2 vols. Los Angeles: LACMA; University of California Press, Berkeley, 1986–88.

Pal, Pratapaditya (ed.). *Master Artists of the Imperial Mughal Court*. Bombay: Marg Publications, 1991.

Pal, Pratapaditya (ed.). *The Peaceful Liberators: Jain Art from India*. Los Angeles: Los Angeles County Museum of Art/Thames and Hudson, 1994.

Palast der Götter: 1500 Jahre Kunst aus Indien. Berlin: Dietrich Reimer Verlag, 1992.

Peabody, Norbert. 'In Whose Turban does the Lord Reside?: The Objectification of Charisma and the Fetishism of Objects in the Hindu Kingdom of Kota'. *Comparative Studies in Society and History*, vol. 33:4, (October 1991), pp. 726–54.

Peterson, Indira Viswanathan. *Poems to Siva: The Hymns of the Tamil Saints*. Delhi: Motilal Barnarsidass, 1989.

Pope, G.U. (ed.). *The Tiruvacagam*. Oxford: Clarendon Press, 1900.

Prasad, B. Rajendra. *Art of South India: Andhra Pradesh*. New Delhi: Sundeep, 1980.

Prasad, H.K. 'Jaina Bronzes in the Patna Museum', in *Shri Mahavira Jaina Vidyalaya Golden Jubilee Volume*. Bombay, 1968, pp. 275–89.

Punja, Shobita. *Divine Ecstasy: The Story of Khajuraho*. New Delhi: Viking, 1992.

Ramacandra Kaulacara. *Silpa Prakasa: Medieval Orissan Sanskrit Text on Temple Architecture*. Translated by Alice Boner and Sadasiva Rathsarma. Leiden: E.J. Brill, 1966.

Ramachandran, T.N. 'The Nagapattinam and Other Buddhist Bronzes in the Madras Museum'. *Bulletin of the Madras Government Museum*. 1954. Reprint. Madras: Director of Museums, 1992.

Ramanujan, A.K. *Speaking of Siva*. Harmondsworth: Penguin, 1973.

Ramesan, N. *Temples and Legends of Andhra Pradesh*. Bombay: Bharatiya Vidya Bhavan, 1988.

Rao, N.S. Nagaraja (ed.). *Kusumañjali: New Interpretation of Indian Art and Culture: Sh. C. Sivaramamurti Commemoration Volume*, 2 vols. Delhi: Agam Kala Prakashan, 1987.

Rao, T.A. Gopinatha. *Elements of Hindu Iconography*, 2 vols in 4. 2nd edn. Varanasi: Indological Book House, 1971.

Ray, Nihar Ranjan et al. (eds). *Eastern Indian Bronzes*. Part I by Nihar Ranjan Ray; Part II by Karl Khandalavala and Sadashiv Gorakshkar. New Delhi: Lalit Kala Akademi, 1986.

Richards, John F. (ed.). *Kingship and Authority in South Asia*. 2nd edn. Madison: South Asian Studies, University of Wisconsin, 1981.

Saraswati, B.N.; Malik, S.C. and Khanna, Madhu (eds). *Art, the Integral Vision: A Volume of Essays in Felicitation of Kapila Vatsyayan*. New Delhi: D.K. Printworld, 1994.

Sastri, K.A. Nilakanta. *The Colas*. 2nd ed. rev. Madras: Madras University, 1955.

Schimmel, Annemarie. *Islam in the Indian Subcontinent*. Leiden and Cologne: E.J. Brill, 1980.

Schumann, H.W. *The Historical Buddha: The Times, Life and Teachings of the Founder of Buddhism*. London; New York: Arkana, 1989

Selected Masterpieces of Asian Art: Museum of Fine Arts, Boston. Boston: Museum of Fine Arts, 1992.

Sengupta, Anasua. *Buddhist Art of Bengal: From the 3rd Century BC to the 13th Century AD*. Delhi: Rahul Publishing House, 1993.

Settar, S. *The Hoysala Temples*, 2 vols. Bangalore: Kala Yatra Publications, 1991–92.

Sewell, Robert. *A Forgotten Empire (Viajayanagar): A Contribution to Indian History*. Reprint. New Delhi: Asian Educational Services, 1992.

Shah, U.P. and Dhaky, M.A. (eds). *Aspects of Jaina Art and Architecture*. Ahmedabad: Gujarat State Committee for the Celebration of 2500th Anniversary of Bhagavan Mahavira Nirvana, 1975.

Sharma, R.C. 'New Buddhist Sculptures from Mathura (Pre-Gupta Epoch)'. *Lalit Kala* 19, (1979), pp. 19–26.

Shukla, D.N. *Vastu-Sastra, Vol 2: Hindu Canons of Iconography and Painting*. New Delhi: Munshiram Manoharlal, 1993.

Singh, Ram Charitra Prasad. *Kingship in Northern India (c.600 AD - 1200 AD)*. Delhi: Motilal Banarsidass, 1968.

Sinha, Kamini. *The Early Bronzes of Bihar*. New Delhi: Ramanand Vidya Bhavan, 1983.

Sircar, D.C. and Sarma, S.R. 'Kapilas Inscriptions of Narasimhadeva'. *Epigraphia Indica*, 33:1, (1959), pp. 41–43.

Sivaramamurti, C. 'Amaravati Sculptures in the Madras Government Museum'. *Bulletin of the Madras Government Museum*. n.s. vol. 4, (1956). Madras: Thompson & Co. for the Superintendent, Government Press.

Sivaramamurti, C. *Early Eastern Chalukyan Sculpture*. Madras: India Press for the Controller of Stationery and Printing, 1962.

Sivaramamurti, C. *South Indian Bronzes*. New Delhi: Lalit Kala Akademi, 1963.

Sivaramamurti, C. *Nataraja in Art, Thought and Literature*. New Delhi: National Museum, 1974.

Sivaramamurti, C. *The Art of India*. New York: Abrams, 1977.

Sivaramamurti, C. *A Guide to the Archaeological Galleries of the Indian Museum*. Calcutta: Indian Museum, 1978.

Skelton, Robert. *Rajasthani Temple Hangings of the Krishna Cult*. New York: American Federation of the Arts, 1973.

Snellgrove, David (ed.). *The Image of the Buddha*. London/Paris: Serindia Publications/UNESCO, 1978.

Snodgrass, Adrian. *The Symbolism of the Stupa*. Delhi: M.Banarsidass Publishers, 1992.

Spellman, John W. *Political Theory of Ancient India: A Study of Kingship from the Earliest Times to circa AD 300*. Oxford: Clarendon Press, 1964.

Spink, Walter. 'On the Development of Early Buddhist Art in India'. *Art Bulletin* 40, (1958), pp. 95–104.

Srinivasa Desikan, V.N. *Guide to the Bronze Gallery*. 1972. Reprint. Madras: Commissioner of Museums, Government Museum, 1994.

Srinivasan, D.M. 'Saiva Temple Forms: Loci of God's Unfolding Body', in Yaldiz, Marianne and Lobo, Wibke (eds). *Investigating Indian Art: Proceedings of a Symposium on the Development of Early Buddhist and Hindu Iconography Held at the Museum of Indian Art, Berlin, in May 1986*. Berlin: Museum für Indische Kunst: Staatliche Museen Preussicher Kulturbesitz, 1987, pp. 335–47.

Srinivasan, D.M. (ed.) *Mathura: The Cultural Heritage*. New Delhi: American Institute of Indian Studies, 1989.

Srinivasan, P.R. 'Bronzes of South India'. *Bulletin of the Madras Government Museum*, n.s. vol. 8, 1963. Printed at Indian Press, Madras for the Controller of Stationery and Printing, Madras.

Srinivasan, P.R. and Aiyappan, A. *Story of Buddhism with Special Reference to South India*. Madras: Government of Madras, 1959.

Starza-Majewski, O.M. 'King Narasimha before His Spiritual Preceptor'. *Journal of the Royal Asiatic Society*, no. 2, (1971), pp. 134–38.

Starza-Majewski, O.M. *The Jagannatha Temple at Puri: Its Architecture, Art and Cult*. Leiden: Brill, 1993.

Stern, Robert W. *The Cat and the Lion: Jaipur State in the British Raj*. Leiden: E.J. Brill, 1988.

Strong, John S. *The Legend of King Asoka: A Study and Translation of the "Asokavadana"*. Reprint. Delhi: Motilal Banarsidass, 1989.

Stutley, Margaret and Stutley, James. *A Dictionary of Hinduism: Its Mythology, Folklore and Development, 1500 BC - AD 1500*. London: Routledge & Kegan Paul, 1977.

Tadgell, Christopher. *The History of Architecture in India: From the Dawn of Civilization to the End of the Raj*. London: Architecture Design and Technology Press, 1990.

Tambiah, S.J. *World Conqueror and World Renouncer: A Study of Buddhism and Polity Against a Historical Background*. Cambridge: Cambridge University Press, 1976.

Tambiah, S.J. 'A Performance Approach to Ritual', in *Culture, Thought and Social Action: An Anthropological Perspective*. Cambridge, MA: Harvard University Press, 1985, pp. 123–66.

Thapar, Romila. *Cultural Transaction and Early India: Tradition and Patronage (I.H. Qureshi Memorial Lectures 1987)*. Delhi: Oxford University Press, 1987.

Tillotson, G.H.R. *The Rajput Palaces: The Development of an Architectural Style, 1450–1750*. New Haven: Yale University Press, 1987.

Tod, James. *Annals and Antiquities of Rajast'han, or, The Central and Western Rajpoot States of India*, 2 vols. 1829. Reprint. London: Routledge and Kegan Paul, 1972.

Topsfield, Andrew. *Paintings from Rajasthan in the National Gallery of Victoria*. Melbourne: National Gallery of Victoria, 1980.

Topsfield, Andrew. 'Udaipur Paintings of the Rasalila'. *Art Bulletin of Victoria*, no. 28, (1987), pp. 54–70.

Topsfield, Andrew. *The City Palace Museum, Udaipur: Paintings of Mewar Court Life*. Ahmedabad: Mapin, 1990.

Topsfield, Andrew and Beach, Milo Cleveland. *Indian Paintings and Drawings from the Collection of Howard Hodgkin*. New York: Thames and Hudson, 1991.

Upanishads, Vastusutropanised. *Vastusutra Upanisad: The Essence of Form in Sacred Art*. Sanskrit text, English Translation and Notes by Alice Boner, Sadasiva Rath Sarma and Bettina Bäumer. Delhi: Motilal Banarsidass, 1982.

Vatsyayan, Kapila. *Classical Indian Dance in Literature and the Arts*. 2nd edn. New Delhi: Sangeet Natak Akademi. 1971.

Vatsyayan, Kapila. *Kalatattvakosa: A Lexicon of Fundamental Concepts of the Indian Arts*, 2 vols. Delhi:IGNCA/Motilal Barnarsidass Pubs, 1988, 1992.

Vaudeville, Charlotte. 'The Govardhan Myth in Northern India'. *Indo-Iranian Journal*, vol. 22:1, pp. 1–45.

Vogel, J. Ph. *Indian Serpent-Lore or The Nagas in Hindu Legend and Art*. 1926. Reprint. Varanasi: Indological Book House, 1972.

Watters, Thomas. *On Yuan Chwang's Travels in India, 629–645 AD*, 2 vols. T.W.R. Davids and S.W. Bushell (eds). London: Royal Asiatic Society, 1904–05.

Welch, Stuart Cary. *Room for Wonder: Indian Painting During the British Period, 1760–1880*. New York: American Federation of Arts, 1978.

Welch, Stuart Cary. *India: Art and Culture, 1300–1900*. New York: Metropolitan Museum of Art/Holt, Rinehart, Winston, 1985.

Welch, Stuart Cary. *The Emperor's Album: Images of Mughal India*. New York: Metropolitan Museum of Art, 1987.

Welch, Stuart Cary and Welch, Anthony. *Arts of the Islamic Book*. Ithaca, New York: Published for the Asia Society by Cornell University Press, 1982.

Wescoat, James L. Jr. 'Gardens versus Citadels: The Territorial Context of Early Mughal Gardens', in Hunt, John Dixon (ed.). *Garden History: Issues, Approaches, Methods*. Washington, DC: Dumbarton Oaks Research Collection and Library, 1992.

Williams, Joanna Gottfried. *The Art of Gupta India: Empire and Province*. Princeton, NJ: Princeton University Press, 1982.

Worswick, Clark and Embree, Ainslee. *The Last Empire: Photography in British India, 1855–1911*. New York, New York: Asia House Gallery, 1976.

Yaldiz, Marianne and Lobo, Wibke (eds). *Investigating Indian Art: Proceedings of a Symposium on the Development of Early Buddhist and Hindu Iconography Held at the Museum of Indian Art, Berlin, in May 1986*. Berlin: Museum für Indische Kunst: Staatliche Museen Preussicher Kulturbesitz, 1987.

Zahir al-Din Muhammad Babur. *Baburnama*. Translated by A. S. Beveridge. Reprint. New Delhi: Oriental Book Reprint Corporation 1970.

Zwalf, W. *Buddhism: Art and Faith*. London: British Museum/British Library, 1985.

Colour Plates

Plate 1: (Frontispiece, pp. ii–iii)
'Shore Temple', Mamallapuram, Tamil Nadu, early 8th century (Photo: Antonio Martinelli).

Plate 2: (Foreword, p. vi)
Image of the Hindu goddess Kali cut into rock face at Vijayanagara, Karnataka
(Photo: John Gollings).

Plate 3: (Gods and Goddesses, pp. 20–21)
Tiruvengalanatha Temple, dedicated to Vishnu, Vijayanagar, Karnataka, 16th century
(Photo: John Gollings).

Plate 4: (Enlightened Saviours, pp. 50–51)
Buddhist monastery, Takht-i-Bahi, Pakistan, *c.* 1st–2nd century (Photo: Michael Brand).

Plate 5: (Auspicious Guardians, pp. 82–83)
Stupa 1, Sanchi, Madhya Pradesh, 3rd–1st century BC (Photo: Michael Brand).

Plate 6: (Royal Image, pp. 102–103)
City Palace, Udaipur, Rajasthan, 1567 and later (Photo: Antonio Martinelli).

Plate 7: (Appendices, p. 150)
Shalimar Garden, Kashmir, founded 1620 (Photo: Michael Brand).